MASTERING THE SEMI-STRUCTURED INTERVIEW
AND BEYOND

D0905234

QUALITATIVE STUDIES IN PSYCHOLOGY

This series showcases the power and possibility of qualitative work in psychology. Books feature detailed and vivid accounts of qualitative psychology research using a variety of methods, including participant observation and field work, discursive and textual analyses, and critical cultural history. They probe vital issues of theory, implementation, interpretation, representation, and ethics that qualitative workers confront. The series mission is to enlarge and refine the repertoire of qualitative approaches to psychology.

General Editors: Michelle Fine and Jeanne Marecek

Everyday Courage: The Lives and Stories of Urban Teenagers
Niobe Way

Negotiating Consent in Psychotherapy
Patrick O'Neill

Flirting with Danger: Young Women's Reflections on Sexuality and Domination
Lynn M. Phillips

Voted Out: The Psychological Consequences of Anti-Gay Politics
Glenda M. Russell

Inner City Kids: Adolescents Confront Life and Violence in an Urban Community
Alice McIntyre

From Subjects to Subjectivities: A Handbook of Interpretive and Participatory Methods
Edited by Deborah L. Tolman and Mary Brydon-Miller

Growing Up Girl: Psychosocial Explorations of Gender and Class
Valerie Walkerdine, Helen Lucey, and June Melody

Voicing Chicana Feminisms: Young Women Speak Out on Sexuality and Identity
Aida Hurtado

Situating Sadness: Women and Depression in Social Context
Edited by Janet M. Stoppard and Linda M. McMullen

Living Outside Mental Illness: Qualitative Studies of Recovery in Schizophrenia
Larry Davidson

Autism and the Myth of the Person Alone
Douglas Biklen, with Sue Rubin, Tito Rajarshi Mukhopadhyay, Lucy Blackman, Larry Bissonnette, Alberto Frugone, Richard Attfield, and Jamie Burke

American Karma: Race, Culture, and Identity in the Indian Diaspora
Sunil Bhatia

Muslim American Youth: Understanding Hyphenated Identities through Multiple Methods
Selcuk R. Sirin and Michelle Fine

Pride in the Projects: Teens Building Identities in Urban Contexts
Nancy L. Deutsch

Corridor Cultures: Mapping Student Resistance at an Urban High School
Maryann Dickar

Gay Dads: Transitions to Adoptive Fatherhood
Abbie E. Goldberg

Mastering the Semi-Structured Interview and Beyond: From Research Design to Analysis and Publication
Anne Galletta

Mastering the Semi-Structured Interview and Beyond

From Research Design to Analysis and Publication

Anne Galletta

FOREWORD BY WILLIAM E. CROSS, JR.

NEW YORK UNIVERSITY PRESS

New York and London

NEW YORK UNIVERSITY PRESS
New York and London
www.nyupress.org

Permissions to reprint include the following:

Tropp, L., & Wright, S. (2001). Ingroup identification as the inclusion of ingroup in the self. *Personality and Social Psychology Bulletin*, 27(5), 585–600. Inclusion of Ingroup in the Self (IIS) Scale, Reprinted with permission of SAGE Publications.

Anne Galletta and William E. Cross, Jr., "Past as Present, Present as Past: Historicizing Black Education and Interrogating 'Integration,'" in *Contesting Stereotypes and Creating Identities: Social Categories, Social Identities, and Educational Participation*, edited by Andrew J. Fuligni. © 2007 Russell Sage Foundation, 112 East 64th Street, New York, NY 10065.

© 2013 by New York University
All rights reserved

References to Internet websites (URLs) were accurate at the time of writing. Neither the author nor New York University Press is responsible for URLs that may have expired or changed since the manuscript was prepared.

Library of Congress Cataloging-in-Publication Data
Galletta, Anne.
Mastering the semi-structured interview and beyond : from research design
to analysis and publication / Anne Galletta ; foreword by William E. Cross, Jr.
pages cm. — (Qualitative studies in psychology)
Includes bibliographical references and index.
ISBN 978-0-8147-3293-9 (cl : alk. paper)
ISBN 978-0-8147-3294-6 (pb: alk. paper)
1. Interviewing. 2. Qualitative research—Methodology.   I. Title.
H61.28.G35 2012
001.4'33—dc23   2012049429

New York University Press books are printed on acid-free paper, and their binding materials are chosen for strength and durability. We strive to use environmentally responsible suppliers and materials to the greatest extent possible in publishing our books.

Manufactured in the United States of America

10 9 8 7 6 5 4 3 2 1

To Leanne, Julia, and Clare,
who each carry a story of strength, wonder, and persistence

CONTENTS

Foreword by William E. Cross, Jr.   ix
Acknowledgments   xi

Introduction   1

SECTION I: SETTING THE STAGE

1 Crafting a Design to Yield a Complete Story   9
2 The Semi-Structured Interview as a Repertoire of Possibilities   45

SECTION II: THE SEMI-STRUCTURED INTERVIEW:
COLLECTING AND ANALYZING QUALITATIVE DATA

3 Conducting the Interview: The Role of Reciprocity
   and Reflexivity   75
4 Ongoing and Iterative Data Analysis   119

SECTION III: SYNTHESIZING AND INTERPRETING
RESEARCH FINDINGS

5 Building Theory   149
6 Writing Up and Speaking Back to the Literature   173

   Afterword: Loose Threads   191

   Appendix A: Sample Protocol for Student Participants   195
   Appendix B: Past as Present, Present as Past: Historicizing
      Black Education and Interrogating "Integration"   203
   Notes   231
   References   235
   Index   241
   About the Author   245

WILLIAM E. CROSS, JR.

With this book, scholars and students who embrace qualitative research methods to excavate new knowledge are introduced to the semi-structured interview. Anne Galletta shows the novice how to break down the interview gestalt into its constituent parts, and then reintegrate the material into a theoretically rich and empirically strong narrative.

Here in one succinct and readable volume, the author discusses (1) the role and importance of qualitative methods in contemporary research, (2) the centrality of semi-structured interviewing to qualitative research, and (3) the critical steps required for the competent and masterful application of the semi-structured interview.

In this book the full potential of the semi-structured interview procedure is analyzed, deconstructed, and synthesized; the discussion is always embedded in real-world examples that facilitate the reader's comprehension and ultimate mastery of the procedure. Importantly, Galletta's interrogation and explication of the basic elements of interviewing are illuminated by concrete examples taken from her substantive case study on school integration. A great deal of the coherence and integrity of this guide is gained by the fact that Galletta draws her step-by-step examples primarily from this case study; a published chapter from this previous work is included as appendix B to enable readers to follow her research and writing journey all the way to the finished publication. Rather than flooding and perhaps distracting readers by a myriad of exemplars, the complex contours of the interviewing process are made accessible through a riveting storyline.

Galletta showcases the importance of context as the backdrop for each participant's perspective (positionality), an identity matrix as the frame for deciphering each participant's complex identity (intersectionality), and resistance as a window into understanding how marginalized people persevere (resilience). With rich exemplars and a delicate step-by-step analysis of the process of conducting and analyzing semi-structured interviews, Galletta offers to readers a compelling methodological guidebook that can easily be applied to their own research.

ACKNOWLEDGMENTS

Words do little justice in conveying my gratitude to those who have contributed to this book and sustained me in its preparation. That said, I open this book with a testimony of my appreciation.

The theoretical and substantive richness of this text is greatly influenced by my work with Michelle Fine. Beginning with my doctoral work at the City University of New York (CUNY) Graduate Center in the mid-1990s, Michelle nurtured my study as a social psychologist and shaped my development as a qualitative researcher, guiding much of the work referenced in this text. More recently, in her review of early drafts of this book, she encouraged contextualization of each chapter through the concrete rendering of my research. Michelle's influence on my writing is vast. Indeed, it is quite evident within this book, which is designed to tell a story while communicating a method. Michelle has been an intellectual anchor, a tireless guide in my efforts to come remotely close to the standard she has set. I am grateful for her critical edge in pressing for social justice and her contagious spirit of hope and possibility.

William E. Cross, Jr., also a faculty member and later the chair of the CUNY social/personality psychology program, has played a central role in my efforts to communicate to the reader the imperative for a fine-grained analysis and the study of complex phenomena through multiple levels of analysis. In particular, he has shaped my discussion of how one's analytical framework might be organized to explore local meaning in relation to social and material practices that shape that meaning, even as human beings contest, conform to, negotiate with, and sometimes undermine these broader influences. It is with Bill's work in mind that I press the reader for analysis that textures human experience. His influence is threaded throughout countless pages of this text.

I owe much to my editor, Jennifer Hammer, at New York University Press. From the start, Jennifer understood the need for a text focused on the semi-structured interview as a versatile and powerful qualitative research method. As reflected in other texts within the Qualitative Series in Psychology, Jennifer understood the need for this work to draw early scholars and veteran social scientists into the rigor and systematic nature of qualitative research, while also addressing the murkier dimensions of planning and conducting a research project. Persistent and responsive, with drafts returned rapidly even while she was on the road, Jennifer read every sentence with care and raised important questions when the text deviated from its purpose. I am indebted to her editorial instincts and her expertise on qualitative research, which crafted a book we both hope will serve readers well.

In addition to the editorial assistance from New York University Press and the reviewers of my manuscript, my efforts to produce this book were furthered by invaluable feedback from the social and clinical psychologist Jeanne Marecek. Jeanne posed critical questions, pushing me toward substance and clarity in my writing. Her guidance was particularly instrumental in encouraging me to attend to the role of inference within qualitative research, the act of drawing meaning from data, and the inductive processes toward generating complex ideas grounded in the lived experience of research participants. She likely would correct me now on the unwieldy construction of this last sentence.

Considerable support for my writing of this book came from James (Jay) McLoughlin, the former dean of the College of Education and Human Services at Cleveland State University (CSU) and the current dean, Sajit Zachariah. I am also grateful to James C. Carl, the former chair of the Curriculum and Foundations department, for his encouragement and support as I worked to complete the manuscript. My colleagues and students at CSU have played a key role in inspiring me and in helping me envision how this text might prove useful to those exploring complex research questions through qualitative methods.

I am grateful for those who assisted me in conducting the desegregation study, which is described throughout the book and serves as a concrete and unfolding story. Contributing to the research on desegregation was Mark Freeman, the superintendent of the Shaker Heights City School District in Ohio, who offered encouragement and provided me access to a rich array of archival material in the district office. The librarians, Kristen Pool and more recently Meghan Hayes, at the

Moreland Room within the Shaker Heights Main Branch Public Library provided exceptional expertise and support through the library's local history collection. My study would not have been possible without the many students and alumni, parents, educators, and community leaders who were willing to participate in my interviews and who informed the desegregation study. The richness of their interviews and the power of their insights made this book about the semi-structured interview possible.

Most significantly, I write with tremendous gratitude for my partner in life and love, Larry. Together we have stretched the 24 hours of each day and have carved out time for our creative endeavors and for each other. As I pressed for clarity in meaning in writing this text, Larry sought precision in harmony, tone, and instrumentation in his music. Working in different spaces of our home and our lives, we found commonalities in our respective efforts, always conscious of each other's role in supporting this work. Patient with my inability to estimate time properly as I worked, Larry's humor sustained me. As I squeezed in my writing between grading students' papers and preparing for the next day's class discussion, he found ways to keep me connected to what it means to be human: music, affection, and his coupling of spices and simple ingredients into complex and satisfying meals.

Also supporting me in spirit and kinship is a family of poets, storytellers, artists, and teachers, possessing in one form or another a powerful creative impulse. My father, Tom, always a skilled observer who takes pen to paper with artistry when life allows for it, followed my work with interest. My mom, Dorothy, listened with care and celebrated every step forward in my efforts to complete the manuscript. Larry's dad, Gene, who is no longer with us, inspired me to continue through his legacy of teaching and love for science, his subject of expertise. Larry's mom, Jean, provided an appreciation for multitasking, a generous heart, and prayers. I am grateful for the strong ties within my family and the spirit of generosity that has sustained me.

Introduction

This book is written for budding social scientists and those more advanced scholars interested in developing or fine-tuning their skills in qualitative research. It is crafted to take you out of the realm of the abstract and engage you in a sustained way in the twists and turns of conceptualizing and carrying out a qualitative research project. This text addresses planning a research design, conducting data collection and analysis, synthesizing and interpreting research themes, and writing up research results. Slices of a completed research project are inserted within this book to illustrate key dimensions of qualitative research in a concrete way as they are introduced. The book's aim is to highlight the ways in which qualitative research builds on a rigorous, reflexive, and action-oriented tradition of social science.

While a number of methods are discussed here, there is a particular emphasis on the use of the semi-structured interview. This method is typically underutilized, yet it has remarkable potential. Characteristic of its unique flexibility, the semi-structured interview is sufficiently structured to address specific dimensions of your research question while also leaving space for study participants to offer new meanings to the topic of study. The focus on the semi-structured interview is complemented in this book by attention to the use of multiple methods.

This book attends to the process of bringing to the surface the multidimensional nature of lived experience. It responds to an imperative for fine-grained qualitative analyses in order to open up new possibilities in understanding complicated phenomena often accepted as unproblematic. The semi-structured interview is particularly instrumental in achieving this type of texturing. It creates openings for a narrative to unfold, while also including questions informed by theory. It also leaves a space through which you might explore with participants the contextual influences evident in the narratives but not always narrated as such.

To illustrate this methodological approach and philosophical orientation, I make use of a real case study—a qualitative study focused on a particular social problem with a long history in education and psychology. Referred to throughout as "the desegregation study," its inclusion is intended to illustrate in a concrete and detailed manner the use of the semi-structured interview within a multimethod qualitative study. By embedding an unfolding research story into rather straightforward "how-to" discussions, the book aims to draw you into the demands and dilemmas of qualitative research.

The overall philosophical orientation of the desegregation study that serves as the running example in this book reflects the critical theory interpretive tradition. Predicated on a desire to explore human relations and structural forces, or what the social psychologist and Jesuit priest Ignacio Martín-Baró (1994) referred to as "limit situations," the discussion of the desegregation study attends to the human condition as a confrontation with both limitations and opportunities. This focus encompasses history as one of several analytical levels in relation to individual experience. The use of the semi-structured interview within a multimethod design in the desegregation study thus reflects an aspiration to not only study social problems but also play a role in disentangling the threads contributing to the problems (Carspecken & Apple, 1992; Collins, 1998; Giroux, 1988; Kincheloe & McLaren, 2000; Ladson-Billings & Donnor, 2005; Lather, 1986; Martín-Baró, 1994; Weis & Fine, 2004).

The narrative within which this book is written is itself multilayered. It reflects a set of commitments to the story it tells about one school district's history of desegregation. In the process of guiding you through the stages of qualitative research, it will illustrate the interpretive process through the inductive nature of qualitative research.

Structure of the Book

The book is organized into three sections, with chapters offering a general discussion of qualitative research methods, particularly multi-method designs and the use of the semi-structured interview, interspersed with excerpts from the desegregation study, which offer concrete examples as to the twists and turns that might occur in your conceptualizing and conducting research. As the structure of the book is intended to reflect the progressive movement of qualitative research methods, the book is best read not as isolated chapters but as a whole.

Section I of the book, "Setting the Stage," introduces the task of crafting a qualitative research design. This section is meant to draw you into a more in-depth understanding of qualitative research through the use of the semi-structured interview.

Chapter 1 focuses on how to formulate your plan to research a particular topic. This chapter includes a discussion of key steps, such as preparing a literature review; conceptualizing the focus of your research through an interdisciplinary study of extant research; constructing a sufficiently open-ended research question; identifying methods best suited to that question; and developing a data analysis plan. The chapter is organized to address all aspects of the research design, including participant recruitment and selection, such practicalities as gaining access to your research setting, and, if applicable, considerations of your relationship with the site under study. The chapter includes a discussion of the specific research-design dilemmas and decisions that arose during the desegregation study as a means of illuminating the kinds of issues you might face in your own work.

Chapter 2 provides an overview of how to construct a semi-structured interview protocol. It underscores the continuum of structure available to researchers, with options to use more or less structure in the protocol, depending on the purpose of the research and the research question. The chapter is designed to assist you in thinking about the development of a protocol and your inclusion of particular segments to address dimensions of your topic. It also highlights the use of tools and resources to draw the participant more fully into the topic of study. Specific tensions evident in the construction of the interview protocol for the desegregation study are highlighted in order to showcase the dilemmas you may confront. The chapter provides a detailed discussion of the deliberations and actual decision making about the types of questions included in the semi-structured interview for the desegregation study, and this demonstrates how such tensions can be worked through.

Section II, "The Semi-Structured Interview: Collecting and Analyzing Qualitative Data," moves the book's focus along to the topics of conducting an interview and analyzing interview data. I address the ongoing and iterative nature of qualitative data analysis and the way in which analysis accompanies data collection, and this process involves a close reading and coding of interview transcripts, reciprocity with one's participants, and researcher reflexivity. The chapters within this section explore how specific thematic codes and patterns emerge and take on increased meaning and theoretical weight. Through the use of examples from the desegregation study, this section demonstrates efforts at researcher-participant reciprocity, researcher reflexivity, ongoing coding of interview data, the emergence of thematic clusters, and the early formulation of a conceptual framework.

Chapter 3 explores closely the nature of interviewing in general as an interaction between two or more individuals, and it discusses the benefits and drawbacks inherent in this method. I attend to the nature of decisions made during the actual interview, and the notion of the researcher as an instrument, reflecting and acting upon the nature of the exchange between the researcher and participant as the interview unfolds. The chapter consists of two sections. The first section focuses on your efforts to achieve reciprocity with your participants. The second section discusses the need for researcher reflexivity to assess the particular methodological and ethical snags that frequently emerge as one proceeds forward with qualitative research. As these decisions are frequently informed by the interpretive tradition guiding one's research design, the desegregation study examples in chapter 3 reflect the critical theory interpretive tradition.

Chapter 4 details the analysis of the data, offering further elaboration on the way in which data collection and analysis occur in an ongoing manner in qualitative research. The chapter details each stage of the analysis, from organizing the data at an early stage to locating thematic patterns. It underscores the way in which qualitative data analysis is iterative, requiring a process of looping back into the data and demanding a close reading of the interview transcripts. The second half of the chapter demonstrates the analytical possibilities available in the movement between *individual experience* within a *relational context* and the *structural conditions* and *historical context* that participants encounter.

Section III, "Synthesizing and Interpreting Research Findings," discusses the critical importance of the final phase of one's research, including synthesizing themes toward interpretation and theory building, formulating this synthesis for a wider public, and engaging significant others in the implications of one's work.

Chapter 5 outlines the progressive movement into synthesizing study findings. It demonstrates several tools that aid in interpretation, including graphic displays, reflective writing, and feedback from critical friends. This chapter underscores the iterative process of qualitative research as you search for relationships across thematic patterns. It discusses the way in which interpretation involves exploring empirical data in conversation with extant theory. The chapter notes the interpretive loops through which you articulate a conceptual framework in response to your research question. It prepares you for drawing together a set of ideas that provides the basis for theory building.

Chapter 6 discusses the steps subsequent to synthesizing one's research findings and positioning the work within the literature. It underscores how writing carries with it ethical demands, challenges of representation, and issues of interpretation and deliberation in responding to your research question. The chapter also addresses the nature of research as inherently an ongoing conversation within and across disciplinary boundaries and communities of interest, and the manner in which research findings have the potential to lead to further theorizing and related research endeavors. Additionally, the chapter notes the importance of finding ways to draw those individuals and groups for whom your study is relevant into a discussion of the findings.

In sum, this text consists of three major sections, covering the stages of research and the use of the semi-structured interview as part of a multimethod design. The strength of this book is that it offers undergraduate and graduate students, as well as those in the professions, a pathway into rigorous, reflexive, and action-oriented research through following the bumps and gains of one particular study. I invite you to *think big* when planning your research, providing you with considerable insight into the qualitative tools that are available to you. We will explore the way in which qualitative research draws social scientists into the depth of individual experience embedded within multiple and overlapping contexts throughout the research endeavor. In so doing, the book illustrates how the notion of "semi-structured" can be fully exploited to attend to complex research topics.

Setting the Stage

1

Crafting a Design to Yield a Complete Story

In this chapter, I will lead you through the process of crafting a research design to respond fully to your topic of interest. We'll address the role of building on extant literature and its influence in shaping your research question, methods, and analytical framework. Here, I give special attention to the selection of methods of data collection, particularly the use of semi-structured interviews. I also illustrate how semi-structured interviews allow for the exploration of lived experience as narrated in the interview in relation to theoretical variables of interest. In concert with archival study and oral histories, the semi-structured interview offers great potential to attend to the complexity of a story in need of contextualization.

In laying out the process of crafting a new study, this chapter draws on the example of my initial approach to the desegregation study, the case study that will be used to illustrate the various pieces of the research process in this book. Through the inclusion of examples from the desegregation study, the chapter lays out a process for approaching a study in a way that is attendant to its local meanings as well as broader spheres of influence. The excerpt below from a journal entry recorded early in my study serves as an introduction.

Journal Entry, Desegregation Study
In the summer of 1998 my family moved to Shaker Heights, Ohio, where we enrolled our daughters in the school system. At a gathering that summer among those living on our block, a group comprising mostly white middle-class and affluent families, I told a neighbor how my family was drawn to the city and school system because of its desegregation history. He shrugged and responded, "Sure, it's great if you want to raise your kid in a place where everybody doesn't look like him."

Clearly, racial diversity is valued in the community, however nonchalantly it was expressed by my neighbor. Support has been high in this community for its public schools, with tax levies typically successful in garnering public support. Yet increasingly I have begun to wonder about what residents in the community understand to be the history of the school system's desegregation. What are their thoughts on racial equality? What does it mean to this community, more than 50 years after the *Brown* decision, for its school district to be racially and economically desegregated?

Historically, desegregated districts faced federal scrutiny during the 1960s and 1970s in terms of equal educational opportunity and reducing racial isolation in their systems. From the 1980s forward these systems saw an erosion of judicial support for policy mechanisms used to reduce racial isolation and increase opportunity and outcomes among students of color. The national context has changed greatly over time. How has the district weathered these changes?

Even now, a national reform agenda measures and penalizes public schools for gaps in achievement between students of color and white students but fails to address gaps in material, social, and educational resources that parallel the depressed achievement. How might equality be facilitated within these broader and more local conditions, and how might it also be thwarted—even within this same institution? Moreover, how do I create a design and tell a story not of a single district, but broader and more far-reaching than any one institution?

The district's desegregation history was my general interest, and I understood this topic to be multifaceted and complex. Theoretically, the work involved multiple domains of knowledge across several streams of literature. Methodologically, it demanded a design that reached across narrative, history, law, and policy. At a fundamental level, it was necessary to explore the experiences of individual students, parents, and educators. However, each "experience" is shaped not only by individual agency but also by the structures within which individuals are situated. In this sense, it was important to study the particular structures of the school district—its policies and practices—that shaped individual experiences of schooling. More broadly, schools and school systems do not operate in isolation but are influenced by a larger milieu of social, political, and economic conditions as well as legislative action and judicial decisions at the state and federal levels. History encompasses each of the three levels, reflecting stories told and stories forgotten.

Beginnings: The Role of Extant Literature

The existing literature should inform your development of a research question, selection of methods for data collection, and formulation of an analytical framework. The strength of the research design depends on the clarity of the research question and the extent to which the variables of interest are articulated. To get there, you will steep yourself in the literature on the topic of interest. This may be accessed through research databases, which offer increasingly sophisticated tools. Searching through these databases, using terms related to your topic, will yield considerable sources, including journal articles, books, reports, and other relevant materials.

Your review of current knowledge about your topic of interest is also influenced by dimensions of your experience, including your autobiography and your understanding of the research context. Perhaps you are curious about alternative explanations to those in the existing literature. You might be dissatisfied with gaps, inconsistencies, or uncertainties in current theories. Perhaps you are aware of an angle of vision missing from the literature. Your observations and experience, grounded in the topic, may suggest elements of the topic absent from the academic discourse. As is evident in my journal entry above, your autobiography and life experiences are often wound into the research. While life experiences and familiarity with the research context may bias the research, they will also offer important insights. With considerable reflexivity, your autobiography and its relationship to the topic have the potential to contribute greatly to the research. This will become more evident in later chapters, which demonstrate how reflexivity, which is the process of examining your influence on the construction of the research design and in carrying out research activities, is achieved. Reflexivity is central to qualitative research: it strengthens the rigor of the design by attending to your thought processes, assumptions, decision making, and actions taken in order to locate and explore ethical and methodological dilemmas.

Social Psychological Study of School Desegregation

In the desegregation study, my disciplinary roots directed me toward a social psychological study of school desegregation as the focus of my literature review. However, it became clear that other disciplines and streams of literature would add depth and breadth to my conceptualizing a research design on this topic. I extended my search to include educational policy, classroom practice, the history of desegregation, and desegregation law. Gradually, three domains within the literature weighed in, influencing my thinking about a research question, framework, and design. Figure 1-1 provides a look at the three domains, or streams, of literature.

My review of the literature shaped an emerging understanding of what I might study in the district's desegregation history. The social psychological literature examined the study of intergroup contact, cooperation, and conflict. Questions emerged in my review of the literature concerning the underexplored role of conflict in the study of desegregation. Considerations of conflict as potentially productive in bringing to the surface persistent inequalities informed how I might study desegregation efforts within the district (Apfelbaum, 1979; Apfelbaum & Lubek, 1976; Pettigrew, 1986). Related to the absence of conflict was the literature in educational policy and desegregation law regarding an increasing emphasis on race neutrality, or "color blindness," and the arguments in its favor that found their way into classrooms (Pollock,

Streams of Literature for a Social Psychological Study of Desegregation

Desegregation History	Educational Policy	Social Psychology
intangibles	opportunity structures	contact theory
race consciousness	busing	conflict/cooperation—material sources
deference to white interests	access	
second-generation segregation	tracking	conflict/cooperation—status and identity
diversity—compelling state interest	educational opportunity	social categorization
race neutrality	academic outcomes	relations of power
	social capital and networks	differentiation and personalization
	standards	
	testing	social mobility vs. social change

Figure 1-1. Streams of literature

2004; Schofield, 1982, 1986a, 1986b) and the courts (Orfield & Eaton, 1996; Peller, 1995).

In terms of desegregation law, evident in my literature review was a pattern during and after the 1954 *Brown v. Board of Education* decision. This pattern revealed a tendency to establish desegregation policy least likely to disturb majority white interests in public education, as noted in the late legal scholar Derrick Bell's convergence theory (Bell, 1995). Bell notes that changes in policy or law concerning racial justice occur when the action taken does not threaten existing relations of power. In the convergence of interests, those disadvantaged before the legal remedy or legislation gain relief; however, the arrangement is such that there continues to be some maintenance of privilege. While the *Brown* ruling reversed *Plessy v. Ferguson* and altered history, it also reflected deference to mainstream white interests. In its 1954 ruling, much of the Court's argument turned on black inferiority without noting its complement: white superiority (Cross, 1991; Jackson, 1998). Additionally, the 1955 *Brown II* "all deliberate speed ruling" permitted great latitude among districts regarding the timetable for implementing *Brown*. In this way, the *Brown* decision moved the country toward racial equality even as it created roadblocks for actually achieving this equality.

For some time after *Brown*, educational leaders appeared to focus on maintaining white loyalty and avoiding a white exit from schools (Hirschman, 1970). In so doing, the leaders maintained financial stability and sustained social connections with middle-class whites and a broad array of institutions—the "intangibles" as noted in *Sweatt v. Painter* (1950). This ensured that schools retained not only material resources but also the social capital and networks necessary for students to fully realize education as a property of power (Wells & Crain, 1997).

Although Supreme Court rulings in the 1960s and early 1970s increasingly articulated the means to achieve racial integration, school districts across the country frequently engaged in change efforts that were less likely to impact white students and their families. Public school systems sustained white loyalty by employing the following strategies: delaying desegregation; implementing token desegregation by retaining racially intact classes and activities; putting black students into remedial or general education academic tracks and placing white students in magnet programs or honors academic tracks; too readily suspending and expelling African American students; laying off African American teachers while retaining white faculty; busing black children more frequently and for longer distances; closing schools that served black students, rather than sending white children to these schools, and addressing overcrowding in predominantly black schools by building new schools deep within black neighborhoods rather than at locations where white and black neighborhoods shared contiguous borders (Jefferson, 1991; Orfield, 1978, 1983; Orfield & Eaton, 1996; Wells, Holme, Revilla, & Atanda, 2009; Whyte, 2003).

Given this historical background, I was interested in exploring whether there were junctures in the history of the Shaker Heights district that reflected a willingness to *displace long-established patterns of race and class privilege* in order to reduce racial exclusion. Or were national trends of reluctance toward altering existing arrangements of white privilege evident in the district's policies and practices? Over a 40-year period, to what extent had opportunity structures become accessible to students of color?

Anticipating that these historical junctures would be evident, I paid careful attention to the emergence of policies and practices that did *not* replicate broader societal power relations shaped by race and class. These structures were likely to move schools and the school district toward facilitating racial equality in terms of educational opportunity and academic outcomes. In doing so, they were less likely to reinforce racial stereotypes and sustain inequality. In designing the project, I anticipated that I would locate these educational structures, which I defined a priori as *transformative.* I also anticipated in my design the emergence of policies and practices that did not include strategies or interventions to reduce racial inequality. I identified these educational structures a priori as *replicative.*

Moving from Literature Review to Formulation of a Research Question

As evident in my discussion of the desegregation study, the literature review plays a key role in your formulation of a research question. Other influences include your experience with the phenomenon of interest. As you work your way through the literature review, maintain a file of useful articles and an annotated bibliography of each relevant source. Your annotation should include a summary of the source and a discussion of the way in which the source is related to your topic. These notes often become the basis for your later writing, whether that be a dissertation prospectus, a grant proposal, a conference presentation, or a journal article. Additionally, the notes inform your thinking about your design, particularly the formulation of your research question.

The research question provides a compass that will serve you well for the duration of the project. It shapes the analytical framework, which drives the data collection and ongoing analysis of data. A research question that is purposeful in its articulation of the phenomenon under study will serve as a reliable foundation in the design of the research. The primary variables of interest should be included in the research question, and each variable should be articulated in a manner that informs both you and the participants. Whether the variable of interest is completely grounded in participant experience or is defined a priori through a particular theory, the language used in the research question should be well developed and clear. Every word in the research question should be purposeful: the leaner the question the better. Sometimes a researcher will pose an overarching question, with a few subquestions that elaborate on the key areas of study.

The Research Question for the Desegregation Study: Empirical and Theoretical Anchors

In the desegregation study, the research question needed to be sufficiently open to enable me to elicit data grounded in the experiences of the study participants. It also needed to offer me and my participants room for exploring the phenomenon under study, while retaining some relationship to the theoretical anchors in the literature. I set out to explore the relationships, structures, and the sociopolitical contexts at work in the district as it desegregated over time. This meant locating the lived experiences of students, parents, and educators across races and class within broader institutional and societal structures over a period of nearly 40 years. The research question and the constructs of interest were formulated from the study of interpersonal and intergroup relations, educational policy and practice, and desegregation law. While the design was deeply social psychological, it was also interdisciplinary. My research question addressed two central areas: the experience of racial equality and the conceptualizations of equality within a desegregated district. The question was as follows: In the context of school desegregation, how have parents, students, and educators across race and class *experienced* and *conceptualized* racial equality?

In this way, experience grounded in participants' narratives would be studied in relation to educational structures, which were the policies and practices that participants encountered at a particular period in the district's history. The theoretical underpinnings of *equality* in the study design were influenced by my literature review. I defined racial equality in the following manner: *providing equal educational opportunities, producing equal academic outcomes, and engendering equal power relations between students of color and white students*. As in my design, in my research question I created a tension between *what participants might narrate* as an experience of racial equality and *my theoretically informed definition of equality*. There was sufficient evidence in the literature to warrant my use of "transformative" and "replicative" as theoretical constructs through which I would analyze educational structures. Nevertheless, I remained open to finding that these theoretical constructs might be complicated by the empirical data and thematic patterns emerging from the study. In this way, the study entertained from the beginning a potential tension between the theoretical and empirical. It offered dialectical space for data and theory to converse (Lather, 1986) as the study proceeded.

Developing a Plan for Data Analysis

In your research design, you will need to include a data analysis plan. The plan details how you will organize your data once they have been collected and how you will draw meaning from them. In planning for your analysis, consider what you are looking for and how you will know you have found it. A good starting point is your disciplinary knowledge base. If there is extant theory as it relates to the terms you have included in your research question, then dimensions of the theory provide clues as to what you will look for in the data. As you move along, you may find that the data related to your research question have complicated extant theory or have introduced dimensions yet unexplored in the literature. You will label these data, using terms that reflect the meaning generated by them. Your analysis plan prepares you for this process and sets the stage for you to code, or name, chunks of data, and later you can cluster these codes as they exhibit relationships with other coded data. This will lead to your conceptualizing a response to your research question.

As noted earlier, you may have found the literature to be dismissive of or to lack important consideration related to the topic of your interest. In this case, your analysis plan may be more open-ended as it relates to theory. The process of analyzing your data remains systematic nonetheless. The plan will lay out how you will work your way through a close reading of the data, looking for thematic patterns, reflecting ideas that emerge, and offering a meaningful response to your research question. As you proceed in your research, this plan will help you to locate instances within the data connected to the topic of your interest.

It will outline how you will document these instances and explore them in more depth in an ongoing manner as the data collection proceeds and analysis continues.

Your articulation of a research question is a starting point and is reflective of what you and others understand *now* about your research topic. The data analysis plan should leave open the possibility that meaning unanticipated at the onset of the research may emerge from the data sources, producing new knowledge grounded in the research context. This is the particular strength of qualitative research as it offers an inductive approach, allowing for an iterative and ongoing pursuit of meaning.

Your analysis plan is also supported by the interpretive tradition that informs your research design. An interpretive tradition provides guidance in terms of the role of the researcher, and it offers a particular view toward inquiry and the generation of knowledge. There may be specific approaches toward data collection and analysis within an interpretive tradition, or the tradition may instead more broadly inform how you think about interpretation. The interpretive tradition also offers guidance as you run into ethical and methodological dilemmas during the research. It reflects philosophical debates concerning knowledge construction and validity claims, and it connects you to a history within your discipline or across disciplines related to the science and ethics of research. It is important to be explicit about the interpretive tradition guiding your research design and to draw on this tradition, particularly in your use of reflexivity, during which you document actions you have taken and decisions made as you proceed in the research, with a careful study of how these events may have influenced the direction of the research.

Desegregation Study: The Theoretical Framework and
Its Influence on Analysis

In the desegregation study, I was guided by the interpretive tradition of critical theory. As a theoretical tradition that offers an orientation for my work, critical theory provides a framework for understanding and studying social relations. These relations are not detached from history or current structural conditions, involving legal, economic,

educational, and social practices, ideologies, and norms. While critical theory attends to the constraints individuals and groups experience,
it frames structural limitations in tension with human agency, making
room for the study of how relations of power are sustained and reinforced as well as how they are countered, played against, and thwarted.
This interpretive tradition has a long history, with origins in the work
of Karl Marx in the 19th century and the Frankfurt School before and
after World War II. Its roots have been complicated and nourished by
an ongoing engagement of theory and practice, particularly critical race
theory, feminist theory, queer theory, liberation psychology, and critical
pedagogy, toward understanding and humanizing relations at local and
global levels.

As an orientation that informed my research design, critical theory
offered a way to study a school district's desegregation history. This is
most evident in my analysis plan. For my data analysis, I studied the
experience as narrated by participants within different opportunity
structures in this district situated within the period of 1965 to 2003. My
analysis also involved a study of the national legal and educational policy context impinging upon the district. Thus the analytical framework
guiding the research was multilayered and textured. The participants'
narratives would be studied within a particular historical period, certain educational structures, and a constellation of relationships as well
as the events, discourse, and trends of a broader sociopolitical context.
Locating lived experience in historical, legal, and policy-oriented contexts would increase the degree of confidence in the interpretations I
would make. The research design would allow for a full exploration of
the complexity of the data. It would provide a critical shift back and
forth between individual experience and structural conditions, allowing for the full realization of the way in which structure and agency are
in frequent tension (Sewell, 1992).

The impact of my review of the literature and my familiarity with
the context of school desegregation are evident in figure 1-2, which
depicts my formulation of the analytical framework and variables of
interest for my study. The review was influential in shaping the outer
core of the analytical frame—the sociopolitical conditions realized
through history that impinge upon schools and communities, including the impact of the law. A second key area in the literature was the

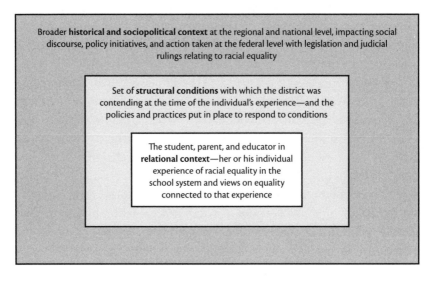

Anticipated Levels of Analysis

Broader **historical and sociopolitical context** at the regional and national level, impacting social discourse, policy initiatives, and action taken at the federal level with legislation and judicial rulings relating to racial equality

Set of **structural conditions** with which the district was contending at the time of the individual's experience—and the policies and practices put in place to respond to conditions

The student, parent, and educator in **relational context**—her or his individual experience of racial equality in the school system and views on equality connected to that experience

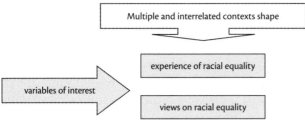

Multiple and interrelated contexts shape

experience of racial equality

variables of interest

views on racial equality

Figure 1-2. Levels of analysis for the desegregation study

study of educational policy and practice in desegregated schools. This formed the middle core of the analysis—the inquiry about educational structures in the district within which students were positioned. It also helped to inform questions in the interview protocol. Third, the literature review included a social psychological focus on intergroup, intragroup, and interpersonal relations. This focus on individual and group experience shaped the central core of the analytical framework, particularly students' relational experience in school—their sense of self in relation to other individuals and groups.

How did these levels of analysis become evident? To a large extent,

they emerged from notes and diagrams I drafted, informed by my literature review. As I read journal articles, book chapters, and scholarly
reports, I penciled in responses to the text within the margins and filled
up notepads to convey my early formulation of ideas generated from
the scholarship. In this way, the literature review is integral to informing and strengthening your research design.

In the desegregation study, then, constructing multiple and intercon-
nected frames of study permitted the research focus to shift from one
frame to the other, moving or oscillating from the local, or individual
level, to the structural and sociopolitical levels (Weis & Fine, 2004).
The framework allowed for an analysis at multiple levels, through
which the data could be assessed for their trustworthiness and consistency in meaning in relation to data from other sources or methods. It
would also allow me to uncover contradictions in the data. Gauging the
degree to which data are trustworthy, often referred to as triangulation,
would not necessarily rule out contradiction. A qualitative research
design allows for a tug in meaning in the data, as will be discussed in
later chapters.

Methods: Guided by Theory, Open to Lived Experience

The nature of your research question guides your decisions about
method. While practical issues, such as limitations in terms of time
and cost and access to sites or participants, enter into considerations
about methods, these should not drive the early design. In your early
development of a research design, it is important to consider the following: What methods show the greatest promise in studying this
research topic? In what way does the interpretive tradition guiding this
study relate to the methods I am considering? What challenges might
arise with my use of a particular method or set of methods? How might
I respond to these challenges and still remain close to the intent of
the research?

Given your consideration of these questions, you may find that while
a certain set of methods would be ideal, you are able to carry out only
a slice of the project, with perhaps the wider array of methods being
part of future research plans. This should be noted, as it will be useful in the future. This documentation of methodological choices and

decisions will lay the groundwork for an ongoing process of reflexivity, as you deliberate why you have acted as you have and what guides those actions. Tracing these junctures in your journey is helpful in addressing questions later as you report back to a wider public about this research.

Qualitative researchers may use a single-method approach, a mix of quantitative and qualitative methods, or multiple qualitative methods. Methods such as participant observation and interviewing—from in-depth interviews to impromptu exchanges amid everyday activities—are frequently employed. The degree of structure within an interview may vary, ranging from unstructured to semi-structured, depending on the nature of your research question and your interpretive orientation. Another useful method, focus groups, allows for the generation of meaning not only with individuals but also with a group of individuals, who will often assist in clarifying and amplifying meaning as well as underscoring nuances and multiple angles of vision. A focus group may precede or follow a round of individual interviews focused on the same topic of study. Surveys provide a different type of format for collecting data, and they may be used in descriptive analysis with a more qualitative approach or move into the quantitative domain through the use of inferential statistical analysis. Performance methods involve participants in the exploration of a topic through various genres of creative expression at the data collection, analysis, and reporting back phases of research.

The array of methods available in the social sciences is often overwhelming as you consider what method is a good fit for the purpose of your research. Your selection of a method may be influenced ultimately by practical concerns, such as time, cost, and proximity to sites and participants. Additionally, the interpretive tradition often informs the choice of the method and the particular way it is carried out. A key criterion is the potential the method offers to explore in a systematic and informed manner the topic of your study.

Desegregation Study: The Multimethod Research Design

In the desegregation study, my efforts to explore *experience* and *conceptualizations* of racial equality within a desegregated district necessitated

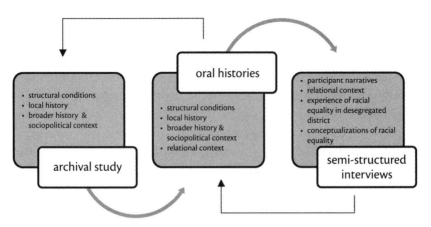

Figure 1-3. Multimethod research design for the desegregation study

methods of data collection that attended to individual experience and context. In terms of context, I looked at the history of the institution and its policy responses over time to its increasingly diverse community. I could then situate individual experience and conceptualizations of racial equality within this context. In my efforts to probe institutional memory, I employed archival study and oral history as methods responsive to the historical, structural, and sociopolitical context. The archival study and oral histories served the design well in terms of collecting data responsive to the two outer layers of the analytical framework. These methods assisted me in analyzing educational structures to the degree that they facilitated racial equality as I had defined it based on my review of the literature.

However, the central core of the analytical framework would have remained constrained had I not pursued a means for understanding the individual experience of students, parents, and educators. This is where the semi-structured interview was crucial to addressing my research question. This method offered insight into individual experience, enabling me to explore participants' narratives of experience and views of racial equality within a desegregated school district. The semi-structured interview promised to yield a more complete story as it related to my research focus. Figure 1-3 illustrates the research design for the desegregation study.

The Semi-Structured Interview: Space for the Empirical and Theoretical

The semi-structured interview provides a repertoire of possibilities. It is sufficiently structured to address specific topics related to the phenomenon of study, while leaving space for participants to offer new meanings to the study focus. It may be used as the sole method in a research design or it could be one of several methods. There is a great deal of versatility in the semi-structured interview, and the arrangement of questions may be structured to yield considerable and often multidimensional streams of data. As a hybrid method, the semi-structured interview can be structured into segments, moving from fully openended questions toward more theoretically driven questions as the interview progresses. The grounded data, elicited early on, provide the context for exploring participants' understanding of the phenomenon under study. A key benefit of the semi-structured interview is its attention to lived experience while also addressing theoretically driven variables of interest.

The semi-structured interview offers great potential to attend to the complexity of your research topic. It allows for the engagement of the participant with segments of the interview, each progressively more structured. It can be carried out in one sitting, or several, and it allows for considerable reciprocity between the participant and the researcher. This reciprocity, or give and take, creates space for the researcher to probe a participant's responses for clarification, meaning making, and critical reflection. A great deal can be accomplished within the semi-structured interview, as long as you give considerable thought to the preparation of the questions included in the interview.

Multiple Methods: Working with Archival Materials and Oral Histories

Developing a semi-structured interview within a multimethod study is one way to *think big* about one's variables and methods for addressing a research question. Multiple methods contribute to the depth and breadth of your analysis, interpretation of findings, and theorizing about the implications of your study. The following section discusses the use of archival study and oral histories in general and in relation to the desegregation study.

Archival Study

Archival materials include newspaper clippings, meeting minutes, maps, charts, tables, photographs, video footage, external studies, and other forms of documentation. Archival data provide a historical record of events, discourse, stakeholders, and images. They draw researchers into both the everyday activities and the significant historical moments of a community or institution or some social unit. Data from archival materials also may directly or indirectly reflect the economic or political conditions and legal matters that impact the setting at various historical periods. Additionally, your study of archival data may inform the development of other data-collection instruments, such as questions and probes within a semi-structured interview protocol.

Resources for archival materials are plentiful. Libraries are a major source of data. They frequently contain specialized collections, as they are often the first institution to which people turn when contributing historical documents. Libraries specialize in organizing and cataloguing archival materials, so a search within a special collection is likely to be productive in terms of locating relevant data. Increasingly, through the use of digital technology, important documents can be scanned and saved for future viewing and analysis. Additionally, there is a cadre of very knowledgeable librarians passionate about and committed to preserving history and making historical materials available to the public.

Another source of archival data is the archival department of the news media, particularly local journals and newspapers as well as regional and national media. Older material is often still contained on microfiche, though it, too, is increasingly being digitized. Newspaper and magazine articles, along with the photographs, maps, and charts they include, provide rich and informative data. These may be accessible through the Internet. Frequently, however, by visiting the archival department itself you are likely to secure the most data and to have direct access to a wide assortment of material.

Should a particular institution or organization be the focus of your study, or connected to your focus, the institution itself is often a major source of archival data. Much invaluable archival material remains within institutions, whether it is organized or not. Recordkeeping is often carried out unevenly, and those with tight budgets and scarce resources are less likely to have an archival department. The looseness of such document organization might result in an institution's reluctance to provide access to an outsider. Confidential material might be mixed up with pertinent letters, meeting minutes, or daily memos. Additionally, archival materials may have been lost or destroyed as institutional policies for preserving archival material may not be in place. Nevertheless, approaching and engaging the institution in your archival study is often fruitful, and it may be instructive for the institution itself.

As you review archival materials, you should create a system for recording key documents as part of the data collection. Primary descriptors of each item should be noted, including the type of item, date issued, stated purpose, pertinent quotes, and relationship to other items. Very important items can be scanned and made into a PDF file for later analysis and possible inclusion in various forms of reporting on the research. Depending on your need for archival data, you can determine approximately how wide a net to cast in terms of collecting archival materials. In the next section I discuss my use of archival materials in the desegregation study.

PROBING INSTITUTIONAL MEMORY: ARCHIVAL REVIEW IN THE DESEGREGATION STUDY

To piece together the district's history in the desegregation study, I used three key archival sources. First, the local newspaper had its archival files, which I reviewed, mostly on microfiche. The newspaper articles provided information on issues concerning the schools and the city itself. They also described the social context of different time periods. Letters to the editor, feature articles, and photographs revealed trends over time and provided very useful data. I also received the local newspaper and the larger regional paper, and I maintained a file of relevant articles from my arrival in Shaker Heights in 1998 onward.

Second, the city had a substantial collection of archival materials in both its public library and its historical society. Many individuals who served on various school or city committees had contributed their documents to these archival repositories. The main branch library, once Moreland School, now houses the Moreland Archival Room, where I spent many days poring over yearbooks, meeting minutes, district reports, school enrollment zone maps, photographs, video recordings, and other sources critical to the district's history.

Third, the district superintendent made available historical documents, correspondence, and other materials. These artifacts were pertinent to the early years as far back as 1965, before and following the voluntary desegregation program in 1970 through the reorganization of the district in 1987. The school system has a long tradition of partnering with outside researchers to study and improve its policies and practices, so the superintendent encouraged me to avail myself of resources that would move the work along. In addition to meeting with several district officials, I had access to a room full of dusty boxes containing documents related to the district's desegregation. It was a feast. There was way too much to look at and I spent a good deal of time wading through documents, some of which were useful. In the end, I would not have approached the task any differently. It was impossible to anticipate which boxes would yield data related to my research question. Nonetheless, it was a significant investment of my time, and it dragged out this phase of the study considerably.

In the desegregation study, the archival review occurred early in the research process in order to document the district's history. Archival material provided information on dates, events, trends, district discourse, and community perceptions. From this, I developed a chronology of the district's desegregation history, and I connected national events related to desegregation law and policy to local events. The chronology provided data for the middle and outer levels of analysis —structural conditions and the historical and sociopolitical context. The archival data informed the development of the interview protocol and provided sufficient historical and policy context to engage participants in questions intended to facilitate my analysis of their narrative in relation to this context. These data also assisted in establishing a pool of possible participants for the oral histories or the semi-structured interviews.

Additionally, archival data suggested thematic codes that might have important analytical weight. For example, archival material contained a great deal of information concerning educational policy and practice in the district. Use of school newsletters, local newspapers, reports on student enrollment data, photographs, and films provided ample material in terms of the educational structures that participants narrated as part of their experience later in the interviews. Figure 1-4 is a sample archival data entry on educational programs and high school facility space that had distinguished students "down there" from "regular high school" and the "normal classroom situation." As will become evident in

Archival item: Film tape 10, (2-2), dated 8/31/78, entitled "Alternative School." One of a series of film segments featuring aspects of the Shaker schools. Located in Moreland Archival Room, Shaker Heights Main Branch Public Library.

Comments: Discussion of alternative school—in high school. Note the use of language "down here," highlighted below, to describe the location of the alternative school in the basement and its components. Interesting emphasis on "caring."

"Down here it seems like they care more," says a black female student featured in the film. A white female student responds similarly. High school principal Paul Murphy states in the film, "We recruit them for the alternative school, try to get them down there to make some kind of adjustment, again to get them back to [the] normal classroom situation. Our ultimate goal is to graduate these students." Also from principal: "The chances of some of these students making it in a normal classroom situation are nil." Also, there are rules "down there" and "they're controlled down there . . ." The narrator points out that the students take some courses in the "regular high school," adding, "They are, after all, a part of that school."

Yolanda McKinney, appears to have leadership role in the program, states: "Most of my young people are very bright kids . . . have ability but not drive." A number of black students are visible, one white male student and two other white students— including earlier featured white female, who says, "Upstairs it doesn't make any difference to them."

Figure 1-4. Sample archival data entry on educational programs and facility space

later chapters, this early pattern of specialization of programs in terms of opportunities, outcomes, and location within a catalogue of course offerings suggested some degree of structural boundary making, positioning students "down there" and "upstairs" within school buildings.

However, the emergence of potential themes and my early rendering of the chronology of the district's desegregation history were incomplete and not sufficiently trustworthy with the archival data as my only source of data. The research design included oral histories as an additional method of data collection and as a way of checking on the data collected through the archives. As noted below, the oral histories provided another major data source for formulating my chronology of the district's desegregation history, and, ultimately, they further textured the context emerging from the archival data.

Oral Histories

Oral histories are rich in perspective, memory, and metaphor. The use of oral histories as a method of data collection preserves knowledge often existing outside of historical documents and secondary sources. They can illuminate a particular historical moment. They also document a culture and a way of life, in order to provide some rendering of time and space that may only be accessible as long as there are individuals to speak about it.

As with all methods, the use of oral history is shaped by the research question and the purpose of the research. These are identified for a participant prior to the first meeting in which an oral history is recorded. Participants are asked to shed light on a historical moment because they possess a particular knowledge sought by the researcher. The extent to which that knowledge is tapped relies on the researcher's ability to listen closely, ask pertinent questions, pursue points of clarification, and give the participant room to generate a narrative. In some studies, the researcher comes prepared with historical reference points, often secured through a study of archival material and through data collected from other oral histories. These points of reference become places from which the researcher and participant can probe history. In other approaches to oral history, the emphasis is more broadly on a time and place, the ways of thinking and doing, and the particularities of the participant's life within the rhythm of daily events and traditions. Oral histories frequently offer participants an opportunity to revisit a significant period of time in their lives, which can be very meaningful to them. In this way, collecting oral histories benefits not only those who access this history in the future, but also those participants who revisit and reflect on some dimensions of their lives.

FORMULATING A HISTORICAL CONTEXT: ORAL HISTORY IN THE DESEGREGATION STUDY

My primary goal in using oral history in the desegregation study was to formulate a historical context in which I could situate participant experience as narrated in the semi-structured interview. In many ways, the oral histories provided me with an opportunity to verify the accuracy of the historical chronology I was developing. This type of validation is also known as a "member check." It helps you check on the meaning of the data you are collecting and the trustworthiness of your interpretation of those data. To accomplish this, I often brought along with me a list of dates, quoted text, and notes from the archives to my sessions with key stakeholders from whom I collected oral histories. I frequently began my session with the individual focused on the developing chronology of the district's desegregation. Opening with considerable "talk" on my part, I then worked through the chronology, in order to check, clarify, explore, and understand the key events and programs and policies in place in the schools and the particular set of sociopolitical pressures upon the district. Most important, I hoped to uncover junctures in the district's history that may or may not have been evident in the archival material, revealing institutional grappling with conceptualizations of racial equality. I referred to these sessions as "conversations" to underscore my pragmatic use of oral history in the research design.

In terms of the oral histories, it is useful to look at the relationship between purpose and structure briefly here. My oral histories, or "conversations," were not designed to explore directly the topic central to my study: the experience of racial equality and conceptualizations of equality. Instead, these sessions were intended to verify as much as possible the district's desegregation history. The session was thus structured according to the chronology of events connected with the participant, reading from excerpts of archival texts in order to jog the participant's memory and to prime the participant for his or her reflections on that particular event or period of time. This approach did not preclude participants from offering their perspectives and interpretations of events. In each "conversation," there were instances during which I created openings for the participant to offer a narrative and an alternative interpretation of the chronology emerging from the archival material. However, the "conversations" contrast with the semi-structured interviews that followed later in my research. As discussed in the next chapter, the semi-structured interview was designed to elicit participants' experiences of racial equality within a desegregated district and their conceptualizations of racial equality. To do this, my semi-structured interview protocol was considerably different from the oral history protocol.

My selection of participants for the "conversations" was guided by two criteria: (1) their active involvement in a particular period of the district's desegregation history; and (2) their likelihood of representing a particular constituency, racial group, and angle of vision. Most of the participants were identified in the archives and many held crucial leadership positions. Unlike the semi-structured interviews, for which I declined use of the snowball technique for gathering names of participants, in the oral histories I gladly accepted names and pursued those contacts. The historical chronology would only be as comprehensive as the diversity of stakeholders and the range of historical moments in which they were most deeply involved. The individuals with whom I met included those who were or had been members of the board of education, district superintendents, elected officials, and community and religious leaders. I had planned to collect 12 oral histories but ended up with 22, some of which required travel to states where the individuals were residing. Some sessions ran an hour in length. Several were as long as three hours. Some were perfunctory. Others clearly offered the participant an opportunity to reminisce about a moment in time during which he or she had labored intensely in some key aspect of the district's desegregation and attention to racial equality.

In terms of organizing the oral history data, I recorded the sessions by audiotape, and I listened to each oral history several times. My transcriptions varied from one participant to another. While some transcriptions were verbatim and were more than 100 pages, other sessions were transcribed somewhat more loosely, following the order of the session but not being transcribed word for word. Sections of a conversation that appeared important to the development of a historical chronology were noted and transcribed verbatim, where exact wording and meaning were important. This approach to transcription runs the risk that something might be missed. A researcher is never fully sure what is "important" early on in the research. As the purpose of these conversations was the construction of a chronology of historical events, the data I sought were in the participants' introduction of new information or information that contradicted, extended, or provided nuance to the archival data.

In addition to helping me to detail the chronology, these conversations also introduced attention to particular junctures in the district's history: the district's first effort to desegregate, subsequent policies to reduce racial imbalance in schools, and efforts to maintain the district's reputation for high academic standards. The history helped to develop the semi-structured interview protocol and it enhanced my ability later to probe participants during the interviews. The context it provided could be referenced during the semi-structured interviews with students, parents, and educators. Further, the data from the oral histories contributed greatly to the analysis, as they informed the structural and sociopolitical levels of my analytical framework.

The oral histories added flesh and spirit to the skeletal chronology. They introduced me to the thought processes, strategizing, and behind-the-scenes activities at work in the district and community regarding school policy and practice. Frequently these stories were not evident in existing documents. Although the archival data provided sufficient information to draft a chronology of district policies and practices, they could not fill in the depth of insight and experience related to these historical moments. The oral histories provided the perspective of those deeply involved in the district's desegregation.

While the oral histories and archival materials provided historical context, the archival data were also instrumental in building a pool of potential participants. The next section discusses an important consideration in your research design: the recruitment and selection of study participants.

Participant Recruitment

Deliberating over specific procedures for identifying potential study participants is not trivial. How one proceeds is very important because it will influence the data collection and analysis. Consider your research question. What individuals are most likely to offer responses relevant to your research question? Where might there be gaps in locating diverse perspectives and experiences as it relates to your research question? How will you fill in those gaps?

Qualitative research does not involve random sampling of participants in the statistical sense. The design is most faithful to the research question when you have formulated criteria for the selection of participants. For example, would the research benefit from the participation of individuals from a particular profession, geographical location, or affiliation? How will you select participants in order to ensure a full representation of perspectives and experience as it relates to your research topic? In order to secure a pool of possible participants, how will you recruit them? For example, you might post fliers in the research context, inviting individuals to contact you should they have an interest in participating. You might approach individuals directly, informed by some dimensions of their experiences that need to be represented in your study. Whether you approach directly or indirectly, you should provide sufficient information about the purpose of the research, the degree of involvement expected of the participant (time and type of activity), and (briefly) how the data will be used. As interest is generated and participants volunteer, you might decide to select one participant over another in order to address the breadth of representation you are trying to achieve in the research.

While the number of participants you determine for your study is often influenced by issues of time, cost, and other practicalities, the most ideal approach is to continue recruiting participants until you feel that the interview data are no longer producing new thematic patterns. In other words, there's a kind of saturation point. When you are limited by time, cost, or other practicalities, it is important to note the areas in which you find that questions persist. This documentation is useful to the wider community that will read your work and for those (including yourself) who will build on it.

To help you document the extent to which participants have contributed to the dimensions you have identified as important to your research question, create a matrix with columns for each dimension of importance and create rows in which to list participants by code names or pseudonyms. This is useful before your participant selection; afterward, you can use it to continue to consider how thoroughly you have achieved participation among individuals offering experience and perspectives in the dimensions important to your research question.

Building a Pool of Participants That Were Representative of the District History and Potential Dimensions of Student Schooling Experience

My original intent in the desegregation study was to recruit participants for the semi-structured interview through the use of "network sampling" (LeCompte & Schensul, 1999), a kind of "snowball" approach. This procedure involves asking each participant, typically at the close of the interview, for a recommendation of other individuals who might also be willing to participate. However, I became increasingly concerned that I would be unable to keep the names of my study participants confidential. As the study moved along, I noted the names of individuals identified during interviews as participants narrated their experiences, but I did not directly ask participants to suggest others.

The greatest source of names of possible participants was the archival data. These data provided more leads in locating potential participants than the namedropping during the oral histories or interviews. In figure 1-5 are notes from my archival study. I had reviewed yearbooks from Ludlow School, during the early to mid-1980s, when Ludlow also served as the site of the district's enrichment program. From these yearbooks, I obtained names and added them to a pool of potential participants. The yearbooks also often provided information regarding potential student participants' club memberships and courses and some approximation, problematic nonetheless, of their racial backgrounds.

The archives not only inspired my list of potential participants, but also clued me in regarding possible emerging themes. In this case, through my archival study I noted early traces of what became a thematic pattern: the impermeability of boundaries between the regular

From: Moreland Library Archival Room, collected 12/20/02, Ludlow School yearbooks, reflecting elements of Ludlow's magnet program. Ludlow served as the elementary school for this increasingly black neighborhood and the site for an enrichment magnet, enrolling students from across the district during the 1980s before district reorganization in 1987.

Comments: There's a pattern here, increasingly clear by third grade and stark by fourth grade: a majority white class and racially mixed (and typically majority black) class, both of which stayed relatively intact through sixth grade. There are seven students who moved between these intact classes in my study of five yearbooks (82–83; 83–84; 84–85; 85–86; 86–87—the last year Ludlow was open).

from majority black classes to majority white classes: two white boys, one African American boy, and three African American girls

from majority white classes to a majority black classes: one African American girl

Figure 1-5. Sample archival entry based on a review of yearbooks

and gifted program and the degree to which the gifted program was racially identifiable. This finding from my archival study was also evident in data from the semi-structured interviews, where students narrated having many of the same friends year after year within the higher course levels in grades 7 through 12. While this may not be unusual as school friendships are formed, the repeated presence of the same core group of students at the highest course levels and at the lowest course levels complicated the narrative of an "open" level system and the district's discourse of student choice and course-level accessibility. Additionally, the way in which the gifted program was predominantly white and the general courses in the high school were predominantly black introduced further questions about how students might understand their participation within the system of course levels and how it might influence their thinking about themselves and others in terms of ability and motivation to learn.

My criteria for participant selection required that the sample be racially balanced and representative of the range of perspectives and experiences in the district. The study of archival data informed my participant recruitment and selection not only through access to names but also through the study of the district's desegregation history, building a context from which "representativeness" could be assessed. In the archival entries, whenever possible, I looked for a match between names listed in the archives and those listed in the regional phone book, which offered some promise I might be able to reach them.

My participant observation in the community and schools extended my reach, particularly in recruiting participants who could narrate more recent experiences of the school district. As a parent whose children attended two different elementary schools, as well as the district-wide upper elementary, middle, and high schools, I had access to the schools and the parent community in a way in which an outsider did not. As I met parents and grandparents of children within the district, some attending school at that time and others who had graduated, I added names to the pool of participants. From this, I selected those who offered representativeness in terms of *race, gender, age, family composition, neighborhood* (an approximation of *socioeconomic background*), and the *nature of interaction* and *use of programs* within the schools.

In the desegregation study, my strategy in recruiting participants was to convey the research goals accurately and to make clear to the individual the value of her or his participation in the study. I prepared a script, because I did not trust myself to remember the points I wanted to convey concisely. Because a good number of participants were identified through the reading of the archival materials, the initial contact was often via a cold call. Few of those I actually reached declined. Nonetheless, there were instances where I left several phone messages but received no reply. On many occasions, however, the individual responded with interest and we were able to arrange an interview. What I was asking of my participants was more than their time —it was their story.

Although I had planned on having 36 participants (12 students, 12 parents, 12 educators), I did not think the breadth of experience had been sufficiently exhausted when I reached that number. There were still gaps in perspectives and an absence of participants familiar with specific historical periods or district policies. In particular, there was a need to collect more data from students and alumni. From time to time during the study, well into the semi-structured interviews, I returned to the archives to locate the name of a possible student participant, aware that the participant sample had a gap in its representativeness. For example, I returned to several current-phase high school yearbooks to locate a student who participated in Semanteme, a poetry club at the high school. Semanteme solicited poems from students each year, reviewed and selected poems, and published them in an attractive monograph, which was disseminated and given considerable prestige. Like the student newspaper, Semanteme was a club that drew mostly white students. I had recently interviewed a black student, from whom I learned about poetry slams occurring in the city and in the high school cafeteria. These slams drew together many black students and appeared to be spaces of creativity and recognition. There seemed to be little evidence of connections between Semanteme and the poetry slams. The parallel worlds of these two artistic endeavors, drawing students from very different race and class backgrounds, suggested the need for further inquiry. Interviewing a student who participated in Semanteme would offer a useful perspective. Figure 1-6 shows a script I prepared for a "cold call" to a student whose name was included in one of the yearbooks and whose family phone number I was able to locate in the phone book.

As I have noted, the key criterion for participants in the desegregation study was that the sample be racially balanced, recognizing that the "social significance of race" in the United States has produced very divergent experiences between blacks and whites (Jones, 1998) and that it represented a range of experiences and perspectives. The study sample reflected the student demographics of the school system. In the 2002–2003 school year, the high school enrollment of 1,717 reflected a student body of 51.1% African American, 1.5% Asian or Pacific Islander, 1.7% Hispanic, 3.1% multiracial, and 42.6% white.[1] A participant's race was established during the semi-structured interview, when

> **Script**: My name is Anne Galletta, and I am a graduate student working on a study on the desegregation of the Shaker schools. As part of my research I have been speaking to students, parents, and educators connected to the schools from the 1960s through the present about their experience with the schools. I've been reviewing yearbooks and looking at clubs and student activities. I called because I noticed in the [year] yearbook [student's name] was quoted as a member of Semanteme. This club's activities were of interest to me, and I wondered if [student's name] would be willing to talk with me about the Semanteme experience as well as the experience as a student in the district?
>
> **Notes**: Got [student's] dad. He took some time to talk with me. Noted the family chose to live in Shaker Heights because of the diversity and wide variety of opportunities. He described theater as one of the opportunities available to students and noted there was sometimes an overlap between those who participated in theater and those in Semanteme. Also told me that Semanteme was "pretty segregated." Before we got off the phone, he also provided me with the names of several other students whom I might contact, although he didn't give me phone numbers, nor did I ask for them. In mentioning them he also noted the colleges they are attending, such as MIT, Yale, and Carnegie Mellon.

Figure 1-6. Script for "cold call" to student, whose name and club participation was noted in high school yearbook

I asked participants, "To which racial group would you identify yourself as belonging?"

My attention to the category of race was questioned by several participants. Their critique of "race" as a category underscored how the study had the potential to reinforce the very inequalities it ultimately sought to redress. Guided by their caution and that of the literature, I approached my analysis and my writing on the research with an expressed understanding that categories of race are best understood as constructions that are formulated in a social context. At the same time, I remained attuned to the material and psychological consequences of these social constructions. Influenced by my study of the literature, I understood these consequences to have differentially impacted the education, employment, and housing, among many other conditions, of blacks and whites. My study of the literature prior to creating my research design had underscored how these formulations and their consequences have a circular, interdependent relationship (Apfelbaum, 1979), whereby social constructions of race shape psychological and material consequences and the consequences, in turn, powerfully reinforce the social constructions (Opotow, 1995; Ryan, 1971/1976).

The sample also was diverse in terms of constituencies or roles, including individuals who were or are students, parents who were actively involved in the school system or were moderately involved or not at all involved, and educators. Several participants represented two groups: either alumni and parents, or alumni and educators. These were particularly rich interviews. Attention was also given to gender and class diversity, as well as the representation of parents, students, and educators from the different schools and neighborhoods in the school system. Standardization of the protocol required that all or most of the parents and students had experience with the high school. An effort was made to include students and/or parents of students who took classes at the different course levels available in the high school and who participated in various academic support and enrichment (special education and gifted education) as well as extracurricular programs.

After a year of interviews and ongoing analysis, my matrix of participants reflected a satisfactory level of representation. While there were some gaps here and there in student representation for a particular historical period, I was able to elicit data from educators employed by the district across some or all of the years of study. My matrix indicated adequate representation of participant experiences and perspectives across race, gender, role (student/parent/educator), as well as other variables, such as neighborhood (an imperfect proxy for socioeconomic background), degree of involvement with the school, and time period most connected with the district. Although more interviews would have produced additional insights, sufficient data had been collected across the 43 semi-structured interviews, 22 oral histories, and my study of archival data. The sampling matrix is provided in table 1-1.

Table 1-1. Sample by Study Phase and Participant Racial and Gender Background

	Educators	Parents	Students/Alumni
Early Phase (1965–1987)	4[a]	11	8[b]
	2 black	7 black	3 black
	2 white	4 white	4 white
			1 biracial
Current Phase (1988–2003)	5	10	12
	2 black	5 black	7 black
	3 white	4 white	5 white
		1 biracial	
Subtotal	9	21	20
	[c]	13 females	12 females
		8 males	8 males
Total	9	21	20 = 50
Students who became parents or educators, providing two perspectives:			– 7
Actual total			43

[a] Educators include teachers and administrators. Some of the educators interviewed had experience in both phases.
[b] The study provides 50 perspectives of students, parents, and educators. Because 7 students later became parents or educators and are repeated in the total number of 50, they are subtracted to provide an actual count of number of participants, totaling 43.
[c] For confidentiality, the gender of educators is not provided.

Gaining Access

How do you gain access to your research setting? In locating participants for the study, how does one proceed? It is important to think carefully about your first approach with individuals in the research setting and subsequent interactions thereafter. Whether you are an insider or outsider, your approach demands consideration of ethical responsibilities, including how to recruit your participants, inform the participants and those who may act in the role of "gatekeepers" of the purpose of your study, and maintain a level of contact and accessibility.

Before data collection begins, those researchers working within a university setting will need to secure approval from their Institutional Review Board (IRB). This process requires the preparation of an application in which the research question, methods and instruments of data collection, and participant sample are detailed. The IRB requires an in-depth discussion of the steps taken in order to protect human subjects.

This entails providing a step-by-step set of procedures for achieving such tasks as protecting participants' confidentiality, not exploiting particularly protected groups such as children and youth, gaining informed consent, maintaining safe storage for data, and other necessary precautions. Frequently an IRB application is submitted and then returned to the researcher with questions from the board concerning particular research procedures. After what can be considerable back and forth between the researcher and the board, the procedures are clarified sufficiently so that the board can give its approval. While this process may delay the researcher's ability to begin the research, and may create particular challenges in designs that are participatory and/or action-oriented, the exchange between the IRB and the researcher has the benefit of fine-tuning or further articulating the research design.

Should your research involve an institution such as a school or community organization as the site of data collection or involve members of the institution off-site, the IRB requires a letter from the institution acknowledging the purpose of the research and indicating agreement for the research to be conducted. This can be secured with varying degrees of ease, depending on the nature of the research, the relationship between the researcher and the institution, and the perceived usefulness (or threat) of the research to the institution. Throughout the research, it is best that you maintain communication with key individuals about the particular steps of the research and overall direction, without compromising the data collection or the participants' confidentiality. An early step toward instilling trust with those who play an institutional gatekeeping role is through discussing and formulating aspects of the IRB application.

Gaining access might require more or less work, but it is nevertheless likely to be complicated, particularly when the research involves an organization or institution that is accountable to a wider public. It is important that you attend to reciprocity with the site, addressing, when possible, the needs and requests of your participants and the key gatekeepers with whom you become increasingly connected. In a similar way it is important to maintain a reflexive stance throughout all phases of the research. The use of researcher reflexivity, a process of reflecting back on one's thought process, assumptions, decision making, and actions taken, allows for the documentation and study of methodological and ethical issues that may emerge. It also involves your study of how subjectivity and bias may influence data collection and analysis as well as how study findings are reported. These important dimensions of reciprocity and reflexivity are further explored in later chapters.

Ethical Considerations of the Researcher's Relationship to the Desegregation Study Research Context

In the desegregation study, there were ethical issues I needed to attend to throughout the research because I was an insider—a parent of children in the schools and a resident of the community. Below is a set of notes exploring aspects of my insider status. These notes point to the importance of maintaining a reflexive lens on your relationship with your participants and, if applicable, the institutions within which you may be intimately involved.

> Having secured approval for my research from the Institutional Review Board of my university, I met with a district official to introduce myself and learn what was necessary for me to begin the research. Because I was not seeking access to students within schools, my request to conduct research was relatively uncomplicated from the district's perspective. There was an offer from the district to identify a list of possible participants, but I declined. I wanted to ensure the confidentiality of my participants and felt a list of individuals from the district office would compromise my assurances. Additionally, a district-prepared list of possible participants had the potential to skew the data in a particular direction.
>
> Early on in the study I was aware of the advantages of my insider status. While I did not need to seek access to school buildings because my work was not ethnographic, there was a clear slice of this study that was informed by my participation on a daily basis as a parent of children in the school system. My informal conversations with other parents, individuals in the community, and teachers often provided further information as I developed a chronology of events in the district over time and, later in the study, as I mused over emerging themes.
>
> As a result, I felt the tug of loyalty on two levels. First, I struggled

with how to conduct the research wisely. Living in the community and engaging with teachers and parents on a regular basis, I understood the complicated give and take between good intentions and dissatisfying consequences, often resulting in inequalities for students of color. More broadly, I understood the district to be one of a smaller group of school systems with a history of attending to racial balance and equality of opportunity between white students and students of color. In this sense, while white and middle-class districts beyond the inner ring of Cleveland enjoyed protection from interrogation concerning their racial and economic homogeneity, this and other diverse districts have been closely watched for failures to address inequalities. With federal efforts to address school accountability through No Child Left Behind, this surveillance has increased. Would my research simply further that interrogation without sufficient consideration of the district's efforts, achievements, and struggles?

On another level, my awareness of my race and class privilege within the district introduced me to another dilemma. Early in the study, while I was still poring over archival material at the district office, two district officials queried me about the study. At some point one interrupted my description with the question, "Do you have children in the system?" to which I responded yes. At that moment it seemed that my having children in the district positioned me differently from a researcher outside the community. Why? On the surface, the question was straightforward. But there was something else at work, nearly imperceptible, something that drew me uncomfortably into the unspoken arrangement of givens within the conversation.

For some time I felt an uneasiness about this exchange and tried to locate the source of my unease. Was the assumption that when all was said and done, I would ultimately protect a system in which I had an investment? Such an assumption, and its implications, rattled me. Bounded by race and class connections, the three of us, white and middle class, had signaled in this moment a particular phenomenon in need of exploration. Could it be that we were the beneficiaries of a system with deep claims in the value of diversity at little cost to our children? Was I sufficiently aware of how I was positioned and the extent to which I shared this allegiance? These were questions in need of exploration.

Summary

As suggested in the introduction of this book, it is indeed a challenging task to construct a research design reflective of your research interests and purpose. Your review of the pertinent literature will inform the development of your research question, as will dimensions of your experience and, if applicable, your knowledge of the research context. Consider what particular interpretive tradition is appropriate for your study and in keeping with your philosophical orientation about the construction of knowledge and ethics of research. In crafting your design, you lay the groundwork in terms of methods of data collection and analysis that will guide you for the duration of the project.

Through a discussion of the desegregation study, I have outlined key components to a research design. My experience has been used here to help you to imagine *some* possibilities in qualitative research and particularly in the use of the semi-structured interview. In the next chapter I will discuss the actual construction of the semi-structured interview. I will introduce ways in which you might capitalize on the versatility of this method in texturing data, thus attending to the depth and complexity of individual lives positioned within overlapping and interacting contexts.

2

The Semi-Structured Interview as a Repertoire of Possibilities

A social institution can be fully understood only if we do not limit ourselves to the abstract study of its formal organization, but analyze the way in which it appears in the personal experience of various members of the group and follow the influence which it has upon their lives.
—Thomas and Znaniecki (1918/1927, cited in Chase, 2008, p. 60)

The semi-structured interview, valued for its accommodation to a range of research goals, typically reflects variation in its use of questions, prompts, and accompanying tools and resources to draw the participant more fully into the topic under study. Semi-structured interviews incorporate both open-ended and more theoretically driven questions, eliciting data grounded in the experience of the participant as well as data guided by existing constructs in the particular discipline within which one is conducting research. Formulating questions and ordering them requires considerable time and trial and error through the field-testing of the protocol, which is the set of questions guiding the interview. Each interview question should be clearly connected to the purpose of the research, and its placement within the protocol should reflect the researcher's deliberate progression toward a fully in-depth exploration of the phenomenon under study.

This chapter focuses on the purpose and construction of the interview and offers one route among many to developing an interview protocol. In order to illustrate the versatility of the semi-structured interview as a method for exploring data grounded in participants' experience as well as those data that are theory laden, the chapter includes a discussion of the development of the interview protocol for the desegregation study. It offers as an example the use of three segments within the interview, moving from very open-ended questions focused on concrete experiences to more specific and theory-driven questions. The use of three segments does not represent a fixed requirement. Your interview protocol may involve more or fewer sections. Moreover, some interviews are carried out in several sessions, reflecting a continuum of structure over the course of the sessions. The examples provided by the desegregation study are not prescriptive but are intended to stimulate your thinking about what is possible in the construction of your interview protocol. This chapter details not only my development of the semi-structured interview protocol but also some experiences I had in using the protocol. It thus offers insight into the type of deliberation that can occur in your effort to respond to your research question through a well-crafted interview protocol.

Opening Segment: Creating Space for a Narrative Grounded in Participant Experience

As you plan the opening segment of your interview protocol, keep in mind several tasks you'll need to accomplish before the interview actually begins. You should begin with a statement of the purpose of the research and an expression of gratitude for the participant's involvement. If the participant has not yet signed a consent form, she or he should do so before the interview begins. This ensures participants' understanding of their rights, including the right to not answer a question and to end the interview should they feel the need to do so. If the participant gives consent to audiotape or videotape the interview, you would turn on the recording device at the same time you open with your first interview question. These are the preliminary steps to consider.

In planning the protocol, the early part of your interview is intended to elicit from the participant the central story that will give your inter-

---

**Opening Segment of the
Semi-Structured Interview**

establish a level of comfort and ensure understanding
of participant rights

move into broad questions that create openings
for participant to begin to speak from her or his
experience

when necessary, probe for clarification

mentally note meaningful junctures in participant's
story to which you'll return later in the interview for
greater exploration and depth

support the flow of the narrative with probes that
guide its direction as it relates to your research topic

Figure 2-1. Opening segment

view direction and depth. The questions are open-ended in order to create space for participants to narrate their experiences; however, the focus of the questions is very deliberate and carefully tied to your research topic. The objective is to guide a participant in conveying an account of an experience as it relates to the topic of study. As this segment is typically the most open-ended, it will elicit data you cannot anticipate in advance. In this sense, the opening segment relies on your knowledge of your topic and your ability to support the unfolding of the participant's narrative. A good deal of your exploration of the topic with your participants is constructed from the material in this first segment of the interview (see figure 2-1). In many ways, it is the richest and most provocative source of data, as it is the narrative that is in place before the use of more theoretically shaped questions follows.

Your attention during this segment of the interview is focused on listening carefully to the unfolding story, probing to ensure portions of the narrative are clear, and noting particular details, events, observations, insights, and emotions within the narrative that are relevant to the topic and that you may want to return to at an appropriate place later in the interview. In many ways, you are formulating a short list of important statements made by the participant that you know will be relevant to questions later in the interview. This also requires some discipline on your part as you allow space for the narrative to develop, holding back some questions until the participant has covered sufficient ground in the opening questions. On the other hand, this is not to preclude your probing for meaning. Your thoughtful questions often serve as helpful guides for participants, so they can focus on the direction of their responses to your question.

Achieving space for data deeply grounded in the participant's experience and angle of vision should be the primary focus of the first segment of your interview protocol. This requires that the questions in the early part of the interview create openings from which you can learn about the participant and his or her experience. Your beginning segment is intended to be the most open-ended in your interview, focused on encouraging a generative narrative, a way into the phenomenon of study *as determined by the participant*. In many ways this early segment is the most important, because it provides the initial narrative to which you will return and build on in a reciprocal manner, engaging the participant in his or her experience in terms of clarification, generating meaning, and critically reflecting as you move forward. While the structure of this early segment and the nature of its questions should be unfettered by theoretical concerns, its intent nonetheless is saturated with theoretical considerations. As in all segments of the interview, your interpretive tradition will influence the direction of your questions and the degree of structure within your protocol.

Consider ways to elicit narratives that are detailed and in-depth. As you move along in this first segment, you may want to offer an opportunity for participants to further explore the topic. How might you use tools and resources that bring to the surface ideas, perspectives, and experiences that might not be immediately accessible to the participant? For example, to assist participants in their recall of an event that may have happened several years earlier, you might use photographs, newspaper headlines, video footage, and other archival materials. Asking your participants to create a map or representation of an experience and then talking about their thoughts and/or feelings regarding the particular phenomenon may also be useful. Such tools facilitate a means through which participants can shed greater light on their experiences and generate meanings about the research topic. They may also yield additional contextual details about the experience that could be discussed later in relation to other questions in the interview. This is particularly helpful when words are not enough—when images, symbols, and artifacts open up new lines of communicating dimensions of an experience. Such tools can evoke conversations that often prove to be analytically rich (Bagnoli, 2009; Sirin & Fine, 2008).

For each question you include in your interview protocol, it is important to be clear about the purpose each question serves. In other words, is the question necessary and how will it contribute to the study of your topic? One way to assess the utility of a protocol is to pilot it in two or three interview sessions, ideally with individuals who reflect some of your criteria for participation in the study. The pilot will give you much to think about in terms of your phrasing of questions, their order, the usefulness of the questions, and the structure of the interview.

Middle Segment: Questions of Greater Specificity

The middle segment of the semi-structured interview may be designed to pursue your topic of study in more depth with the participant. This is achieved in different ways, depending on your analytical framework and the interpretive tradition that guides your work. Regardless of these variations, the middle segment will draw from what you have already learned from your participant in the opening segment of the interview, and it will move the interview along, with an eye toward eliciting data of greater specificity and, perhaps, broader contextual levels.

This middle piece of your protocol involves consideration of questions that will ensure your research topic is adequately explored. While the first segment of your interview protocol used questions sufficiently broad to move the participant into her or his story, the questions in this next segment attend to the nuances of that story, either through questions structured into the protocol or through a series of probing questions constructed by the researcher as the interview proceeds (see

---

**Middle Segment of the
Semi-Structured Interview**

attend to nuances in the narrative thus far

shift into questions that are more specific as they
relate to your research question

loop back, when appropriate, to participant's
narrative material as it connects with specific
questions

explore further participant's responses noted as
meaningful in the opening narrative

extend your probes beyond clarification to meaning
making on the part of the participant toward the
research topic

Figure 2-2. Middle segment

figure 2-2). The intent is to create space to explore the complexity of your topic, and the depth you achieve is largely dependent on the effectiveness of your opening questions in the first segment of the interview, further guided by your probes.

Questions of increased specificity are typically put on hold initially: they can be more informed once the participant has talked about her or his experience as it relates to the research topic. Questions in the middle segment are more suited farther along in the interview after some degree of trust has been established and some reciprocity between the researcher and participant has been attained. These are not personal questions designed to make the participant feel vulnerable; instead, they are somewhat narrower than the first set of questions and more comfortably located well after the opening narrative provided by the participant. Should these more specific questions be included too early in the interview, they may shortchange the participants and the researcher of the emergence of data grounded in the perspective and experience of the participants.

Concluding Segment: Revisiting the Opening Narrative for
Important Theoretical Connections and Moving toward Closure

The final segment of your interview protocol offers an opportunity to
return to points in the participant's narrative that are still in need of
exploration. Whether you carry out your interview over several days
or in one setting, you should design your protocol with space in which
to connect back with earlier ideas expressed by the participant. More
nuanced questions or those that reflect the theoretical areas of focus
in your study are more fitting for this segment of the interview. In this
way, the data that are grounded in lived experience and those addressing theory might converse.

The movement from the opening narrative to more in-depth and perhaps theory-laden questions in the final segment illustrates the range of
possibilities available with this method. Both in your formal questions
and in your prompts, you are supporting your participant in generating
meaningful responses. You have an opportunity to engage the participant in clarification, meaning making, and critical reflection, particularly as it relates to more abstract and theoretically driven questions.

However you structure your interview protocol, the final segment
benefits from and builds on the data emerging from earlier questions
in the interview (see figure 2-3). As the interview progresses, you are
increasingly engaging in meaning making with your participants. How
is the lived experience as narrated by your participants informing your
phenomenon under study? Is there a story, metaphor, or a particular
phrase pregnant with meaning within the interview that needs further
exploration? Are there contradictions in the participant's narrative that
might be raised with care? As elsewhere in the interview, you proceed
in a manner that invites depth but attends to indications on the part of
the participant that the topic has been exhausted, is inaccessible, or is
off-limits. This can be difficult to ascertain. It relies on your ability to
probe and open up areas the participant may not have directly considered while also reading body language, facial expression, and tone of
voice to determine a participant's desire to move on to the next question. A useful way to gauge the situation is to close out each major area
of questioning by asking, "Anything else?"

**Concluding Segment of the
Semi-Structured Interview**

pose questions that may reflect theoretical
considerations—offer participant opportunity to
explore opening narrative in relation to theory-driven
questions

where possible, return to those stories and metaphors
in need of further exploration

look for opportunities to explore contradictions

work toward a sense of wrapping up and indicating to
participant the interview is nearing completion

ask participant for additional thoughts or final points

thank participant and emphasize his or her
contribution to the research

Figure 2-3. Concluding segment

As you approach the conclusion of your interview, your protocol should be structured to allow for closure. Design your questions toward the end of the protocol to allow for a kind of wrapping up. As you end the interview, your focus should be lighter and less intense. Always conclude by asking the participant if he or she has anything further to add. There may be something your participant has to say and this is the space for her or him to formulate final thoughts. Finally, indicate to your participant the value of his or her contribution to the research.

In the next section, I discuss the ways in which the interview protocol was developed for the desegregation study. The use of three segments attended to the development of a narrative that was sufficiently open-ended, with shifts toward specificity in the second segment, followed by an opportunity to explore the data grounded in lived experience, as it emerged in the first segment, in relation to questions of theoretical significance. This section includes a discussion of my planning for the protocol, but it also highlights examples from actual interviews to underscore the ways in which the sets of questions and probes were useful in eliciting meaningful data and ways in which they were problematic. The types of questions and the use of supportive tools are intended to illustrate the versatility of the semi-structured interview, and the continuum of structure that is possible in designing a protocol closely aligned to your research question. A sample interview protocol from the desegregation study is located in appendix A.

Creating an Opening: Constructing the First Segment for the Desegregation Study Interview Protocol

In constructing the first segment of the interview, I sought an opening through which I could invite the participant to narrate his or her years of schooling in the district. This narrative would become the material the participant and I would work with as we moved into the more theoretically driven questions. There would be periodic opportunities farther into the interview to loop back and draw on instances within the participant's narrative that might be relevant to the question at hand. Thus, the semi-structured interview would be progressive in the way that the second and third segments built on the first. It would be grounded in the empirical data—the lived experience as narrated by the participant—and increasingly engaged with theoretically driven questions and prompts toward generating meaning. Additionally, the interview would draw not only on the data elicited during the interview but also on archival and oral history data already collected in the study.

Well-versed in district history, my objective was to develop a protocol that would give sufficient depth and complexity to individual lives within this district at particular junctures in its history. This necessitated a protocol that effectively invited participants to speak about their schooling trajectory. In the case of student participants, I sought to elicit their stories of favorite teachers, opportunities they accessed and those they did not, meaningful learning experiences, adult and peer relationships that facilitated their academic success, and those relationships and educational policies and practices that constrained educational opportunity.

> **Anne:** Before we begin, I wonder how you would describe the community of Shaker Heights to someone who doesn't live here?
>
> **Nika:** I would say it's pretty cosmopolitan, . . . but then at the same time it's kind of segregated, . . . certain areas, I mean, I can see why they are the way that they are, you know, the more affluent areas are predominantly—white, and the middle-class areas are pretty mixed. Some are more black or more white than others, but I don't know—I don't know why that is. Maybe I'm too young to know why or maybe people just prefer . . . There's mostly African Americans, . . . one block up and one block, you know, behind my street, but then like two blocks up, it gets—it starts getting more mixed.
>
> **Anne:** And that's really a historical neighborhood, I mean, that's a neighborhood that . . . has a tremendous history as being one of the first areas in Shaker Heights that was integrated.
>
> **Nika:** 'Cause my mom grew up [there] . . .
>
> **Anne:** Uh-huh, wow, OK. All right. Elementary schools. Where did you go?
>
> **Nika:** I went to Shaker K through 12 . . .

Figure 2-4. Early excerpt from interview with Nika

In the dialogue box (see figure 2-4) is an excerpt from my interview with Nika, a young woman who is African American and who attended the high school in the mid-1990s. This first segment with Nika illustrates an open style of questioning, designed to encourage the participant to speak from her experience. Also evident here is my insertion of comments as they relate to her narrative. While such comments may yield relevant data, they also run the risk of producing few connections or of actually distracting the participant from her narrative. In the case above, my comment regarding the integration history of the Ludlow neighborhood, where Nika resides, was productive. Nika then linked her mom to the history of Ludlow, where some of the earliest efforts at changing real estate and mortgage-lending practices occurred to facilitate racial integration in housing. This was an important moment, and I tucked it away to return to it later in the interview. We pressed forward, as I asked Nika to talk about her elementary school experience.

As you can see in the exchange, the first segment was designed to elicit a narrative concerning Nika's experience of schooling. It began most broadly, getting some background information, and I then asked her to describe the community of Shaker Heights. The protocol then moved into Nika's experience of the school system. This next section was also open-ended, and it allowed Nika to narrate her educational trajectory, from kindergarten through high school graduation. This section focused on her experience of the schools attended within the system.

While the high school experience was the primary focus, the accumulation of experiences leading up to high school was a necessary backdrop for understanding what contributed to the high school experience. Many probes were provided to explore fully each "leg" of the journey. Probes attended to structural dimensions (educational programming, including gifted/enrichment, tutoring, special education, and remedial programs; educational policies and practices; co-curricular and extra-curricular opportunities) as well as relational considerations (relationships with educators; relationship with peers; the nature of friendships after leaving elementary for upper elementary and middle school; relational experiences within the course-level system).

To illustrate the way in which this open-ended segment of the interview was designed to capture dimensions of schooling to which I might return in later segments, I draw again from my interview with Nika. She had narrated her experience in Ludlow School where she had participated in the district's gifted program, which was open to Ludlow students and which served as a magnet school for students across the district. This arrangement was established in the early 1980s as part of the district's ongoing two-way desegregation plan, which allowed for transfer across schools in order to reduce racial imbalance, particularly at the elementary school level but later including the junior high schools (reflecting the grade configuration before the district reorganized in 1987). Nika talked about her elementary school experience, telling me, nearly five pages into the transcribed text, "My whole schooling was pretty advanced. I was always on like an accelerated track . . . I never really had classes with many African American students." Nika spoke about how much she gained academically from the gifted program and later, in 7th through 12th grade, from the advanced courses. However, there is a juncture in her narrative during which she situates the racial

> . . . it's like they [the students removed from the ad-
> vanced course] were, like de-tracked. . . . They never took
> AP. . . . There was one black boy . . . [tap, tap, tap], . . . but
> the rest of the kids, they just stayed in that [regular] class.
> . . . It was from that point, . . . that's when I saw, like, the
> light, I saw really what was going on in that whole school
> system. It's, like, they showed their face pretty much, and,
> I mean, if you don't really, if you don't get hit like that,
> then you're naïve, you don't even know, and you just let
> it go. You don't do anything because you think there's
> nothing to do. You think you're in the right place and
> you're not.

Figure 2-5. Data emerging early in interview and revisited
later in interview

isolation in the district's advanced courses as systemically problematic
and, consequently, a cause of shock to her. This juncture was communi-
cated through her narrative of an experience in her early adolescence,
which appears 20 pages into the transcribed text of the interview.

Nika told me that early in the school year she was removed from
an advanced course with several other students by a school administrator who announced "we were in the wrong class, that we were supposed to be in the other [course] . . . and the other kids in the class
knew that wasn't the enriched class." All of the removed students were
African American. Nika defined this juncture in her years in the district as a moment when she "saw the light" in terms of racial inequality
in the district. The narrative of "shock" as a result of one experience
or an accumulation of experiences of exclusion in the school system
emerged in my analysis as a pattern evident in a number of black students' experiences. This thematic pattern ultimately informed my analysis. Nika's narrative is included here in the dialogue box (figure 2-5)
to convey her view of what transpired in this experience, particularly
for the black students who did not assert their proper placement in the
advanced course. Nika's narrative underscores how data emerged in
the first segment of the interview, through the participants' narrative
of their schooling experience, to which I could later return within the

interview for further exploration. The point at which I would return to such data often took place in the third segment, which was more explicitly focused on participants' conceptualization of racial equality.

The Use of Tools to Further Explore the Narrative

In the desegregation study, I also used tools in the first segment of the interview to facilitate the participants' narration of their high school experiences through their creation of a relational map. Through the use of simple, almost crudely prepared materials, representing social groups within the high school, I asked participants to map out the social landscape. A large oval-shaped piece of paper board allowed for a physical representation of the social landscape. Small circles were used to symbolize social groups that made up the student body. Participants were asked to identify these groups according to their own labels and descriptions.

This form of relational mapping, the naming of groups and positioning them in approximation to one another, created a space for participants in which to narrate their thoughts on their high school experiences, and it produced openings through which additional questions could be asked. The mapping tool led to greater thought and explication on the part of the participants than if they had simply been asked to respond to a question about the social groups within their high school. Additionally, it provided more background information and participant commentary to be drawn on later in the interview, as questions became increasingly abstract. This enabled me to reach back into the narrative elicited through the mapping and make connections, ask additional questions, seek clarification, and note contradictions.

In using the mapping, my hope was to produce some concrete rendering of the high school social landscape. Ultimately, I sought to recreate as much as possible the way in which the participants viewed self and other within the high school. I prompted participants to think about clubs, classes, social cliques, and other group formations. I began this section with the following questions:

> Could you use some of these materials to provide a sort of map of the
> social landscape of the high school? You'll notice I have a big circle to

represent the high school, and then many smaller circles to represent groups that were a part of the high school. Could you use these smaller circles here to show the various groups of students that you think made up your high school?

Following this, I asked participants to position these groups in relation to one another. Sufficient time and probing were provided to explore the extent of connection or distance among social groups in the high school, as well as the perceptions and experience of participants toward these groups. As participants created their relational maps, they talked about the groups and relationships they were representing with the circles. I also asked what particular classes or extracurricular activities brought groups of students together and what set the groups apart.

During their creation of the relational map, I asked participants to locate themselves on the map. They did this by placing a small rectangular sticky note that read "self" close to or at a distance from the designated groups, depending on the relationship of each group with the student being interviewed. Students were then asked to indicate which groups had the greatest influence on the social landscape. The depiction of these groups was framed with two different colored pipe cleaners that represented strength of voice and opinion at two levels: (1) influence of a group on adults making decisions about policies and activities in the school, and (2) influence of a group among peers. Toward the end of this part of the interview, participants were asked to identify the racial composition of the groups. Small rectangular stickers were applied to groups as designated by the students. The options were predominantly black/African American; predominantly white/European American; racially mixed. The location of self in relation to the groups and the participation of these groups in the social landscape of the school informed my use of probes in the later interview segments. Additionally, the participants' view of their relationships with the groups they identified and the racial composition of these groups also provided useful data. A portion of a white student's map, Mark, who was attending high school at the time of his interview with me in the early 2000s, is provided in figure 2-6.

To illustrate the way in which the mapping revealed students' relational experiences, I highlight here an excerpt from an interview with

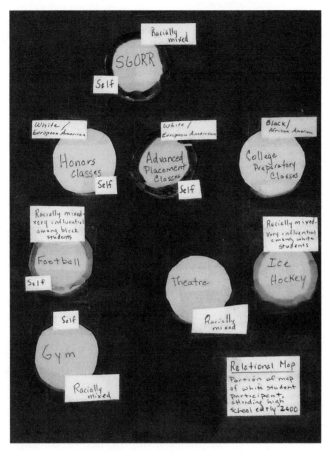

Figure 2-6. Relational map from interview with Mark

Karan. Karan is a white student who attended the high school in early 2000. While her strength was in the arts, Karan struggled academically and was provided with a tutor during high school. She was also often one of a few white students in the college preparatory courses in high school. In the excerpt in the dialogue box (see figure 2-7), I asked Karan about what draws groups together and what keeps them apart. In speaking about what influences separation, Karan referred to the course levels and her experience in the majority black college preparatory courses. Her perfunctory response reveals how normative the racial composition of the course levels was for her. While she notes the impact of the course levels in separating groups of students, she also

> **Anne:** Are there classes or extracurricular activities that bring different student groups together?
>
> **Karan:** I think student clubs more . . . student council . . . and the Student Group on Racial Relations.
>
> **Anne:** Are there any classes or extracurricular activities that are effective in separating kids?
>
> **Karan:** Just I think the AP and honors. . . . The CP is for mostly blacks, and honors is for mostly—white
>
> **Anne:** And kids who contradict that, . . . black kids who go into honors and the AP classes, white kids who go into the CP classes, . . . what experiences do they have?
>
> **Karan:** I think—I'm a white student in the CP classes and it's—it's—the *same*. I think, I mean, yeah. I don't think it really matters. I mean you might not have as many friends, but you're fine.

Figure 2-7. Relational map question: What draws groups together? What keeps them apart?

assures me, in a manner reflecting considerable ambivalence, that being one of a few white students in one's classes is "fine."

Informed by the critical theory tradition, I understood that social relationships are often shaped by a combination of structural conditions and individual agency, and by the intersection of group memberships that inform one's sense of self in relation to others (Collins, 1998). By looking at groups identified by the participants and their relationships to these groups, I hoped to come closer to an understanding of participants' experiences of racial equality. There was not a direct line available in this analysis. Instead, the use of the mapping provided a relational context from which I might draw as we moved through the rest of the protocol into later, more specific questions asked of participants regarding their experiences and understanding of racial equality. Additionally, the *talk* that emerged as participants named and placed groups on the map, along with positioning their "self" sticker, revealed important understandings on the part of the participants about their

high school experiences. The data from this *talk*—mine and theirs—
were often unanticipated, highly complex, and rich in material that the
participants and I would return to throughout the interview.

The Middle Segment within the Desegregation Study Protocol: Toward Greater Specificity

In the desegregation study, the middle segment was designed to further explore my research question on the *experience* and *views of racial
equality* among students, parents, and educators over the nearly 40-year
period of the district's desegregation. To do this, I used questions that
responded to my theoretically driven definition of racial equality, which
included facilitating equal educational opportunity, producing equal
academic outcomes, and engendering equal relations of power between
students of color and white students. It was necessary to ask participants about their experiences and to find the right questions to encourage them to be specific.

As my study was guided by an analytical framework that positioned
individual experience in relation to the educational structures in which
they participated, and in relation to broader sociopolitical trends, the
interview protocol was supposed to elicit the data necessary to inform
those levels. This middle segment was designed to provide greater clarity on participants' high school experiences, informed by their opening
narratives. It also asked them directly about three key areas related to
realizing the full benefits of the school system: expectations, opportunity, and access to information. These data would then be compared
and contrasted by race largely, but also by other dimensions. In this way,
the questions in this middle segment provided material to discuss high
school experiences in greater specificity. It also would inform the third
segment of the protocol, designed to explore the participants' views on
racial equality in the school system.

The research also necessitated that students self-identify by race,
because my analysis would compare student experience by race. In
this segment, I began with the question, "Could you tell me what racial
group you identify yourself as belonging to?" Additionally, to learn
how closely students felt connected with students in their racial group,
I used Linda R. Tropp and Stephen C. Wright's Inclusion of Ingroup

in the Self (IIS) scale (Tropp & Wright, 2001). This scale measures the degree of connection participants feel toward those who share the same racial backgrounds (their racial ingroup) and toward those who do not (their racial outgroup). The IIS scale consists of seven pairs of circles, initially at a distance from each other and then increasingly closer and overlapping, with the final pair nearly fully overlapping. Participants were asked first about the strength of their connections with their racial ingroup: "What set of circles would you select that best represents the strength of your own sense of connection with this group?" If the student self-identified as black, he or she would be given a set of circles representing "self" and "other black/African American students." Participants were then asked the same question with another scale that is similar except it reflects their sense of connection with their racial outgroup. For the student self-identifying as black, she or he would be given a set of circles representing "self" and "other white/European American students." My use of the IIS scale was not intended for quantitative analysis. Rather, it engendered useful discussion on the part of the participants about their racial identity and relationship with others within and across race.

It is helpful to look more closely here at my rationale for including the IIS. As I have noted, it was not for the purpose of quantitative analysis. I selected the scale because it would help me understand the degree of connections students felt toward each other in terms of race. In particular, the IIS arrangement of circles in varying degrees of relationship to each other, a continuum moving from separate to overlapping, was effective as a visual for getting participants to talk about their relational experiences by race within a desegregated high school. A replication of the IIS scale is located in appendix A within the desegregation study interview protocol.

Early on while conducting interviews, I followed the IIS scales with a question about where these ingroup and outgroup connections were strongest: at school, at home, or within certain community spaces. After my interview with Keith, a black student attending the high school in early 2000, I realized if I asked the question somewhat differently, I would get more information at the school level. I revised the question to ask about where *in school* the connections to one's racial ingroup and outgroup were strongest. Keith's focus on where in school

> **Anne:** [*after Keith selects the highest level of connection with black students on the ISS scale*] Any place in particular in school where you feel most connected?
>
> **Keith:** Gym [*he laughs a little*] and then—maybe some of my classes.
>
> **Anne:** OK. [*slight pause*] What classes? Any in particular?
>
> **Keith:** History.
>
> **Anne:** And why is that?
>
> **Keith:** Most of the black kids are in my class, ... and English, there is—only one white kid in that class.

Figure 2-8. Question following the inclusion of Ingroup in the Self (IIS) scale (Tropp & Wright, 2001)

his sense of connections were strongest for black students underscored the value of this narrower question solely about school both for ingroup and outgroup connections. My earlier interviews had yielded data on relationships in school but not as efficiently, because this revised question focused more specifically on the school experience. In figure 2-8 is a portion of my interview with Keith.

By phrasing the question as to where in school the sense of connection was strongest to a participant's racial ingroup and outgroup, I could elicit data on activities, classes, and spaces in the high school that brought African American and European American students together, those that kept them apart, and those that students viewed as spaces for ingroup gathering and cohesion. In this way, the IIS also collected data on students' experiences with their racial outgroup, such as the extent to which they felt they had contact and social affiliation, where that contact and social affiliation took place, and what it meant to them. This provided additional data on participants' school experiences as well as data on relational and structural arrangements within the high school that produced a social psychological space of sameness or difference.

[*interview with white teacher*]

Anne: I've been asking the people I interview what racial group do they identify themselves as being a member of?

[*pause*]

Ted: What a silly question.

[*speaking at the same time*]

Anne: White, European American; black, African American.

Ted: What a silly question. . . . There is no such thing as a racial group. People culturally are reflective of a background. And I think that's one of the tragedies at Shaker, that a number of African American kids are culturally—who use the power language, and culturally accept certain value patterns—are referred to as "white." There is no such thing as a racial group. There is your background, where you come from, what your value system is . . .

Anne: Um-hmm. OK, well then, then you might find this useless but, um, this is a set of Venn diagrams to give me a sense of your connections . . .

Figure 2-9. Ted's response to question on racial identity

The responses among some students, parents, and educators to the racial identity question were informative and provided additional data on participants' experiences and perspectives. Ted, a white educator in the district for many years, critiqued the utility of a question about participants' racial identification, as indicated in the excerpt of my interview with him in figure 2-9. A number of parents, African American and European American, also declined to self-identify by race. Their reasoning came from the feeling that individual differences defied any kind of categorization, a response that was more common among white and black parents who had children in the system in the late

1960s through the 1970s, with three parents (two white and one black) declining to make choices. A fourth parent, who was African American and whose child attended school in the early 1980s, also chose not to respond. This parent pressed me to think further about the way in which categories of "white" and "black" are social constructions, and she pointed to the "limited and constraining effect" of these constructions. At the same time, she felt that there were discrepant experiences for white and black students in the school system, but she noted that focusing on "race" had detrimental consequences as well. Instead, she stressed a wider analysis of "structural domination arising from the constraints of the prevalent social, economic, and political context."

These responses among participants produced useful and humbling moments, and they appropriately underscored the manner in which race is socially constructed. At the same time, I felt that the question concerning how one identified by race remained sufficiently connected to my research question. I also found the use of the IIS scale to be purposeful. While it inserted itself uncomfortably into the interview, it nonetheless created a pause in the narration and yielded considerable moments of questioning, degrees of resistance, and launching points from which experiences that spoke to racial identity could be accessed. Particularly for students, it opened up the space for them to narrate their understandings of self and others and to explore relationships across and within race and to locate spaces and experiences in the high school where racial group membership was salient. While I was conflicted about reinforcing an essentialized view of race, the social and material consequences of its construction were evident in the interview, archival, and oral history data, warranting my continued use of this question about racial identity and my use of the IIS scale.

My deliberation over whether or not to include these questions is illustrative of many moments during the research where I felt torn over issues of theoretical imposition, researcher bias, and other ethical and methodological dilemmas. These junctures within the research are important to note. As you move along in your research you are likely to experience concerns about your use of a protocol question, a particular prompt, or some other decision made during your research. These moments should be documented and studied, a process known as reflexivity that is central to qualitative research. Reflexivity allows you to look back at what happened and to consider the ways in which the research may be influenced by actions you have taken or assumptions you have made. Reflexivity may also inform your analysis and reveal additional considerations as you carry out your research. Chapter 3 highlights the ways in which reflexivity strengthens qualitative research in exploring these types of uncertainties.

Also within the middle segment, I included six closed-response questions, accompanied by Likert-scale responses. Likert scales provide participants with a set of 4 or 5 responses reflecting degrees of agreement or disagreement, from which they select one response. Included among these were questions about the extent to which the following was achieved: the high school shared similar *expectations* for students as their parents; students benefited from educational *opportunities*; and *information* concerning those opportunities was available. The question on opportunity is highlighted in figure 2-10.

Like the IIS scale, these Likert-scale questions were not intended for quantitative analysis. Instead, they helped to clarify and elaborate further the students' experiences by creating a situation in which they had to select a specific measure for each of these areas of schooling.

In this middle segment, the last in this series of Likert-scale questions packaged "experience" together and asked participants to compare their experiences with those within and outside their racial ingroup. This question, highlighted in figure 2-11, was placed strategically after the other closed-ended questions. It benefited from the accumulation

---

I want to ask you about educational opportunities for you in the high school.

Educational opportunities provide students with the kind of teaching, courses, and opportunities to study and discuss academic work with their peers that are necessary to prepare them, academically and socially, for college and a career. Educational opportunities include academic classes and extracurricular activities.

How much did you benefit from the opportunities available in school?

☐ a great deal   ☐ a good amount   ☐ some   ☐ a little   ☐ none

Figure 2-10. Question on educational opportunity

Comparison of Self to Ingroup

How *similar or dissimilar* would you say your experience as a student in the high school was to the experience of other [*indicate person's self-identified race here*] students?

☐ very similar   ☐ somewhat similar   ☐ similar   ☐ somewhat dissimilar
☐ very dissimilar

Comparison of Self to Outgroup

What about [*indicate other major racial group (white or African American or biracial) here*] students? How *similar or dissimilar* would you say your experience was to their experience?

☐ very similar   ☐ somewhat similar   ☐ similar   ☐ somewhat dissimilar
☐ very dissimilar

Figure 2-11. Questions on comparison of experience of self to ingroup and outgroup: Likert-scale response

Kate was initially uncertain how to respond to the question on her experience of educational opportunity compared with African American students. She said she was "not sure" and asked me to repeat the question. Then she said, "very similar," then "well, wait a minute," and then "yes, because they had the same opportunities I did." In her comparison of the self to her outgroup, then, Kate viewed her experience as "very similar" to black students as a result of the opportunities she viewed as equally available.

Figure 2-12. Kate's response to question comparing student's experience to that of racial outgroup

of responses thus far. It also provided material to which I might return when I asked participants about their views on racial equality.

To illustrate the complexity of these data, I have included in figure 2-12 my notes from a telephone interview with Kate, a white student who had attended the school in the early 1980s. As with other study participants, Kate's discussion of "opportunity" lent itself well to the next set of questions within the concluding segment. Because my question on views of racial equality was the most abstract and most informed by theory, it came in the final segment.

Situating Lived Experience within Abstract Notions of Equality:
The Third Segment of the Desegregation Study Interview Protocol

In the desegregation study, the final segment included open-ended questions pertaining to students' conceptualizations and experiences of racial equality. I opened this portion of the interview by reading aloud a statement reminding the participant of the *Brown v. Board of Education* decision in 1954. I included this background information in order to impose some degree of theoretical orientation, including historical decisions impacting racial equality in education. The text I used is provided below:

> In 1954, the *Brown v. Board of Education* decision of the Supreme Court ruled that public schools that were racially segregated and operated under a "separate but equal" premise were unconstitutional and "had no place in public education." (*Brown v. Board of Education of Topeka*, 1954)

Following the *Brown* prompt, I asked participants to talk about what racial equality in public education meant *to them*. In this way, the primary variable of study was initially explored through the participants' definition. However, the insertion of the reference to *Brown* situated this segment of the interview in a history of legal and social contexts relating to school desegregation. Next, I asked participants to talk about a personal experience or observation they had of racial equality or inequality in the district. In my use of this third segment, I found that the participants' selection of an example of racial equality or inequality, or an indication that they had no example, provided crucial data. Often at this point I might reference an experience narrated earlier in the study, and I would ask if that experience offered insights into racial equality in the school system.

The elicitation of grounded data as they related to the participants' views of racial equality in the school system was then followed by a theoretically driven set of questions, guided by a definition of racial equality as facilitating equal educational opportunity, equal academic outcomes, and equal relations of power. By including these questions, the protocol allowed for insight into the participants' views of equality *directly narrated by them* as well as their responses to *a view shaped by the study's theoretical variables*. It also created space for the possibility that the definition of racial equality as theorized in the research design *may or may not correspond* with what the participant offered as the meaning she or he gave to racial equality.

My protocol branched in different directions after the question on racial equality. For parents and educators, I delved into equality of outcomes. I provided a "snapshot" of national data trends over 30 years, a visual that charted the narrowing and widening of the gap in test scores between black and white students from the National Assessment of Educational Progress (NAEP). To situate the discussion more locally, I provided two more visuals. The first of these compared test results for Shaker Heights students with a national norm for the Stanford Achievement Test for 1991–1992 (Stupay, 1993). The second chart used the Stanford Achievement Test results for the same year, but it compared the performance of white students to black students in the district. I asked participants to talk about what they thought about the data, what concerned them, and what questions were raised in viewing these data. My intent was to move the conversation about racial equality beyond opportunity and toward a consideration of outcomes.

In developing my interview protocol for *students and alumni*, however, I did *not* include the NAEP outcome data. While the gap in standardized test scores between white and black students offered an opportunity to discuss inequality of outcomes, it also had the potential to leave unanswered many questions about factors contributing to the gap. In my reading through archival materials and talking with parents and educators, I was aware of several intense periods of conflict when data on "the black-white achievement gap" were presented with little depth or with no emphasis to communicate that individuals in both racial groups defy group patterns. I felt conflicted about presenting these data, *particularly to high school students and recent graduates*, in the last section of a one- to two-hour interview. In such a situation, I knew I would not be able to assist the youth in the necessary scrutinizing of stereotypes about achievement and motivation that often emerge in participants' encounter with these data. I never felt completely satisfied with this decision. Nonetheless, I was unwilling to present the set of charts depicting the gap in a strictly one-dimensional manner in my concluding segment with white and black high school students or recent graduates.

In addition to opportunity and outcomes, I also sought to draw the participants—students, parents, and educators—into a conversation about how equal relations of power might facilitate equality. In a statement that referenced the historical advantage whites have had in education, I asked the following: "In what way would you say the school system has made efforts to create more of a balance between blacks and whites in terms of social influence or power?"

My question here was deeply theoretical, informed by my review of the literature and the analytical framework that emerged from that review. When participants indicated there were efforts within the district to reduce the historical advantage of whites, or a failure to do so, I asked them to talk further about this. Again, this question was sufficiently abstract and relied on my ability to draw on participants' narratives for possible examples of the disruption of privilege. In case an example was not evident, I also included some points in the district history to which I could refer, should there be little to draw from in a participant's narrative. Additionally, *the question left open the possibility that the participant might reject the premise of the question entirely and would believe that racial equality in the district had been achieved.* As such, this question was best positioned in this last segment of the interview, during which the participant and I had hopefully achieved a level of comfort with each other and a sufficient narrative had been produced for the participant to articulate his or her view on racial equality as different from that which I was offering.

This final segment was particularly informed by my use of the critical theory interpretive tradition. It created what the critical theorists Phil Carspecken and Michael Apple (1992) and others refer to as dialogical data generation, which involves "data generation that proceeds through establishing an intensive dialogue between the researchers and those researched" (p. 548). The questions in this final segment, then, facilitated an exploration of the participants' definitions of racial equality *not only* as informed by particular experiences in the school district *but also* in relation to a particular theoretical frame concerning racial equality as it relates to public education. This segment represented the greatest infusion of theoretical influence. Deliberately placed well after the first two segments, which focused on eliciting data grounded in the participants' experiences of the school system, this final segment was designed to interject existing theory on this topic. In this way, I sought to engage participants in ideas that may or may not have been aligned with the meaning they had given to their experience and their views on racial equality.

In other interpretive traditions, the inclusion of questions so draped in theory would be viewed as influencing the participant in a manner that compromised the authenticity of the data. Introducing a particular view of racial equality within a protocol specifically designed to study lived experience seems counterintuitive and certainly problematic. However, as constructed within the semi-structured interview, this last section was conceived as an opportunity to understand better the extent of "fit" between the data elicited in the interview and the existing theory guiding the research question as well as the analytical framework of the study. Through the insertion of this dialectical process, I would ultimately be prepared to modify existing theory or to build new theory.

From this discussion of how I conducted semi-structured interviews as part of the desegregation study, we can consider some general tips that may apply in planning your interview protocol. These include structuring the interview early on with ample room for participants to narrate their experiences. From this opening narrative you can move into more specific questions, following up on the narrative and/or introducing questions guided by a priori theoretical considerations. It is helpful to view the interview as organized into segments, moving toward more abstract or theoretical questions as the interview progresses, while creating space to loop back into material narrated earlier on. Some researchers opt to conduct their interviews across several days, allowing time for the researcher to study the data and develop additional questions. This also allows the participant time to respond with more deliberation and depth.

Summary

We have discussed the development of a protocol for a semi-structured interview and have underscored the versatility of this method. The semi-structured interview offers researchers a way to attend to lived experience and pursue questions from extant theory. As noted earlier, the questions in your interview protocol are shaped by your research question, analytical framework, and interpretive tradition. Your protocol may involve the use of supportive tools to further elicit ideas, perspectives, and experiences that may not be immediately accessible to the participant. The inclusion of images, artifacts, or opportunities for the participant to create a representation or a relational map may generate additional dimensions of lived experience.

The structure of your protocol need not be divided into sections but it generally benefits from generous space early on for the participant to construct his or her narrative, increased specificity toward clarification and meaning making as it relates to your research question, and progressive movement toward more abstract and theory-laden questions later in the interview. These latter questions, asked too early, before the researcher and participant have explored dimensions of participant experience and gained some trust, may shut down the flow of responses during the interview or result in superficial responses. Moving toward closure in the interview, the research should invite the participant to add any final thoughts and should wrap up the interview by reminding the participant of the value of her or his contribution to the research.

As with qualitative research in general, the semi-structured interview protocol is designed to be cumulative and iterative. It creates the space for a continuum of structure. What the participant narrates and how that narrative unfolds inform the remaining segments of the interview. The questions you prepare should progressively lead the participant into a full consideration of your variables of interest. How you guide your participant through the protocol is another crucial aspect within qualitative research. In the next chapter, consideration is given to your role in carrying out the interview.

The Semi-Structured Interview

Collecting and Analyzing Qualitative Data

3

Conducting the Interview

The Role of Reciprocity and Reflexivity

To do this type of research [the researcher] must pay the
price of intense awareness of self and others and must con-
stantly attempt to define relationships which are ordinarily
taken for granted.
—Dollard (1949, p. 20)

Central to this chapter is an exploration of the ways in which you might
conduct a semi-structured interview in a manner that is productive
for both you and the participant. A common thread across qualitative
research and its diversity of interpretive paradigms is attention to the
role of the researcher. This is particularly true when the semi-structured
interview is used as a data-collection method. Here, it is fundamental to
reflect and act upon the nature of the exchange between the researcher
and participant. You may prompt the participant, rephrase questions,
and make changes according to the interview situation. In this manner,
the idea of *researcher as instrument* is a frequent point of emphasis evident in qualitative research.

This chapter offers a closer look at the way in which the semi-
structured interview provides space for reciprocity between you and the
participant and for reflexivity in terms of dilemmas encountered within
the research project. These dilemmas are methodological, theoretical,

and inevitably deeply ethical as you reflect back and recalibrate elements of the data collection and analysis. This chapter explores closely the nature of interviewing, in general, as an interaction between two individuals, with the benefits and drawbacks inherent in this method.

By discussing a number of interview excerpts and vignettes from the desegregation study, I underscore here the unpredictability even within a well-planned protocol. The chapter consists of two sections: the first focuses on efforts to achieve reciprocity with your participants and the second focuses on the need for reflexivity to assess the particular methodological and ethical snags that frequently emerge as you proceed with your qualitative research. These processes play a role across many interpretive traditions within qualitative research. The theorizing as to research purpose and the means through which reciprocity and reflexivity might be achieved reflect the particular orientation of these traditions. The focus on reciprocity and reflexivity provides an important backdrop for anticipating a discussion of data analysis and interpretation.

Approximating Reciprocity: Engaging Participants in Clarification, Meaning Making, and Critical Reflection

Key to effective interviewing is the researcher's attention to the participant's narrative *as it is unfolding.* Well-informed judgments on the part of the researcher are important as to when and *when not* to interrupt the participant as he or she responds to a question. Guiding the participant within open-ended questions takes some anticipation of possible routes he or she may travel in responding, and you must ascertain what further inquiry is appropriate and often necessary. It also takes some spontaneity and guesswork, as you come upon junctures in the interview that potentially offer a deeper understanding of the participant's narrative.

In this way, your role is to keep one eye on where you are and the other on where you're headed. Contributing to your interviewing skills and decision making is the depth at which you have explored the phenomenon of study, particularly through your ongoing immersion in data collection and analysis. As thematic patterns emerge and are explored and labeled as codes, you will become more attentive to further evidence of these patterns in future interviews. However, *this strategy should be kept in check*. It is important not to overload an interview with excessive attention to your search for converging and diverging thematic trends in the data. This approach has the potential to dull your sensitivity to what is said *and* not said during the interview. It also may slant your questioning in pursuit of confirming evidence. In general, then, it is best to focus the interview on the task at hand: eliciting from the participant the meaning he or she gives to the focus of study and capturing that meaning as accurately as possible.

As there is some degree of risk in the decisions you make over the course of an interview, you will need to revisit decisions and reflect back on the consequences of those decisions. Qualitative research therefore involves reflexivity. This reflexivity is intimately bound up in all phases of the research, often contributing in substantial ways to the resulting conceptual framework.

Carrying out your interview relies on two orienting tasks: the first is to listen closely to the participant for points in need of clarification and further generation of meaning; the second is to locate and place on hold points in the interview to which you may return later for elaboration or on which you may invite the participant to critically reflect. These processes reflect the reciprocity you as a researcher offer the participant during the interview.

In discussing researcher-participant reciprocity, this chapter draws on the work of the feminist theorist Patti Lather (1986). Lather refers to reciprocity as the "give and take, a mutual negotiation of meaning and power" (p. 267). This give and take occurs in communicative space, which is the space of engagement between the researcher and participant. It also occurs in conceptual space, which is the space of engagement between data and theory. Both incite a dialectic between contrasting ideas, alternating explanations, and multiple angles of vision. At the heart of this dialectic is the notion of reciprocity—creating an exchange between the empirical data as it is collected and analyzed and the theory embedded in one's questions, framework, and design. Sometimes that means a conceptual tussle during one's analysis; other times it means an interviewing process that not only documents and records but also interacts and engages with participants, who bring to the interview experience and knowledge. Because participant experience and knowledge are shaped by a set of conditions, possibilities, and constraints, your interview may involve some form of analytical interruptions for the purpose of working out the tensions between the theoretical and empirical.

Reciprocity also is facilitated according to the structure of your interview. Some interviews are spaced out over the course of several sessions. This allows you time to concentrate fully on the various segments of your interview. It also creates space for you and your participant to think more deeply about responses to interview questions, to revisit points from a previous session, with ample time to construct meaning. Other interviews take place in one sitting but are structured to create openings for an unencumbered narrative on the part of the participant as well as more direct questions regarding the study focus.

In the following sections we will discuss several types of communicative and conceptual reciprocity, using three approaches: clarification, meaning generation, and critical reflection. This discussion is not intended to be exhaustive, because there are other forms of engagement between the participant and the researcher and/or between data and theory. The discussion weaves together general statements regarding each form of reciprocity with excerpts from interviews I conducted for the desegregation study.

Carrying Out the Interview and Approaching Reciprocity within the Desegregation Study: Participant Engagement in Clarification

In general, a frequent form of participant engagement in the semi-structured interview is intended to achieve clarification and understanding. This is crucial, as your understanding of the participant's response may be inaccurate. Engaging for clarification ensures, as much as possible, accuracy in interpretation. It also gives space for further elaboration and depth in terms of the focus of the participant.

In the desegregation study, the first segment created space for an opening narrative. In this segment, as we have seen, I asked several broad questions that guided a student in telling me a story about his or her schooling experience, or that helped parents to talk about their children's experience. This section of the interview required that I follow the narrative as it was presented and interrupt when necessary for clarity, additional information, and a layer of complexity that may have not been immediately accessible. Probing for clarification is instrumental in adding meaning and depth to the data.

In order to look more closely at asking for participant clarification, I highlight an example from an interview with a white parent in the desegregation study. As noted earlier, the interview protocol for the desegregation study began with a question or two about the background of the participants, and then I invited them to talk about the community and each phase of their schooling, from elementary to high school. In the transcription excerpt below, I had begun the interview with one of the standard opening questions on the protocol: "Could you tell me, were you born in Shaker Heights or did you move here at a certain point with your family?" As was typical for my interviews, one of the participants, Mary, narrated her experience for a considerable period of time. In my transcripts, there are five pages of transcription in which Mary provided me with information without any prompts. As Mary was headed in the direction I had sought, I refrained from interrupting, creating the space for as much detail and perspective as I could secure in this first segment of the interview.

As a result, early in the interview, I was already fairly well informed about Mary's entrée into and early parenting years in the city. In this first segment of the interview I learned that Mary's professional background is in education and that neither she nor her husband was born in Shaker Heights. They moved to a white middle-class neighborhood centrally located within Shaker Heights after her husband took a job in Cleveland in the late 1960s upon his completion of an advanced degree at an Ivy League institution. Mary had begun to tell me of her dissatisfaction with the traditional education her oldest child was getting in kindergarten in a district school located in their neighborhood. She then shifted into a new narrative on her involvement in the late 1960s with the district's desegregation plan at the elementary school level. On the surface, her abrupt shift seemed like a digression but, as becomes evident in the transcript, her referencing the district's desegregation plan of 1970 is actually quite connected to her story about her dissatisfaction with her daughter's education. Furthermore, it responded directly to my research question on participants' conceptualization of racial equality. In the transcription below, there are illustrations of my engaging Mary in clarification of her experience, seeking elaboration or further depth into her experience and views.

MARY: And I was not very happy with the experience she [the 5-year-old daughter] had because it was lots of coloring and pictures and that kind of thing and that's not how she had been raised, so her pictures never got put up because she didn't stay inside the lines.

ANNE: Oh, my God.

MARY: So she was feeling badly and I was applauding, saying "Well, great, you're not to stay inside the lines," but at that same time then—so this was now—'69 . . . you may want to correct me on the dates . . . The board of education came up with the desegregation plan, and the first plan was—that only African American children would be transferred from Moreland School to other schools.

ANNE: Right, the one-way busing.

MARY: Right, one-way busing, and—we were part of a group of citizens that went to the board of education and said, "Now, you know, this is not the way it should be . . . white people should also be involved in transferring their children . . ."

ANNE: [interrupting] Were you—

MARY: [continuing] ". . . to aid desegregation."

ANNE: Were you a formal group, or was it just kind of—had it come out of the meeting in February when the superintendent first presented the plan, and then people began to formulate [a response]? Or did you know about the plan earlier? I mean, did people know about that plan?

MARY: I don't remember those details, but it was a fairly formal group in that, you know, people who felt strongly about this met over a number of months.

ANNE: You did?

MARY: And then took a recommendation to the board of education or to the superintendent who was then Dr. Lawson, I believe.

ANNE: Right—that's what I have, yeah.

MARY: And, um, so out of that input from citizens grew the Shaker Schools Plan.

ANNE: Uh-huh, and let me just backtrack on that one, um, I'm really interested in how people say, "This is not fair because the onus is on the black families."

MARY: Um-hmm, um-hmm.

ANNE: You know, and—especially, um, if a group of white parents are saying that, um, they know what they may be encountering—in terms
of their white friends . . .

MARY: Um-hmm, um-hmm.

ANNE: . . . who might be like "Geez, let's just, let's do what we have to do
and be done with it and not, you know, try to complicate the matter
further," so I, I guess if—was it a hard time for [this group of white]
people? You know, or was it just a, you know, did you strengthen
each other as a group, um, or—

MARY: Oh, I would say definitely, and, I think as a mother, I was a little bit
more apprehensive about it than my husband was, although I knew
it was the right thing to do, and I think the other part of the equa-
tion is that we were not completely happy at our home school, our
neighborhood school, and we knew that the faculty at Moreland had
a reputation of being creative.

ANNE: Ohhhh.

MARY: And you know willing to sort of, you know, be out there in trying
new things . . .

Through my efforts to engage Mary in clarification, data collected
from the archives and oral histories on the debate about equality related
to the district's first proposed desegregation plan were further vali-
dated. Additionally, I also gained insight into the thinking among the
white parents in the district who supported the idea of desegregation
but opposed the manner in which the district had proposed it be carried out—as a one-way busing plan. This one-way plan, presented to
the Board of Education in February 1970 by Superintendent John Lawson, involved transporting students in grades 4 through 6 from Moreland School, which was predominantly black, to predominantly white
schools in the district. As suggested here, the argument for a two-way
plan, voluntary for all, emerged from the conceptualization of racial
equality as involving *both* white and black families.

Mary's telling of the story shifted from her discussion of her dissatisfaction with the way that the teacher was unwilling to exhibit
her daughter's artwork on the classroom wall, because it failed to stay
"inside the lines," to the district's desegregation plan announced in

February 1970. This excerpt, then, couples a critique about racial equality as not addressed in desegregation with a critique of teaching and learning. These two dimensions of Mary's experience contributed to her decision to add her daughter's name to a list of white students who would be bused to the Moreland School the following year in order to address racial isolation in the predominantly white and predominantly black elementary schools within the district. Embedded in Mary's story is also a consideration of access to quality education, which Mary understood to be located within Moreland School, the focus of the district's desegregation plan.

Probing for clarification is important for ensuring accuracy of the data. Asking a participant to elaborate on a point (e.g., "Could you tell me more?") is likely to yield more details and may offer additional insight. It also buys you time, should you need to think through additional questions while the participant is further explaining a point. In another excerpt here, I asked a participant for multiple points of clarification. Lynne is a black parent from the Ludlow area, a predominantly black neighborhood. She is also an alumna of the district. Lynne narrates the struggle of her sons who attended school in early 2000.

LYNNE: But it's very different, I found, for girls than boys.

ANNE: Yeah, I think so.

LYNNE: I mean, I know in gender it is [different in general, but] for African Americans, it's very different.

ANNE: Uh-huh.

LYNNE: Yeah.

[*Slight pause*]

ANNE: I don't want to make any assumptions about what you're saying. Do you mind . . .

LYNNE: Well . . .

ANNE: . . . expanding on that a little bit?

LYNNE: Well, here, I'll give you an example . . . when we went to the Honors Assembly at the end of the year.

ANNE: At the high school?

LYNNE: At the high school, um-hmmm. Now, I don't remember specifically, but I would say [my daughters] got 3.5 and above for honors, but . . . there was nobody: No African American male at that 3.5 and

above, and in [other honor assemblies she attended] there may have
been nobody or no more than 2 or 3.

ANNE: Right, 3.5 and above.

LYNNE: Yeah, and only a handful of 3 points and above. Now there were
a few more females. But the difference in lack of African American
males with academic achievement was—significant.

[*Slight pause*]

ANNE: So then, how does that affect your sons?

LYNNE: Um, my oldest son left Shaker after 10th grade.

ANNE: Oh. [*slight pause*] OK.

LYNNE: My youngest son is about to go into ninth grade, and I don't know
if I'm going to keep him at Shaker.

ANNE: OK, [*writing*] not sure for ninth grader. OK, and your ninth grader
has been in the middle school.

LYNNE: Um-hmm . . .

ANNE: In the advanced classes?

LYNNE: Um-hmm.

ANNE: Is he alone or are there other black males in the classes?

LYNNE: [*makes breathing sound, like a laugh, or exasperated sound, or
muted cough*] There's a couple, although in his English class, this year,
he wanted to get out of it, because he was the only African American
in his English class, yeah, he wanted to get out of it. But I made him
stay, and he didn't do well. In his science class, there were two other
African American males. There probably were some females, but he
doesn't talk about them [*laughs a little*]. Um [*tap of pen*], he felt like
the teacher used—used to discriminate against them.

ANNE: Um-hmm—aga—against all the black students or just the—

LYNNE: In his class, the African American males.

ANNE: OK.

LYNNE: 'Cause he'd come home and say things like, "She doesn't believe me
when I tell her something," and he'd say, "We got it all right and she
thought we cheated," stuff like that . . .

In asking Lynne to elaborate on her point about gender and race, I created space for details regarding her observation of the low numbers
of high-achieving black males in the district and her discussion of the
implications that this had for her sons' academic success. This section

of the interview also verifies a thematic pattern reflecting distance and even mistrust between teachers and students; this pattern arose in interviews with black parents, particularly in talking about their sons, or in interviews with the young men themselves. In the language of another African American parent whom I interviewed at another time, "prove yourself!" captured this sense of betrayal narrated by black parents about their sons' experiences.

Engaging Participants in Generating Meaning

Another level of participant engagement is for the purpose of uncovering the meaning of some dimension of the participant's talk during an interview. While engaging participants in a process of clarification allows you to have increased confidence about the accuracy of word usage, engaging participants in generating meaning takes the interview below the surface of words, expression, and metaphors to the *meaning* participants give to their narratives. This is particularly important because the interviews may introduce meanings you did not anticipate. The introduction of new meaning contributes to your interpretation of the data and your efforts to respond to your research question. Frequently the source of surprise, participants' generation of meaning is likely to complicate your analysis, and it is often the source of new analytical codes and the restructuring of an emerging conceptual framework.

Creating space for unpacking meaning will contribute to the accuracy of your analysis. It may also set the stage for you to reintroduce participant meaning of a particular event or phenomenon later in the interview in an effort to position it in relation to other interpretations of the same phenomenon, theoretical or empirical.

Further drawing from the desegregation study, I provide an excerpt below from my interview with Michael, a black parent whose child attended the district in the 1970s. At this point in the interview, I pursued a question originating from my study of archival and historical data about the district's effort to desegregate at the elementary school level in 1970. My study of the archival data had found there to be considerable opposition to *any* form of desegregation among a vocal group of white parents. However, as noted in the previous transcription excerpt with Mary, there was also opposition among a group of parents, some of whom were white and others of whom were black, who supported desegregation but questioned the inequality inherent in a busing plan that involved black students only.

To some extent I had come prepared to explore this dimension with Michael, as I had located his name in the archives as playing a role in the debate over Moreland's desegregation. I selected him as a participant for his particular experience at that time in the district's history. In my interview with Michael, I held back initially from asking direct questions until he told me a considerable part of his story, unstructured by my questions or interjections. Michael's interview was conducted before Mary's, and each offered an angle of vision shaped by race and their engagement with others in raising concerns about the inequality imposed on the black students and their families in the district's desegregation plan. These two interviews and several others, along with more archival analysis, provided insight into the experience of individuals within an institution engaged in the question of how educational structures might facilitate racial equality.

Below, I am trying to understand the nature of the opposition by a multiracial group of parents from Moreland toward the district's desegregation plan. I asked Michael about his thoughts regarding the Board of Education meeting on February 10, 1970, when the superintendent offered a proposal for desegregation at the elementary school level. Michael's interpretation of the district's stance and his use of "ultimatum" in place of "plan" generated new meaning absent in the study until this interview. Here, I draw on the archival and oral history data that had prompted a question in my mind as to why there appeared to be tepid support within the African American community of Moreland School for the desegregation plan proposed in February 1970.

ANNE: Were you at that meeting by any chance, that board meeting?
MICHAEL: Yes.
ANNE: In February?
MICHAEL: Yes, I . . .
ANNE: What do you remember about it?
MICHAEL: I remember that it was kind of heated . . .
ANNE: Yes.

MICHAEL: . . . and we were given an ultimatum.

ANNE: Huh.

MICHAEL: "Take it or leave it."

ANNE: This is the plan.

MICHAEL: Yeah, yeah.

ANNE: Wow! Because I remember, um, talking with someone, a white person, who was at the meeting—and mentioned that, you know, of those black parents that were attending, nobody stood up in support of the plan. At that point I didn't realize that the plan was really a deviation from what a lot of black parents really wanted.

MICHAEL: You mean didn't support which plan?

ANNE: The Board of Ed's plan.

MICHAEL: Oh, oh yes.

ANNE: Which you're saying was like an ultimatum . . .

MICHAEL: Oh, yeah.

ANNE: . . . and this person who was saying was kind of mystified, "Well, isn't this what they were asking for, it's integration," you know?

MICHAEL: Um-hmm.

ANNE: And I was kind of mystified, too, but I'm beginning to understand now, that from what you're saying, what some other people were saying and the archives, there was a difference of opinion about how integration should be achieved.

MICHAEL: Right.

ANNE: And so possibly the reason why no black parents stood up, beside the fact that it may have been a very heated session, as you said . . .

MICHAEL: Umm.

ANNE: . . . was because there wasn't a wellspring of support for this particular plan.

MICHAEL: Right.

ANNE: OK.

While the "ultimatum" was clear to Michael, it had been far less clear to me in my study of the archival materials. And the interviews thus far, as well as most of the district reporting at that time, had not sufficiently reflected the point that this "voluntary" district plan did *not* seem voluntary for the parents of Moreland. In this sense, the interview with Michael played a role not only in clarifying but also in generating significant meaning on how desegregation may not necessarily yield racial equality. This became all the more clear in a subsequent section of the interview, several transcription pages later, as indicated in the excerpt here, during which I sought Michael's perspective to understand better the views among African American parents at Moreland.

ANNE: There's not a lot about all of this. Basically in the chronology of events there is this presentation in February, and then some recognition of a flurry of activity and then a revised plan in May or June, which reflected voluntary cross enrollment, but there's very little—

MICHAEL: Well, there would be—

ANNE: talk about what happened.

[*Both speaking at the same time*]

MICHAEL: there would be—

ANNE: in between [*laughs a little*].

MICHAEL: There would be voluntary cross enrollment, if we could get enough volunteers.

ANNE: Right.

MICHAEL: The burden was put on us . . .

ANNE: OK [*suddenly very serious*].

MICHAEL: . . . to go to the other schools, the other parents, and solicit . . .

ANNE: OK [*like it's dawning on her*].

MICHAEL: . . . volunteers.

ANNE: All right.

ANNE: So then—

[*Both speaking at the same time*]

MICHAEL: And if—

MICHAEL: And if we could get enough volunteers to meet a quota or whatever their figure was, they would consider the plan.

ANNE: OK, voluntary only if you get the numbers. Now you had to get the numbers from black parents and white parents, right? If you were doing . . .

MICHAEL: Well, . . .

ANNE: . . . a cross-enrollment.

MICHAEL: . . . we were strictly concerned about white parents coming to Moreland: that was our biggest concern. There were a considerable amount of black parents that wanted, you know, their children to be bused, to the other elementaries, but our real task was to get . . .

ANNE: Ummmm.

MICHAEL: . . . white parents to volunteer their children to come to More-land School.

As Michael notes, the original one-way plan meant that for the students in fourth through sixth grade, the entire student body would be bused to schools outside their neighborhood, essentially shuttering the upper elementary section of their school. Several groups of parents raised questions about this plan, including a multiracial group from Moreland and a group of white parents whose children attended other elementary schools. This confluence of parent pressure ultimately succeeded in convincing the district of the benefits of a two-way plan that kept all grades at Moreland open and created in this school what I later analyze as a desegregated site of educational privilege.

While the above form of participant engagement reflects some aspects of clarification, there is actually something deeper happening here. In the interview, Michael and I are engaged in generating meaning from his experience. This complicated the use of "voluntary" in my analysis of archival and oral history data. Here, I probe for greater depth in terms of a chronology of events. However, what is interesting is that my openness to meaning making that has already been established in the interview (as illustrated in the first excerpt) may have facilitated Michael's willingness to reveal more about his perspective. In this second excerpt, Michael speaks directly to the parameters of the debate on equality as it related to racial integration.

This shift back and forth between me and Michael underscores the purpose of engaging participants in meaning making as one conducts the semi-structured interview. Creating space within the interview for the participant to challenge, question, and discuss with you dimensions of the topic of study is invaluable to your research. It is central to the interpretive process. At times it can be humbling to the researcher, as in the exchange here, which occurred later in my interview with Michael.

MICHAEL: The parents in Moreland were given an ultimatum that you take what we've offered you and that's it! At a later date, we came up with

the percentage of whites in this school and that school and everything, ok, so, the volunteer thing did involve black parents. Also,
all black parents didn't have to volunteer to go because I didn't. So,
there was some resistance to that, you know, kind of like ha, ha, ha,
go ahead and do it if you can—to us—go ahead and find enough
[white] volunteers.

ANNE: OK . . . I've been curious about those pressures that, um, were on
Shaker Heights and that contributed to it going into a voluntary
direction, because sometimes a—

MICHAEL: Not, not a voluntary. Originally, it was a mandatory . . .

ANNE: A mandatory . . .

MICHAEL: . . . program.

Occurring one-third of the way into the interview, and well after the
interactions excerpted earlier, Michael once again reminded me of the
way in which "voluntary," as a discourse in the district, was contested
by those for whom it most greatly applied: the predominantly black and
working-class students of Moreland School. This interview in particular, and the meaning generated for the data through my interaction
with Michael, was crucial in my theorizing about the tensions within
the community in conceptualizing racial equality.

The generation of meaning may occur as a result of a question you
bring to the interview, as when I deliberately sought Michael's knowledge of a particular moment in the district's history. At other times,
however, meaning making with the participant may be unplanned,
emerging through the participant's narrative.

To illustrate this, I draw from an interview with Matt, a student from
the 1970s who is white. Matt's parents supported the desegregation of
the district through the cross-enrollment plan, and they sent Matt to
Moreland when he reached the fourth grade, the grade at which white
students could be bused. My interview with Matt was important in providing a perspective of a student who was an early participant in the
two-way desegregation program.

In this excerpt, Matt is talking about his first year at Moreland and
his experience of "feeling very isolated" that year. He highlights an incident on the playground, where he used a disparaging word that was
interpreted as racist by the black students with whom he was playing. In

this excerpt, Matt communicates to me his shock over the response of the black students toward his actions.

> MATT: I remember my fourth-grade year as being, as feeling very isolated, and unhappy, not myself feeling integrated into the Moreland school . . . and there were some problems on the playground. I remember one particular problem, where it—probably [as] a fourth grader I was in a kickball game, on the playground, and got into an argument about something, and I used the word "bitch" . . .
>
> [*Slight pause*]
> [*Anne laughs a little.*]
>
> MATT: . . . in a heated argument with another black boy, and he thought it was a racial slur, and all of a sudden I was surrounded and the target of, um, you know, violent posturing and a little bit of pushing and shoving. But it wasn't just he and I anymore, it was me against the community, with the community around me and I thought—it still sticks in my mind as a cultural ignorance. I had no idea that it was going to be taken as a racial issue, I didn't intend it that way but I learned quickly that I had to be more careful, and, I think, it encouraged me to be less—out there.
>
> ANNE: Ummmmm—you mean—spontaneous?
> MATT: Yeah.
> ANNE: OK, more, more cautious.
> MATT: Yes, very much so.

Something about Matt's wording, "I had to be more careful" and "it encouraged me to be less—out there" struck a chord with me. In Matt's consideration of how he responded to this situation, and its effect on him that first year at Moreland, I found his description of his response to have resonance, although I couldn't put my finger on a connection. I wanted to understand the process he was narrating, and so I engaged Matt in generating some meaning around this experience.

At this point in the interview, I felt it important to learn how Matt's experience on the playground and his response to it influenced his views on racial equality. Typically in my interviews, I held off from asking questions like this until much later. But something caused me to press forward. Below, still continuing from the same excerpt, I probe to understand Matt's response to this event. The probe is not very well thought out but it is enough to generate further exploration between Matt and me regarding this experience. He illustrated how his first year at Moreland created a contradiction for him in how he understood his relationship with black youth and his views regarding racial equality.

ANNE: Did, did you resent—you know, did you find that it complicated your—um, your view of blacks and, you know . . .

MATT: Yeah, yeah.

ANNE: Um-hmm.

MATT: Because, ah, to back up for a minute, my block had some people who were [*pause*] who reacted very negatively to a program that my mom was involved in. It was a program where inner-city Cleveland kids would spend a portion of their summers . . .

ANNE: Ohhhhh.

MATT: . . . in Shaker Heights, or other suburbs, and we had adopted a kid, called [*name*] and we're still, we're still in contact. Our street included some very hostile parents who would not let their kids cross the street and play with us, um, they were concerned about, you know, bugs and lice [*speaks quietly*] and don't let their girls touch or play—or do anything with them.

ANNE: Right, right.

MATT: And—so that was my first real exposure to, um, that sort of, ah, racism, and it was a great lesson for me as a young kid because I loved this guy. We played together, and there was a nice group of boys on our side of the street that just had a great time, all summer long, and it was clear that that was the right thing and that what [those across the street] were doing was the wrong thing. To me it was very clear.

ANNE: Yeah.

MATT: Black and white, and, so, I became sort of, a staunch supporter, early in my life [*laughs a little*] of the benefits of integration, at least treating people equally, and so then to go in fourth grade and feel like because I was white I was being treated differently in a community that was black, did complicate my views of racial . . . [*I'm quite certain he said "equality" here, but he speaks it very quietly, his voice drops down as he ends this sentence. Unfortunately, I did not follow up later with him on this point. However, because Matt returned to this*

point in the final segment of the interview, I was able to draw consider-
able meaning from that portion of his narrative.]

These data that emerged as a result of engaging Matt contributed greatly to my analysis of students' experiences of racial equality and their views on this topic. Matt's interview in particular raised my awareness of an experience of dissonance narrated by some white students within what I later analyzed as desegregated sites of educational privilege. It was significant to me that in Matt's interview the narrative about dissonance itself was not shut down, nor was there flight from it, but instead he reflected a willingness to explore this experience. As I moved along in the study, a group of black students also narrated some level of dissonance, although within a very different set of conditions. In the following excerpt, which is later in Matt's interview and during the third segment, which is more structured and abstract and explicitly focused on views of racial equality, Matt discussed his views further. Through these excerpts from his narrative, it is evident how the More-land experience in particular shaped Matt's understanding of equality in the district as complex, as not having been achieved, and yet as offering the potential for growth at the individual and institutional level. Matt's notion of "stretching" stuck with me and influenced my analysis of the relational and structural dimensions of the student narratives. It informed my understanding of how students' conceptualizations of racial equality were shaped by their locations in particular educational structures and within certain conditions.

MATT: When I was at Moreland, you know, fourth grade I felt isolated, fifth grade was better, by the end of—by the middle of sixth grade, I felt comfortable enough to run for student council president.

ANNE: Ohhhh.

MATT: And they felt comfortable enough to elect me and I think that says more, ah, as much, certainly, about my comfort level . . .

ANNE: Um-hmm.

MATT: . . . at the school, a general feeling of acceptance, and being will-ing to risk and bring my identity into a leadership role in a school where two years before, I felt, it was the last place I ever wanted to be. I think it's a real testament to the familiarity and exposure and

> the benefits of integrating, stretching yourself in areas where you're
> uncomfortable, long enough, and sticking it out long enough . . .
> ANNE: Sticking it out, yeah—
> MATT: . . . to become integrated into that—environment.

Engaging participants in generating meaning as it relates to their narratives increases the trustworthiness of your data. It is also a form of reciprocity. It draws the participant into attending to ideas he or she has put forward in the interview. These ideas, often conveyed in stories and symbolic language, such as Matt's discussion of an experience of social and intellectual "stretching," have the potential to generate thematic patterns across interviews.

Drawing Participants into Critical Reflection

An additional manner in which you might probe more deeply during the interview is through the critical engagement of the participants on some dimension of the narrated experience. This degree of engagement is guided by dimensions of critical theory, one of many interpretive traditions you may consider in carrying out your research. Involving your participant in critical reflection in the space of the interview is in keeping with the overarching purpose of critical theory. It supports a view of knowledge as grounded in human experience, and it reflects tensions between human agency and structural conditions. To get at lived experience, critical theorists analyze data in a manner that attends to the relationship between the individual and his or her context, theorized as posing constraints and opportunities reflecting relations of power.

As noted earlier, the critical theorists Phil Carspecken and Michael Apple (1992) describe the role of dialogue between a researcher and participant. Carspecken and Apple underscore this dialogue as instrumental to exploring the participant's experiences in relation to broader social and systemic patterns. This dialogue creates space for the participant and researcher to reflect on the emerging narrative as lodged within layers of complex structural, historical, and relational dimensions (Carspecken & Apple, 1992, p. 512). The process of engagement around "thinking" and "consciousness" is central to the critical tradition and owes much of its articulation to the work of the Brazilian educator and critical pedagogy theorist Paulo Freire (1970/2000). Such engage-ment provides an eye for "cognitive alternatives" in societies highly stratified by forms of difference accorded valuative status, as theorized by the social psychologists Henri Tajfel and John Turner (1979). It also reflects the work of the social psychologist and Jesuit priest Ignacio Martín-Baró (1994), who used public opinion polls to offer Salvador-ans a way to "confront their own image, to see their own opinions and attitudes objectified" and "to examine with a more critical eye the con-trast between what they are living and thinking and what the prevailing discourse is pronouncing" (p. 192). For each of the works cited here, there is a deliberation concerning method toward "opening pathways to building more just and human historical alternatives" (Martín-Baró, 1994, p. 197).

Within the semi-structured interview, then, there is space for re-searchers and participants to engage in a critical reflection of the data. At appropriate junctures during the interview, opportunities may arise for the researcher and participant to inquire into the connections between the participant's experiences and a constellation of human relationships, institutional structures and discourse, and broader socio-political considerations.

As the interview unfolds, there may be moments where the researcher is aware that the participant's narrative offers a particular angle of vision that is considerably different from the theoretical framework or orienting theory driving the research design and analysis. Within the parameters of a semi-structured interview, there is room to explore this gap *later* in the interview, and well after the participant has narrated his or her experience. The later segments of the semi-structured interview allow room for the researcher to pursue questions that critically engage the researcher and participant in exploring the participant's experience through another angle of vision, informed by theory and perhaps other data emerging out of the research.

Engaging the researcher and participant in critical reflection dur-ing the interview itself reflects a form of "dialectical theory building" (Lather, 1986, p. 267), and it yields further texturing in the analysis and interpretation of the findings. As in the case of engaging the participant and researcher in clarifying and in the generation of meaning, creat-ing space for critical reflection within the semi-structured interview

provides some degree of reciprocity between the researcher and participant, between data and theory, and it contributes greatly to the generation of major coding categories and the interpretation of the data.

To illustrate reciprocity in the form of critical reflection, I include
another excerpt from the desegregation study. This interview was with
Jill, a white student who graduated in the late 1990s. In approaching
some form of critical reflection with Jill, I raised a question concerning her narrative of experiencing racial inequality in the upper elementary school in the district. It is useful to look at the interaction between
Jill and me during this third and final segment, well after we worked
through the first two segments. At this point in the interview, I had
asked Jill a question from the protocol, "Could you give me an example
of racial equality or inequality as you have observed or experienced it
in the school system?" In response, Jill returned to an earlier narrative
of her struggle at the district's upper elementary school due to hostility she and several other white students experienced from black students in her class, in which she and her white peers were a minority.
She referred to this as an illustration of racial inequality in response to
my question.

ANNE: . . . something that happened where you said, "Gee, that's really
racial equality" [or] . . . you may have had a moment where you had
a concrete experience . . . where you really clearly saw inequality and
it troubled you. I'm trying to get images, stories of how people have
seen things happen in their lives—which they saw as really being an
instance of racial equality or a real instance of racial inequality.

JILL: Well, I think my [upper elementary] experience would be a good
example of inequality, socially speaking, because it affected the educational setting definitely.

ANNE: [*quietly*] Right.

JILL: Um.

[*Pause*]

ANNE: Inequality in the sense that the individuals who were suffering from
the inequality were the minority, which would have been the white
students? Is that . . .

JILL: Yeah.

ANNE: . . . what you're referring to?

JILL: Yeah, it was, a very interesting, this class was probably 20 black students and 4 white students. I mean, race was a huge issue that year because the students made it so known [*slight pause*] and made it such an issue.

ANNE: Was, you know, was it around resentment of any particular aspect?

JILL: They were just, the black kids in my class, mo—most of them, tended to, they just hated the white kids . . .

ANNE: Uh-huh.

JILL: . . . because we were white, and because we were smart.

ANNE: Uh-huh.

Jill's narrative in the early and middle segments of her interview had revealed her consistent access to educational opportunity and academic outcomes. This evidence did not de-legitimate her experience of inequality. However, I wanted to revisit the narrative with her and to explore with her how her experience might be tied to patterns of inequality evident in the archival and oral history data, as well as interview data. These thematic patterns revealed how black students were excluded or were on the periphery of sites of education privilege. Notions of "white and smart" needed further critical reflection, and I hoped Jill and I might work this through a consideration of the larger structural inequality that likely contributed to the tension between the students and which complicated the view of this event as a form of racial inequality for her. There was room during the last segment in the interview, well after Jill had responded to very open-ended questions about her experience, to pursue this alternative line of analysis with Jill, to understand her thinking further, and to see what such an engagement might yield.

JILL: And—

ANNE: Were all of the white kids being pulled out for the advanced course, was that . . .

JILL: Ah—

ANNE: . . . when you say "because we were white and we were smart" um—

JILL: I was the only one pulled out for math. I think we were all pulled out for language arts.

ANNE: Uh-huh. Do you think that aggravated it in any way?

JILL: Probably.

ANNE: Uh-huh—ok—um—

JILL: It was sort of like, "Well, why are the white kids getting the opportunity to pull out and take other classes?"

ANNE: Right, right.

JILL: And, honestly, I don't know what was going on in their minds.

In this segment of the interview, Jill did not question her view of herself in relation to these students and to the educational structures in which she was participating—and from which the black students were excluded. At one point during my probing, there was an opening of possibility, where Jill expressed a consideration of the experience of those excluded from the advanced classes when she says, "It was sort of like, 'Well, why are the white kids getting the opportunity to pull out and take other classes?' " At the same time, the extent to which she appears willing to understand further the perspective of the black students in her class, and perhaps more deeply explore inequality, was limited. This was evident in the statement immediately following her expression of possible reasons for the black students' resentment, when Jill concludes "And, honestly, I don't know what was going on in their minds." It is at that point that the engagement of critical lines of reflection shuts down.

In another example of critical engagement, I was listening to Carol, a student from the 1980s who is black, talk about her senior year in high school. Seeing no need to stay in school all day with each of her four courses alternating with study hall periods, Carol asked her guidance counselor to line her courses up consecutively in the morning to allow Carol to finish her school day midday instead of the traditional time of dismissal around 3 P.M. Below, I explore with Carol what I increasingly came to see as a kind of benign neglect on the part of her guidance counselor—not an outright act of exclusion but a failure to draw her into a full realization of the education for which the district is known.

CAROL: And I did go to her [counselor] and I said, "Is there any way I can get all of my classes first through fourth period and leave after fourth period?" And she did change it. So I had first period math, second period I think I had history, third period it was English, and I forget —fourth period was probably gym, or something . . .

ANNE: And that was a real benefit for you to be able to leave and . . .

CAROL: Yes, yes it was.

ANNE: OK, 'cause you think of the issue of equality and then you think well [pause] thinking about students today, if it's a financial need then you don't want to deprive a student.

CAROL: Right, but it wasn't even a financial need. I just liked my job 'cause I worked in a supermarket then.

ANNE: But you know as a parent, like thinking of your own daughter . . .

CAROL: Right.

ANNE: . . . when she's in high school, and if she says, "Well, I want to leave at this period."

CAROL: Right.

ANNE: You know, well, of course, college now and everything, it's more and more competitive, but you might have second thoughts, and I don't know maybe you wouldn't but . . .

CAROL: I don't know because my schedule, when I got my schedule in the mail, I had like first period math and then it was like study hall, study hall . . .

ANNE: Right, but what I'm wondering is why your counselor wouldn't have said, gee, if you really like math, here's another, this teacher's a great economics teacher, or . . .

CAROL: Um-hmm, she didn't, she didn't. She changed my schedule from when I was there from fourth period.

ANNE: Right, right, which you, you appreciated.

CAROL: Right.

ANNE: Um, you see where I'm going with—

CAROL: I understand what you're saying.

Because her narrative fit a pattern in the data, I attempted to raise with Carol the possibility that the counselor's ease in making the schedule change might reflect a broader phenomenon of inequality. I was aware of a tension between Carol's narrative of her experience and my study of emerging patterns in the archival, oral history, and interview data. I felt compelled to explore an analysis at the structural level with Carol because I *anticipated it was the line of analysis I would offer in my study.*

As noted in my discussion of the development of the interview protocol for the desegregation study, I planned the third segment of the interview to include the most abstract of my interview questions— questions focused on participants' conceptualizations of racial equality. Often in this third segment, the participants would return to an experience they narrated earlier in the interview, or I might reference an experience they had narrated. This permitted us to revisit the experience, to give it greater contextualization by exploring the complexity of relationships within educational structures at particular moments in the district's desegregation history. I was never fully satisfied with how I facilitated this level of participant engagement. However, when I did *not* make the attempt, I felt the reciprocity I had offered the participant was thin. I was conscious in those interviews of having not found a way to draw the participant into a critical reflection of his or her experience and conceptualizations of racial equality.

This form of reciprocity, of engaging participants in critical reflection during an interview, is fraught with risk. It could shut down the participant, create a level of defensiveness, or steer the participant toward answering questions in a manner the participant perceives you to favor. It is best, therefore, to delay this type of researcher-participant exchange until much later in the interview (or interview process, should your interview be spaced out over several sessions).

Many researchers, guided by other interpretive traditions, would eschew this level of researcher-participant engagement. While it offers an effort to get at meaning, it imposes a particular line of analysis and decenters the participant's authority as the narrator. Keep in mind your research question and research purpose as you consider the nature of reciprocity in the researcher-participant relationship and interaction. This will help you to respond in a deliberate and purposeful manner as you encounter participant responses rich in their potential for complex analysis.

The interactive nature of the semi-structured interview creates space for such complexity. Reciprocity in general, and critical reflection in particular, is facilitated by the following: close listening to the participant's narrative, ongoing and iterative analysis of the data, and working out the tension between data and theory. This is evident in my notes below, documenting a telephone interview with Lorraine, a student from the 1980s. Lorraine, who identified as black, described her advanced course levels, participation in many extracurricular activities, and postsecondary attendance at an Ivy League college. Below are my notes from the third segment of my telephone interview:

> I then went into the third section of the interview . . . [asking her] "Thinking now, what does racial equality in public education mean to you?" She said she "feels really strongly about integrated school systems. But as an adult it needs to be [a] really good school system." She went on to say that she wouldn't care if it's an all black school, it's the quality of education that counts and "is the most important factor." She noted something like in an integrated school the quality of education for black students is "often not happening." I asked her if this was the case in Shaker Heights. She said that there was "no question in my mind" that the "opportunity was there," adding "how easily accessible it felt to people was not clear to me—I wasn't in that position."

During the first and second segments of the interview, Lorraine had narrated her consistent access to educational opportunity and academic outcomes. She was very active in extracurricular activities. Her straightforward account of the advantages of the Shaker system contrasted with other narratives of black students, those who had also experienced its advantages but who narrated an accompanying experience of dissonance from acts of exclusion during their years in the system. Lorraine's narrative also differed from those black students who narrated a consistent experience of exclusion.

Because Lorraine had narrated so few instances of inequality, I had inserted my question "Was this the case in Shaker Heights?" to see if this was an oversight and she would now find in this question an opportunity to narrate her views. Her qualified response, that the "opportunity was there—how easily accessible it felt to people was not clear to me —*I wasn't in that position*," opened up analytical possibilities for me in studying the relationship between two key dimensions of my research question: participants' *experiences of racial equality* and *conceptualizations of equality*. While I did not pursue this further with her, it nevertheless contributed greatly to the research. This single line, particularly the use of the word "position," became a powerful analytical lens from which my conceptual framework was formed. From Lorraine's statement concerning positionality, I drew important interpretive meaning. This may have become clear to me without having asked her this question, but Lorraine's response certainly provided the beginnings of my conceptual framework. In my notes after the interview, I wrote the following:

> This was the first time Lorraine linked opportunity with equality and conceded the possibility that opportunity might be perceived and accessed differently by race. It also reinforces her point that the reason she can't say whether it felt accessible to other people is because she took nearly all advanced placement (AP) courses and had little experience at level 3, the college preparatory level. Also, it ties in to her earlier point about her experience not being "typical" of a black student, because of her being only in AP classes where the curriculum and instruction were far better, according to her. This reminds me of her earlier statements, such as Shaker was a "very good high school for kids like me." Lorraine ended her points where she for the first time linked opportunity and equality with a statement, and she was pretty emphatic here, that she was "not against tracking" but she wished it was "more equal." The only other time she alluded to inequality was in discussing her cousin's placement by the school at the college preparatory, or level 3, courses, when in actuality her cousin had the prerequisites and the academic preparation for the advanced courses. While Lorraine noted her aunt's intervention, she suggested that something like this could happen to other black students. However, she does not return to this point in the interview in order to draw on it in her discussion of equality in the system.

This interaction between Lorraine and me allowed for some degree of critical reflection. However, because this was a telephone interview, I was reluctant to risk much engagement. Telephone interviews are more constrained than an interview in person. They are typically shorter in length. There is also no access to other cues often so rich in meaning and helpful in communicating—body language, facial expressions, and the sound of one's finger tapping on the table to make a point, or the weight of a hand coming down hard with a thud to convey the force of one's statement. There are multiple points of entry that I might have pursued had we met in person. Below are notes from one of the final segments of my interview with Lorraine:

> . . . I asked Lorraine if she could talk about an instance when she saw or experienced something and thought that it was an instance of racial equality—or racial inequality. She paused and then said, "I'm at a bit of a loss." Then she told me, "I understand I was not typical." I asked at this point if that was because of her experience as a black student in the AP levels or because she was from an interracial family? She thought a bit and said "both." She continued, "Clearly, there were other black kids in the classroom at AP levels, but [the] teachers may not have seen me as a black student. As an adult, I perceived this."

Just prior to this last segment of the interview, Lorraine told me she grew up in an interracial family. Earlier in the interview, in response to the question "Could you tell me what racial group would you identify yourself as belonging to? Lorraine had said "black." It was not until we were in the third and last segment of the interview, where we focused on racial equality in a more explicit manner, that Lorraine spoke about her interracial family. I had known about Lorraine's family background before the interview but felt it was up to Lorraine to tell me this or not.

In her completion of the Inclusion of Ingroup in the Self (IIS) scale, Lorraine noted that her sense of connection was stronger among whites, although she traveled with a racially integrated peer group that incorporated not only AP students but also students from several extra-curricular activities. She also noted, "I didn't really develop a strong sense of identity as a black woman until I went to college." The complexity of Lorraine's experience and her views on equality were such that in a face-to-face interview I might have sought to create an opening to discuss her experience further. Short of this, what I was left with were some efforts to probe toward critical reflection. However, in my thank-you letter to Lorraine, I offered some degree of critical analysis. Below is an excerpt from my letter to Lorraine, in which I put in writing what I understood to be her key points, with the hope that she might contact me, should there be a discrepancy or a flaw in my tentative interpretation:

. . . you emphasized that the quality of education is most important, indicating that an academically competitive predominantly black school would be more important to you than an integrated school of lesser quality. In terms of Shaker, you noted that you valued the levels system, but you wished it were more equal. You also noted that while you felt the educational opportunities existed, you were not sure how accessible those opportunities appeared to black students . . . During our interview, you also cautioned me that your experience at Shaker was not a typical experience. This is a phenomenon you described as coming to understand more clearly as an adult. You spoke about being from an interracial family . . . You noted the possibility that some of your teachers may not have perceived you to be a black student. I understand this to mean that the potential for stereotyping and distance may have been reduced by their misperception. This was helpful to me in better understanding your experience and also the context in the high school . . .

Drawing participants into critical reflection was particularly helpful in understanding participants' conceptualizations of equality. It helped me explore the narrative of opportunity in relation to the narrative of racial equality. Lorraine's introduction of one's "position" shaping one's understanding of access and equality led to the idea of *positionality* in my analysis. In this way, engaging my participants in clarification, generation of meaning, and critical reflection furthered my analysis of the data, increasing their depth and complexity.

In each of the excerpts provided from the desegregation study, I have outlined ways in which reciprocity plays a substantive role in qualitative research, in particular within semi-structured interviews. There are many other possible ways to achieve reciprocity between the research and participant. What they share in common is the set of demands they place on the researcher to attend to the nature of the interaction and meaning making as the interview progresses. Given these demands, you frequently find yourself re-attuning (Kohl, 2009, p. 309) and, to use the language of the GPS technology, "recalculating." These highly interactive moments within the interviews yield rich and compelling data that propel the researcher into analysis and interpretation. They also introduce the need for researcher reflexivity, a process of looking closely at what has transpired in the interview or the research in general. Reflexivity allows you to attend to researcher bias and the way in which your decisions may have interfered with the data collection as well as other phases of the research. The next part of this chapter discusses some ethical and methodological dilemmas arising from this highly interactive and in-depth engagement of participants, particularly in the semi-structured interview.

Researcher Reflexivity: Reflecting on Researcher Bias and Recognizing Early Themes in the Process

As we have seen, the semi-structured interview offers great latitude in data collection. Its hybrid nature allows for variation in types of questions and in data-collection tools and materials. At the same time, the interaction between the researcher and participant has the potential to yield disjunctures in meaning and intent. There is considerable unpredictability in interviewing, which can introduce ethical and methodological challenges that complicate the study. To respond to the challenges of carrying out interviews, the researcher must bring a level of reflexivity concerning what transpires during the interview between the researcher and participant.

It is useful here to reintroduce the idea of a researcher as an instrument. As the primary instrument, the researcher extends questions and pursues ideas conveyed in the participants' responses, probes particular statements, and encourages, as well as sometimes shuts down, participants' responses. No researcher conducts interviews free of interference, such as a misplaced probe, an expression of emotion relating to a participant's story, or an exploration of a theme that is emerging but that may not serve that particular interview well. As a result, reflexivity within research is imperative. Through reflexivity, the researcher looks within the research activities, as well as within the relationship between the researcher and her or his participants, in order to locate potential interference. Interference is likely to alter the data and your interpretation. Reflexivity requires the researcher to be vigilant, always anticipating ways in which research methods and ethics may be compromised. Interference of some kind is predictable in both quantitative and qualitative research. It is best to document such interference, so that it is a part of the overall analysis and consideration in your discussions of the limitations of the research. At the same time, it is also important to note that interference, when viewed through a reflexive lens, may be instructive to the research and on some occasions may reveal dimensions important to the research question.

The vignettes below from the desegregation study illustrate the ways in which semi-structured interviews have the potential to yield moments of surprise. These vignettes are included to underscore the issues that might arise, particularly but not exclusively in qualitative research. Often buried within an ethical or methodological dilemma is further rendering of a key idea. Reflexivity allows further opportunity to explore an emerging theme. What follows is the first of three scenarios that discuss concerns that I encountered in carrying out my interviews.

Vignette One: Saving the Exchange

One of my early interviews in the study was with Dan, a white resident who grew up in Malvern, an affluent neighborhood in the city, in the late 1950s through the mid-1960s. Upon high school graduation, Dan attended an Ivy League college, and he then returned to Shaker Heights to raise his family. In the excerpt that follows, I asked Dan about his experience with dance schools, which he told me he attended as an adolescent.

Sometime later, while transcribing the interview, I stopped the audiotape, reread the section I had just transcribed, and replayed the tape. Listening to the exchange, I was struck by the direction this segment of the interview had taken. Why wouldn't I let Dan finish his statement? What was behind my repeated efforts to support, even protect, these dance schools and those attending them, including Dan, from questions about exclusion? This pattern of interaction is evident in the following excerpt:

ANNE: Now just a question on . . . the dancing school. Were there, were there black students as well who attended that?

DAN: No.

ANNE: So [the dancing school] was more cross Shaker, cross schools . . .

DAN: Yes.

ANNE: . . . but still predominantly white.

DAN: Right, it was all—white.

ANNE: Uh-huh.

DAN: And there was also a division between, ah, religions at that time [late 1950s], too.

ANNE: Right.

DAN: So that the dancing school primarily—actually, there was a full division, because there was a Jewish dancing school. There was Baxter's . . .

ANNE: Uh-huh.

DAN: . . . which was pretty much WASP, and then there was also a Catholic dancing school.

ANNE: Wow! That's fascinating.

DAN: Yep.

[*Slight pause—Anne is writing down dance schools*]

DAN: But there was no distinction, other than . . .

ANNE: Yeah.

DAN: . . . I mean there was, but as far as I was concerned it didn't matter.

ANNE: Yeah.

DAN: You know, it just . . .

[*Both speaking at the same time*]

ANNE: Right.

DAN: I feel into that . . .

[*At the same time*]

ANNE: People gravitated . . .

DAN: Exactly.

[*At the same time*]

ANNE: . . . towards their particular . . .

DAN: Right.

ANNE: . . . um, religion, or . . .

DAN: And in none of the, those dancing schools were there black kids.

ANNE: OK.

[*Slight pause*]

ANNE: OK, um, and then the sports, but the sports . . .

DAN: Sports, obviously, were wide open.

ANNE: Yeah.

In this conversation, I did not pause or ask for further clarification, and my expressions of affirmation were legion. My use of "yeah" or "right" was a listening device I tried, not always successfully, to change to "um-hmmm" and to reduce in frequency in my later interviews. Nevertheless, the occurrences of my affirmations and their timing were striking and deserved critical reflection.

As noted earlier, this first section of the interview was designed to elicit the participants' lived experiences and the meaning participants gave to those experiences. As Dan narrated the phenomenon of the dance schools in the late 1950s in Shaker Heights, he was also describing an important aspect of the city's social context. This was a section of the interview in which I needed, as the interviewer, to be quiet and listen and to provide an opportunity for the participant to narrate his experience fully. Minimizing interviewer comments at particular moments during an interview is a skill that develops over time and through one's reflection of the interview process. Such reflection can be achieved by gaining experience in interviewing skills prior to conducting the research. Practice at interviewing will develop increased discipline in maintaining some distance as the interviewer, and it helps you develop an antenna toward interference.

As I transcribed the interview, a question jumped out at me. Why did I not let Dan finish his statement? What was I thinking? Strategically, what was the purpose of my interruptions? These are important questions because each interview question, probe, and interjection should be purposeful. If a researcher cannot answer a question about the purpose of an interjection, then he or she must explore more deeply potential meanings in the interaction. In searching through the exchange, it appeared to me that I was reluctant to give Dan the space to articulate his view. Below is a reflection I wrote as I explored possible reasons for and consequences of my actions at this juncture of the interview:

> Strangely, I am reluctant to let Dan "go there" and yet at the same time, my expressions of assent suggest I am already there with Dan. I am struck at how effectively I derailed the conversation with Dan when it got too close to narrating racial or religious exclusion. Indeed, I actually feed Dan the lines about exclusion being "natural" and acceptable, when I say "people gravitated towards their own particular, um, religion."
>
> Yet at the same time there is some edginess in our back and forth, as if both of us know that those excluded might not see it that way. In

this sense, there is an unspoken smoothening of the wrinkles caused by our acknowledgment that Catholics at one time, Jews later and African Americans consistently were not present among the groups of students participating in these dancing schools.

Finally, after a pause, where all of these possible critiques sit silently between us, I "save" the exchange from the potential of exploring these issues by noting that sports in the public schools were not exclusive by race, religion or any other distinction. With questions about exclusion behind us, we move forward in a discussion about his participation in the sports program at the high school.

Wow. In my replaying the audiotape and transcribing my interactions with Dan, it's unnerving to think of how we carried this out together —a kind of dance or performance of denial and protection. Denying privilege and exclusion, we also protect the notion of a just system of inclusion. And we reinforce this context through terms of normalcy and inevitability.

Still nagging at me: what else might I not be allowing to surface and be articulated?

As the psychologist John Dollard (1949) noted in his study of race and racial relations in *Caste and Class in a Southern Town*, researchers must be attentive to what is unfolding between themselves and their participants. How does the tone of the interview, or the words spoken— including the pauses and interruptions—provide clues to better understand the social phenomena present in the interview and, more broadly, in the research? A reflexive look at the interactions in the interview, and the outcomes of those interactions, adds further texture to the data. Important questions then get raised, which often have relevance to the conversation between theory and data that are likely to emerge early on in qualitative research.

In this interview, *exclusion and privilege* are evident as codes in the research. These codes have an empirical grounding, as they appear in this and other interviews. Since the ideas related to privilege and exclusion were evident in the literature review that informed the research, these codes also have a theoretical base. In qualitative research, potential codes and clusters of key codes frequently begin to emerge as the research moves along through regular revisiting of interview data, along with the study of these data in relation to data collected through other methods. Some codes are discarded as you move along in the research. Others will take shape, further refined by the frequent looping back between analysis and data collection in an iterative process.

Vignette Two: Encountering Dissonance

A second example of the need for reflexivity in the desegregation study also illuminates ongoing and iterative coding in qualitative research. Evident here is a process articulated in what I later analyzed as *encounter*, which was narrated primarily by students in desegregated settings in the high school. While the idea of encounter captured the experience of white students and students of color, it had different trajectories and consequences for students by race. In this section, I link my experience as researcher with that of white students narrating "encounter" in their semi-structured interviews.

The interview involved Deborah, a graduate from the middle to late 1970s. Deborah told me her father was black and her mother was white. She narrated critical incidents as a student in the early years of desegregation through the Shaker Schools Plan, as well as the ways in which she encountered exclusion through teachers' and students' acceptance of racial stereotypes about her. At the point in the interview protocol in which I ask participants to identify the racial group to which they identify themselves as belonging, I neglected to ask Deborah the question.

My own assumptions about Deborah's race and her family background began as soon as I met her—before our interview. I learned that she grew up in Shaker Heights, lived in the Moreland area, which was predominantly black, and was bused to a predominantly white school as part of the voluntary Shaker Schools Plan. I understood her to be African American, and I assumed that her family moved to Shaker for many reasons but certainly among them its schools. I was not entirely right, nor was I entirely wrong. But I clearly had prepared an interview protocol based on a preconceived set of assumptions.

Fairly early in the interview, Deborah's narrative began to depart from the stereotypes I had assigned her. I learned that the greatest influences in Deborah's life were her mother's friends. Her mother was white as were her friends, and they were partnered with African American

men, as was Deborah's mother. Deborah was not close to her white or
her black relatives till later in life. Her "family" was this tight-knit circle
of friends of her mother, and it was this group with whom she spent her
holidays. What she was telling me, then, was that she grew up in a setting where distinctions between people's racial backgrounds were very
blurred, and there were no boundaries. She noted the following later in
the interview about her father:

> My dad is this very—tall black man, he's very black, and he fits into
> the black culture very well, but he doesn't see this black/white thing.
> It doesn't pertain to him either, you know, so, I think that's where I—
> it didn't pertain . . . He doesn't care that the political ground is that he
> should go with this black candidate—a candidate to him, is whomever,
> and so, you know, that's how I was raised.

Deborah was not only telling me that she was raised without an awareness of distinctions between race, but also that her cultural upbringing
was more white than black, and certainly her level of comfort was high
among whites. She told me her neighbors were friendly and supportive
of her mom and that she played with the kids in the neighborhood, so
she was not separated from black families and black culture. They simply were not within her immediate family experience. Similarly, attending a predominantly white school through the Shaker Schools Plan
provided her with another white setting in which she felt, for the most
part, comfortable.

I heard all this and took it in, but what I did not fully comprehend
was that while she might not have "seen" herself as white, she felt deeply
connected to other whites and white culture. The problem was I still
"saw" her as black. At one point during the interview I realized that
I had failed to ask Deborah to self-identify by race before completing
the Inclusion of Ingroup in the Self (IIS) scale (Tropp & Wright, 2001).
When I had given her the IIS scale to complete, I had first handed her
the scale (as her *ingroup* scale) on the strength of her connections to
African Americans. My error became apparent to me during the second segment of my protocol, when I asked her to compare her high
school experience with those within her racial ingroup. Deborah began

to speak about culturally being at ease with whites because of her family experience and her biracial background. At that point I paused and told Deborah that I was struggling because I had not prepared the interview for the experience of a biracial student. What disturbed me most, however, was that the experiences of exclusion she narrated, which were rooted in people's perceptions that she was black and their racial stereotypes about black people, reflected the kind of behavior in which I myself had engaged. The following excerpt provides some insight into our interaction during this part of the interview.

ANNE: OK, how similar or dissimilar would you say your experience as a student, um, reflected the experience of, um—you know, ah, let's see, let's start first with African American students. How similar was your experience . . .

DEBORAH: Um.

ANNE: . . . to other African American students?

DEBORAH: I probably, my perception as an adult would probably be that it was probably easier.

ANNE: Right.

DEBORAH: I fit in a little bit easier. My perception is that the black kids may have had a little harder time because it was definitely a white—community, the school itself.

ANNE: OK, all right—you know—eh, I have to stop here, um, you're being very good with me [*Deborah laughs*], eh, because I—one of the questions I wanted to ask you before when we did the, the, um, racial identity . . .

DEBORAH: Um-hmm.

ANNE: . . . um, was, I wanted to ask you to indicate how you would describe yourself.

DEBORAH: As a stu—when I was a student?

ANNE: Now, I wanted to, you know . . .

DEBORAH: How would I—

ANNE: In the interview, would you, you know, would it be multiracial, you know, what—

DEBORAH: I would definitely describe myself as multiracial. I would definitely describe myself as that, but most of my influence was

Caucasian. Growing up, the people my mom surrounded us with, and my friends in high school, and my friends in college, and now my friends as an adult are mostly white.

ANNE: The reason why I stopped is because I—my interviews have been largely up to this point—either you're white or you're black, and so, so, I'm, I have to honest, this is new.

DEBORAH: This is a new field [*laughs*].

ANNE: So, so, for me to do this interview, I'm, like, OK, well—

DEBORAH: Yeah, "how do I?"

ANNE: And I apologize for that but it's—

DEBORAH: Oh, no, it's—

ANNE: It's also, it's also, it's a good point for me to stop and say, OK, well, wait a minute.

DEBORAH: Yeah.

ANNE: This is very im—you know, a significant and particular point of view that you're bringing to the research.

As a result of my realizing my error, I was experiencing a high level of dissonance as I was asking the interview questions and simultaneously contemplating my own complicity in behaviors Deborah had attributed to whites who excluded her. The experience was a powerful moment, again, of being surprised by my own ability to access stereotypes without even realizing it. The moment underscored the privilege of having "*no idea*" of one's complicity in acts of exclusion and *the struggle that is absent without such an experience*. As I sought to reconcile my actions with my sense of self as a white person as nonracist and just, I found the behaviors I had critiqued in others were there within myself.

My pausing during the interview provided what I later analyzed as a social-psychological "space" of encounter. For me, this moment involved my "shock" of learning that I needed to subject my sense of self as a white person and a just person to scrutiny. As I moved along in my analysis of data, I found that some white students narrated similar experiences. Some of these white participants narrated some encounter with an understanding of their involvement, however indirect or direct, in racial inequality. This *encounter* with a view of their own privilege as a result of their skin color unsettled their previous views of equal educational opportunity. In the reflexive process, my understanding of what transpired at this juncture in the interview created a similar sense of agitation.

As evident in the transcription excerpt above, I paused in the interview and noted to Deborah that I had not prepared a protocol for participants who were biracial. I hoped in taking the time to address this during the interview that I would create space for an exchange between Deborah and myself in which we could explore how her experience demanded that I adjust the data collection and the analysis. In this way, I was able to explore the mechanisms of inequality that were at work even as we engaged in the interview. As a result, the research benefited, as did my own understanding of my role as a white researcher pursuing black and white and biracial participants' experiences and views of racial equality in the district's desegregation history. The pause in my interview also enabled Deborah to talk at greater length about the changes over time in her understanding of the experience of inequality for black students and families, as well as the experiences that developed her views on racial injustice.

Sometimes when I finished an interview, I was already caught up in a key theme I felt was emerging from that particular interview. Such a "hunch" needed time and further analysis before it would take shape as a formal code; however, it often germinated into a substantive idea that yielded a code or cluster of codes. In the case of my interview with Deborah, I became aware during the interview of a phenomenon unfolding. Through a reflexive process subsequent to the interview, I analyzed the relationship between this phenomenon and important theoretical work on the encounter phase of racial identity development (Cross, 1991; Helms, 1990). The theoretical work proved to be useful in explaining the process I had experienced. The ideas generated in my reflexive writing later informed my conceptualizing of the encounter experience as narrated by some black, white, and biracial students. Among the white students in the group I found connections between their narratives and what took place between me and Deborah.

Vignette Three: Act of Disloyalty

This last example of the reflexive process examines my interjection of a point of view into an interview. The participant, Anthony, an African

American young adult, had been a student in the district in the 1980s. During the interview, I had asked him to talk more about what he meant when he said he had been "challenging" to teachers. He cited this as an underlying cause for his failure to graduate from the high school.

Early in the interview, Anthony had spoken of his discomfort and sense of racial isolation in the district's elementary gifted magnet program to which he was bused from his neighborhood school. He described, after this experience, withdrawing from the gifted program and generally disconnecting from school. I was puzzled about his increasing disengagement from school, given his high standardized test scores and his strong academic achievement early in school, his narration of his parents' involvement in his schooling, as well as the history of college education in his family and their middle-class background.

Two additional sources of information played a role in my puzzlement. First, in my interviews with a number of African American parents, the parents had described the ease with which educators stereotyped their sons. This contributed to my interest in clarifying what Anthony meant by "challenging" and what kind of teacher-student interactions went on in his classrooms. Second, my insider knowledge as a parent in the community played a role in my raising this question with Anthony. I drew from dinner-table conversations with my children, white students in honors classes, who attended the high school and who sometimes narrated their own observations of the ways in which high-achieving white male students frequently challenged their teachers.

Guided by these two additional sources of data—one from within the study and the other from my insider knowledge, I had moved the interview in a particular direction to explore this specific issue of Anthony's understanding of what "challenging" his teachers meant.

ANTHONY: . . . I didn't get along with my teachers because I'm very, ah, challenging toward the teacher, and people with degrees and masters, are looking at this kid, like, "Well, who's *he* asking all these questions?" You know, and ah . . .

ANNE: Even though . . .

ANTHONY: . . . it could . . .

[*At the same time*]

ANNE: . . . they get . . .

ANNE: [*laughing slightly*] I'm sorry but, even though they get those kind of
    questions, from—white students as well, but maybe it's just—

ANTHONY: Oh, I wasn't even thinking . . .

ANNE: It's just a different . . .

ANTHONY: . . . it was racial.

ANNE: No, I know, but it bothers me sometimes, when I hear, because kids
    challenge teachers no matter what racial group they're in . . .

ANTHONY: Um-hmm.

ANNE: . . . but they do it differently, and so teachers will accept, they can be
    more, a white teacher might be more accepting of . . .

ANTHONY: I see what you're saying.

ANNE: 'Cause I've seen it in my kids, you know, my kids will come home
    and talk about, you know, an uppity white student who will correct
    a teacher constantly, and that's acceptable, do you know what I'm
    saying?

ANTHONY: Uh-huh.

ANNE: Um, I didn't mean to interrupt you.

ANTHONY: No, I see what you're saying.

ANNE: I, I, do see sometimes that happens.

ANTHONY: Um-hmm.

ANNE: Where it's the *manner* and the *ways* that—young people question
    adults.

During the interview, however, I recall being completely unprepared
for what Anthony suddenly narrated immediately after I voiced my
opinion, as stated above, "where it's the *manner* and *ways* that—young
people question adults." Our exchange is as follows:

ANTHONY: [*speaking more rapidly*] I remember, I remember, now that we're
    talking about that, when I was at Ludlow, my mother, ah, told me
    that a teacher told her, I questioned her or told her something, I cor-
    rected her from something. And my mother told me, the teacher told
    her, like, your son is asking me questions and I'm the teacher, who is
    he to be asking these—

ANNE: Yes.

ANTHONY: I remember my mother bringing me, that out, and, and they
    had told her, that they wanted me to take, or go see a psychiatrist, a
    school psychiatrist, or something . . .

ANNE: Reallllly?

ANTHONY: . . . or, whatever, see, at Ludlow, I remember this now, and, ah . . .

ANNE: Um-hmm.

ANTHONY: . . . but my mother told them, "No!"

ANNE: Right.

ANTHONY: [She said,] "There's not anything wrong with my son" . . .

ANNE: Right.

ANTHONY: . . . you know.

ANNE: Right.

ANTHONY: I remember my mother telling that, that they wanted me to see
    a school psychiatrist.

In re-listening to this interaction between Anthony and me, I was
uneasy that I had raised these points with him. In terms of the interviewing method and ethics of conducting interviews, I felt very troubled
in listening to how I introduced an interpretation of Anthony's experience that he himself had not put forth. My insertion of this interpretation seemed in retrospect wholly inappropriate. Below are my thoughts,
recorded in a reflexive manner in order to document the occurrence of
this event and to better understand it:

Why did I raise this point with Anthony? Where did it come from? It
seems as though it's a complicated mix of outburst on my part, but also
intentional provocation. Clearly, I was disturbed listening to the experiences of exclusion that Anthony had narrated, and maybe the other narratives by African American parents were within psychic reach. Was this
deliberate on my part—intentionally raising the issue and using a particular interpretation of his experience to elicit a response?

Something else bothers me about this exchange. There's some other
layer of discomfort—a subtle undertow of disquiet. Feels like disloyalty, barely perceptible but still there, toward my racial ingroup—the
white students I narrated as "uppity" and the white teachers I narrated
as racially and culturally biased in a more favorable way toward white
students.

At the same time, I can't help wondering, did my expression of disloyalty create the space for Anthony to narrate his memory of something he appeared to have forgotten until that point? Could this be possible? He became so animated, so engaged with a memory that seemed to have escaped him until that point in the interview. Would this story have emerged without my interjection? What do I do with data that are important to the research but that have as the elicitation and source the researcher's interjection of bias?

Anthony's narration of his teacher's suggestion that his "challenging" be addressed by a school psychiatrist provided important data. It raised questions about Anthony's experience and his teacher's assessment of his behavior. It also offered potential links between Anthony's experience and that of other African American students encountering some form of conflict with their teachers. Black parents narrated similar observations, particularly about their sons' experiences. In this way, an interjection on my part created an ethical dilemma, about which I continue to feel deeply ambivalent, even as it yielded additional depth and texture to my data analysis.

Summary

This chapter has provided a closer look at the way in which the semi-structured interview provides space for reciprocity between you and the participant and for reflexivity in terms of dilemmas encountered within the research project. These dilemmas are methodological, theoretical, and inevitably deeply ethical as you reflect back and then recalibrate elements of the data collection and analysis. The chapter has explored closely the nature of interviewing, in general, as an interaction between two individuals, with the benefits and drawbacks inherent in this method.

In addition to offering ethical challenges, attending to events within the semi-structured interview frequently reveals substantive clues about the codes and thematic clusters, or categories, emerging from the data. For that reason, these events prompt both important reflexive exercises and provisional analytical iterations. Efforts at researcher-participant reciprocity as well as researcher reflexivity are both necessary ingredients of qualitative study. As the semi-structured interview mixes both empirically and theoretically guided questions, there is great potential for moments when the researcher might engage the participant in some degree of texturing the data, unpacking commonplace discourse, and exploring dimensions of experience. These junctures occur *within* the interview, requiring researcher-participant reciprocity, and also require reflexivity on the part of the researcher *subsequent* to the interview. Both reciprocity and reflexivity offer the researcher an encounter with emerging analytic themes. This generation of themes and exploration of their meaning will be discussed further in the next chapter.

4

Ongoing and Iterative Data Analysis

We are not talking a language of cause and effect. This is too simplistic . . . there are multiple factors operating in various combinations to create a context . . . Identifying, sifting through, and sorting through all of the possible factors showing the nature of the relationships does not result in a simple "if . . . then" statement. The result is much more likely to be a discussion that takes the readers along a complex path of inter-relationships, each in its own patterned way, that explains what is going on . . .

—Strauss and Corbin (1998, p. 130)

In qualitative research, data analysis occurs alongside data collection. In this way the analysis is ongoing, as you note thematic patterns emerging in the data. Data analysis is also iterative, requiring you to return frequently to your data for further study in order to ensure meaning. With each loop back, you become further steeped in the data. With interview data, this absorption may be likened to the depth of engagement between the participant and researcher during the interview. Now these individuals are no longer physically before you. However, their experience and angle of vision are present in the data as central ingredients for your data analysis.

This chapter outlines key steps in qualitative research for analyzing data. There are variations in the analytical frameworks that researchers bring to their research, often reflecting a particular interpretive tradition. In this chapter, the focus is the *centrality of the empirical data*. The first section of this chapter discusses the analysis of interview data in general, followed later by illustrations of data analysis from the desegregation study. In particular, these later sections demonstrate the analytical possibilities in the desegregation study for movement between *experience* within the *relational* context students narrated and the *structural opportunities* in which students participated, as well as the *historical context* during which they attended school.

General Considerations in Preparing to Analyze your Data

Data analysis demands ample time and reflection. From conducting the interview and reviewing the data, often through the process of transcribing an audiotape or videotape and ensuring the accuracy of the transcription, each step draws you more deeply into the participants' lived experience. The process is also dependent on your attention to the organization of the data. In studies involving multiple methods, additional levels of analysis are included not only within and across interviews, but also across data sources.

Throughout your research, you will continue to reflect on the extent to which you are responding to your research question. Some data may offer an initial lead in your analysis; however, the significance of the lead may not be sustained, yielding a kind of analytical dead end. *Nevertheless, it is best to keep the data analysis fairly loose in its construction early on, entertaining many analytic possibilities.* For example, an idea from the data might take several permutations before it is fully accessible. Additionally, it is necessary to consider what else is emerging in the data that may not respond directly to your research question but may yield information that is important to the study. Finally, some data may be very compelling but clearly in need of a separate study, perhaps as a follow-up to your current research project.

Analytical Steps: Beginnings

It is important to take time to absorb the data through a progression of analytical steps. Upon completion of an interview, several core ideas as well as additional questions may be evident to you. It is useful to make note of these ideas and questions shortly after the interview (see figure 4-1). Also relevant in that reflection are any thoughts about the interview process itself, particularly junctures in the interactions that transpired

```
┌─────────────────────────────────────────────────┐
│ ┌─────────────────────────────────────────────┐ │
│ │                                             │ │
│ │               Beginnings                    │ │
│ │                                             │ │
│ │   complete a postinterview reflection       │ │
│ │                                             │ │
│ │   organize and store data                   │ │
│ │                                             │ │
│ │   establish inventory for recording thematic codes │ │
│ │                                             │ │
│ │   check on accuracy of interview transcripts │ │
│ │                                             │ │
│ └─────────────────────────────────────────────┘ │
└─────────────────────────────────────────────────┘
```

Figure 4-1. Beginning steps in analysis

between you and your participant that should be taken into consideration in the analysis of the data and in ongoing data collection through subsequent interviews. As discussed in the previous chapter, which outlined lingering thoughts, anxieties, and questions evident to me either during or subsequent to the interview, these reflexive writings were instrumental in the analysis of the data, as they introduced important ideas that shed light on the research question and the research process.

The next level of analysis is the organization of the data. Data from semi-structured interviews may be collected through many sources, such as audiotapes, videotapes, photographs, mappings, notes, and performances. Organizing the data so that it is accessible for analysis is a first step. This includes providing some labeling process that does not attach participant names to data-collection instruments as well as storage of the data in a secure location—typically reflective of your promise of confidentiality to participants in your consent form. Audiotapes or videotapes are transcribed and then transcriptions are checked for accuracy. This is a very time-consuming task but necessary to build confidence in your data analysis and interpretation of the findings. In distilling data in some form from its original source, the authenticity and accuracy of that distillation is imperative. The distilled data now serve as the reference for analysis and interpretation.

In taking such steps as reading, organizing, and transcribing, you are already engaging in early analysis. Certain themes that address your research question will become evident. Other themes are striking in and of themselves. Analysis involves locating and labeling these thematic patterns, which reflect ideas evident in the data. These ideas represent a core level of meaning and are often referred to as *codes*. Codes should be documented. This can be accomplished by recording codes as they emerge and then exploring their meaning. Your documentation of codes may be maintained through the use of a software program, memos to yourself, a folder of your written thoughts alongside excerpted interview text, a collection of yellow sticky notes in the data sources (particular pages of transcripts, photographs, mappings), or any combination of these forms of recordkeeping. Your documentation also highlights instances within the data that generated a new direction in your analysis through your discussion of the meaning you have attached to a code. Throughout the process it will not be unusual for you to place "notes to myself" in an electronic file titled just that, as well as on the perimeter of your computer screen, across your desk, or beside your bed. These are the road signs on your analytical journey.

As indicated at the outset of this chapter, it is useful early on in your data analysis *not* to pursue the relationship between data and theory. *Although theory is already embedded in your interview questions and the structure of the interview*, you can remain most faithful to the lived experience of study participants by immersing yourself in the data themselves: the stories, images, metaphors, pauses, and emotions narrated by the participants, as well as the interactions between the researcher and the participant. Through the close reading of the data, certain expressions and ideas are likely to emerge, evident through the particular use of language among participants to convey their experiences. These are important to note. They should be recorded and included in documents *affiliated with the respective interview* and also listed within documentation of the patterns emerging *across the interviews*.

The purpose of this early recordkeeping of thematic codes is primarily *descriptive*, although the construction of meaning you assign to each code occurs through waves of interpretation. Naming or labeling the code should be done carefully to reflect the data from which the code emerged. A code may be one word, as in "pioneer," or several, as in "duality is my reality." Other descriptive information about the code includes an elaboration of its meaning (thus far), how it is used, where it can be located, and what, if any, relationship it may have to other codes that have been recorded. "Relationship" need not be addressed

Code name

Meaning

Exemplar / Most clear or compelling example of this code

Other instances

Relationship to other codes (if any)

Ongoing status of code in analysis

Figure 4-2. Key ingredients in documenting thematic patterns as codes

immediately. To do so might be premature. It may take considerable analysis before relationships among codes are evident. Figure 4-2 provides an example of recordkeeping for each new instance of meaningful text, formulated as a code, as it emerges in the data. While qualitative data collection often generates data rich in meaning, keep in mind the guideline that your search for codes in the data should bear some relation to your research question.

Identifying a code, where it came from, what ideas it puts forth, and, over time, how it is related to other codes is central to the analysis. Tracing your analysis increases the rigor and transparency of your research. Investment in data organization and recordkeeping provides many returns in terms of easy access to data and the ability to follow an analytical thread as it increases or weakens in strength.

As you analyze your data, you are likely to accumulate multiple and sometimes overlapping codes. While many will remain relevant for the duration of the study, others may fall by the wayside as the data collection progresses. A considerable number of codes may emerge that do not necessarily respond to your research question. It is wise to note these and explore them for some time. However, should they fall short of the explanatory power as it relates to the purpose of the research, they are likely to be set aside. A smaller but substantially stronger set of codes will develop. These codes will be grounded in your data and they will relate to your research question in a substantive manner. The decision to narrow your list of codes should be documented, with a clear indication of what's in and what's out and why. The documentation is important for at least two reasons. First, it traces the analysis from beginning to end, making you accountable to the process. From time to time, you, your participants, and a wider community for whom the research topic is important will inquire about your analysis. Such inquiries are more readily addressed through your coding documentation. Second, now and again a code, presumed not useful or relevant, may be retrieved for its potential to shed new light on some dimension of your topic not anticipated or understood earlier in the analysis.

It is important to keep in mind that the frequency of a code is a consideration of its usefulness but not a requirement. It is unwise to discard what may appear to be an "outlier." These codes should actually be taken seriously. Because qualitative research is less focused on the quantity of data, with more attention to the meaning generated by the data, each code should be recorded and studied for its relationship to the research question and other emerging considerations in the analysis.

On a purely practical note, you should maintain a consistent routine for keeping track of your ongoing data analysis, including attention to day, month, and year. As the analysis proceeds, you are likely to copy and paste portions of text to new files as codes are eliminated, combined, or altered. Retaining earlier files that are all well labeled and dated is extremely important. It is easier to try out new ways of defining and organizing codes when you have confidence in your ability to retrieve earlier files. One day of analysis may be substantially different from the next in terms of a leap in meaning, so the tracking of the analysis is invaluable. This process plays out again later in your synthesizing of thematic patterns and in your writing, as the ability to formulate a collection of ideas is facilitated by having access to the building blocks leading to that level of interpretation.

Early Meaning Making in Interpretive Waves

As your interviews are transcribed and other sources of data studied, the list of codes becomes more fine-tuned. Gradually some codes emerge as durable in their frequency and meaning. Sometimes a code

Early Meaning Making in Analyzing Data

read closely within each interview

locate and document meaningful text

attend to expressions of meaning such as images, metaphors, stories

assign names, or codes, to capture ideas related to the text

look for thematic patterns across interviews and across other data sources, if applicable

Figure 4-3. Early meaning making

of great substance emerges but is not widely reflected in the data. Other times a code is frequent but may show significant variation, leading to multiple codes in relation to each other. Additionally, the names or labels given to codes may change. Codes initially named according to a section in the interview protocol frequently get replaced by in vivo codes. These may be words, phrases, or metaphors actually used by the participants, or they may have emerged in your interpretation of the data and from your naming the code to reflect the interpretation (see figure 4-3).

The language of the participants, often stark and vibrant in meaning, powerfully conveys dimensions of their experiences as they relate to the topic of your research. Expressions, symbolic language, images, understandings, ideas, stories, and emotions are central to the analysis, starting out singularly from one interview and gathering conceptual strength as they reappear in other interviews and data sources. These data are coded and explored for what meaning they offer in and of themselves and in relation to your research question. Because these codes emerge in vivo, produced from the interviews, they offer insights grounded in the lived experiences of one's participants.

Throughout the data-collection period, you will move from a focus on each interview *as its own entity* toward consideration of data across the interviews. Within and across the interviews, you are locating instances of meaning and finding data substantively related to your research question. You also will be comparing and contrasting your data and developing early hunches about ideas that are emerging from this process. Your data analysis can be facilitated by asking the following questions:

> *Within the single interview*: What is the experience this participant narrates? What is the meaning this participant gives to his or her experience? How is that meaning conveyed through the semi-structured interview?
>
> What other points from the interview stand out in particular? What questions remain as they relate to this interview?
>
> How do data from different segments within the interview relate? Are there dimensions from different segments of the interview that reveal connections and, in doing so, provide greater thematic depth? Are there contradicting data from different segments of the interview; if so, how might they suggest a more layered representation of the participant's experience?
>
> How do the data from this interview address the research question?
>
> *Single interview as it relates to other interviews (and possibly other data sources)*: In what way are these data related to data from other interviews: confirmatory, extending, nuancing, or contradictory? If your study uses multiple methods, in what way are the interview data related to data collected through other methods?

The process moves from the particularity of a single interview to particularities within other interviews. Patterns are noted and studied, as are the commonalities and contrasting dimensions in the data. In multiple method designs, the analysis proceeds across data sources from the various methods. Here, the analytical space is extended, as meaning emerges across methods involving other sources of data, such as archives, focus groups, performances, and surveys.

As you move along in your analysis, you will begin to entertain ideas about the relationship between thematic codes. Connecting one code to another will extend your meaning making and may offer greater insight into the focus of your study. This clustering of codes under a broader

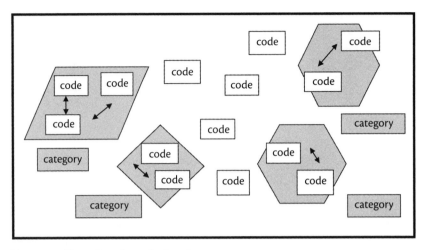

Figure 4-4. Thematic codes and categories

theme, or *category*, often sheds new light in your interpretation of the data. Categories reflect the earliest stage of synthesizing the ideas generated from relationships among codes. The clustering of codes is represented on the code chart in figure 4-4.

You may want to return to your participants to discuss emerging themes. This is often referred to as a member check. It can be achieved in a session subsequent to the interview, or following your analysis of many interviews. The member check provides you with a way to test the "fit" of your interpretation in relation to that of your participants' understanding of their narratives. Your interpretive framework may encourage a member check, and it may be part of your research design. On the other hand, you may not use member checks at all in your study. Whether you include member checks or not, you will find the strength of your analysis relies on the close and systematic study of the data. This increases the trustworthiness of the ideas that you locate and document as codes and categories.

As the relationship among codes is explored, and thematic clusters, or categories, are formulated, you will continue to assess the codes' viability in responding to the research question. Increasingly you will test out ideas about relationships among codes as thematic clusters or categories, moving the research into an increasingly more abstract phase (see figure 4-5). You may also begin to more directly interpret data in

More Interpretive Waves

entertain interpretive possibilities

allow for a conversation between data and theory

move forward in interpretation, and loop back into
data toward responding to research question

Figure 4-5. Ongoing interpretation

relation to theory. Moments of theoretical imposition emerge, soon to be followed by empirical contestation. In an often bumpy fashion, you will move along in drawing greater meaning from the data, in increasing conversation with theory.

Engaging more deeply in interpretation is not necessarily a distinct step, nor is it linear. You are likely to return to more coding, if needed, and to additional efforts at clustering codes and searching for meaningful relationships. This movement back and forth, characteristic of the ongoing and iterative nature of qualitative research, allows for considerable play among ideas and strengthens the emerging conceptual framework that will inform your study.

To recap, you bring to the data analysis your understanding of the research question, your experience with the topic under study, and your increasing exposure to ideas as they emerge in the data. As you identify and document codes, your interpretation takes on greater meaning. Some codes will share connections, and you will create thematic categories. To illustrate some of the steps in qualitative data analysis, the second half of this chapter discusses how themes emerged in the desegregation study.

The Desegregation Study: Early Analysis of Data from Archives and Oral Histories—Historical and Structural Context

In the desegregation study, my earliest exposure to thematic patterns occurred through the study of the archives and oral histories. Because it was necessary to have considerable context at hand before conducting the interviews, I collected archival and oral history data first, followed by an initial analysis of those data. Doing so provided historical and policy context as well as a pool of potential participants for the semi-structured interviews.

Because one purpose of the archival study and oral histories was to develop a chronology of events related to the school district's desegregation, a major form of organizing these data was through a timeline. My analysis led me to organize data on the district's desegregation history into two time periods. The early phase, from 1965 to 1986, encompassed the district's efforts to respond to increasing racial and economic diversity in the schools. The current phase, from 1987 to 2003, consisted of those events occurring after the district reorganized its schools and included more recent events, policies, and practices. My decision to organize the timeline into two phases was a result of my analysis of educational change processes over the course of the entire 1965–2003 time period. It also reflected my analysis of local history and policies in relation to trends at the national level.

The archival material and oral histories introduced thematic patterns and provided a contextual landscape. Recall the diagram conceptualizing the analytical framework in chapter 1. To study participants' experiences of racial equality and their views of it within certain educational settings and at particular historical moments in time, my analysis necessitated context at the individual, institutional, and sociopolitical levels. Within the archival and oral history data were moments of angst, delight, anger, excitement, and turmoil associated with educational change. A study of context at multiple levels allowed me to see change that replicated relations of power accorded to race and class as well as change that disrupted those power relations. In my analysis of these data, then, I was able to formulate a complicated context involving history, educational policy, and intergroup relations and to use this as an analytic landscape within which I might locate study participants.

EARLY CODING DEVELOPMENTS

An early code emerging from my analysis of the archival data and oral histories was that of *boundaries*. Originally evident in data related to housing, it had its most direct application in my study of schooling experience. Fundamentally, Shaker Heights was a "planned community," incorporated in 1912, with restrictive covenants in place until sometime after they were ruled unconstitutional in the 1948 *Shelly v. Kraemer* decision (Weeks, 1968, pp. 8–9). The city was referred to as the "City on a Hill," a place of status and privilege. Accessing this privilege was off-limits to people of color until the mid-1950s. This historical context revealed a city defined by geographical boundaries where privilege thrived through exclusion. The code *boundaries,* informed by the related codes of *privilege* and *exclusion,* took on further meaning, and in doing so generated important ideas in response to my research question.

While nearly every code used in my data analysis had its origin in the archival material, not all codes from the archival material had analytic resiliency. For example, the notion of Shaker Heights as a model of racial integration was frequently coded within my analysis of archival data. Noted in figure 4-6 is an advertisement run by the Ludlow Community Association, which was founded in 1957, to market the area, largely to white buyers, to preserve racial integration as more African American families purchased homes in Ludlow (Weeks, 1968, p. 53).

This code, *model of racial integration,* however, yielded little substance as the study moved along and offered only modest connection to other codes. While it was noted in the oral histories, it was not sufficiently resonant in the semi-structured interviews. It remained a part of the historical narrative but offered little potential for sustained meaning as it related to my research question.

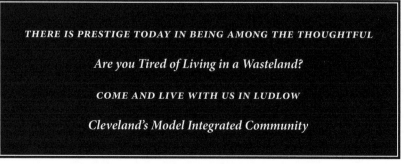

Figure 4-6. Early code from archival data

Archival Item: "Woodbury inaugurates individual pupil-scheduling" (1966, October). *The School Review*, p. 3.

Comments: Item notes that there will be changes in course scheduling at Woodbury Junior High School with the establishment of homogeneous classes by grade point average, standardized test scores, and teacher recommendation. Excerpt below stresses achievement of racial integration and maintenance of academic standards. Also reflects boundaries in "opening of educational gates."

This latest aspect of change at Woodbury takes its place in the record of other changes at the school. Woodbury, as the community knows, has participated in a dominant change of current history: the opening of educational gates to Negroes. Privileged thus to participate in the present, Woodbury has quietly achieved a racially integrated school population.

Has this change affected educational standards at Woodbury? The answer of evidence is a clear no.

See also "Board re-districts junior high schools" (1966, June). *The School Review*, p. 1. See also "Students in ninth grade English are divided into three different levels. Two groups in level three—the enriched or 'honors course'—are this year learning . . ." (1966, September). *The School Review*, p. 3.

Figure 4-7. Sample archival data entry catalogued under connecting codes: *supporting diversity* and *maintaining standards*

What did begin to take shape as a code, not unrelated to the pride that the community took in labeling itself a "model" of racial integration, was a coupling of two strong sentiments within the school district as it experienced increasing racial and economic diversity beginning in the mid-1950s. This involved expressions valuing "diversity" on the one hand and upholding "standards" on the other. There were parallels regarding standards in housing—with an emphasis on property values and property upkeep—but within my focus on education, the corollary was academic standards. In figure 4-7 is a sample entry from my archival data files, an excerpt from the district's newsletter in 1966, cataloguing early on in my study this coupling of the two codes: *diversity* and *standards*.

Coupling *diversity* and *standards* to illustrate the meaning that educators and parents gave to these words involved thinking beyond the discrete words themselves toward a more fully developed idea expressed in the relationship between the words. This is the analytical process through which you tease out meaning from the data. Gradually, codes become increasingly multidimensional in meaning, facilitated by code clustering when ideas share some connection. As noted earlier, this is a process through which thematic categories emerge, offering conceptual resilience and ties to your research question. Other codes that reveal little connection and remain discrete or detached may eventually become less prominent.

This relationship between diversity as a value in the school district and as a threat to maintaining academic standards would further develop over the course of the study as I analyzed district policies and practices evident in the archival material, oral histories, and semi-structured interview data. Thematic patterns in these data would reveal efforts to end exclusionary practices and policies, thus transforming educational structures through which diversity might flourish. Connected to these efforts were other policies and practices that were described as intending to maintain standards. However, the latter policies often appeared to contribute to the exclusion of students by race and class. The relationship between these two codes, *supporting diversity* and *maintaining standards*, revealed an important pattern in the district's desegregation history. This pattern became increasingly prominent and moved me closer to finding a relationship between empirically coded data and codes developed theoretically for the study before it began, reflecting transformative and replicative change.

Also noted in figure 4-7 is my cataloguing of related items and themes. Under "comments" is a notation of the way in which this excerpt from the archives also reflects the code of *boundaries* through the language of "gates" and "opening." Student enrollment data from the mid-1960s revealed a considerable increase in the number of African American students attending district schools, particularly in the Moreland and Ludlow neighborhoods. Boundaries were "opening," not only geographically in terms of the city and its neighborhoods, but *structurally* in terms of access to the educational system. Archival data reveal increased use of course leveling, or academic tracks, including advanced courses and courses to remediate or individualize instruction,

Archival Item: First videotape listed in the series of films on Shaker schools. This tape, "How Do Our Children Stand?," is tape #9 (2-1), dated 8/23/78. Located in Moreland Archival Room, Shaker Heights Main Branch Public Library.

Comments: Videotape begins by introducing viewers to a classical Greek class in Shaker High School. Footage of 10 white students, lots of discussion, no raised hands, just college-level type of participation. Focus moves to high school assistant principal Al Zimmerman, who discusses the advanced placement and honors program. Footage moves to Ludlow Elementary Special Projects program. Narrator describes the program as a "delightful foray into creative thinking." Footage of blackboard, with words listed: sensitivity, synergy, serendipity. Footage of children in Special Projects classroom, seated in a circle: 3 white and 2 black elementary-age students.

Superintendent Jack Taylor speaks about Shaker's strengths, and adds, "Another important factor" and refers to Shaker's increasing racial diversity. Taylor notes some people are concerned that the standard of excellence in Shaker schools would not continue. Dr. Taylor notes that the Shaker schools are 40% minority "and our test scores continue to go up."

Figure 4-8. Sample archival data entry recorded under connecting codes: *supporting diversity* and *maintaining standards*

emerging in the mid-1960s. While school newsletters indicate that the district offered a small number of advanced placement courses as early as the mid- to late 1950s, newsletters and other data sources from the mid-1960s suggest there was acceleration of structural change within the schools' curricula and instruction subsequent to that time.

Using school newsletters, reports on student enrollment data, data from oral histories, and later from interviews, a cluster of codes began to emerge. Previously *boundaries* referred to *geographical* borders that were permeable to some and impervious to others. However, boundaries as *structural*, created through policies and practices resulting in differential experience by race and class, emerged as an additional meaning within this code. This extension of the code into two dimensions (and later three) pushed *boundaries* into a more encompassing and broader analytical level, that of *categories*. Figure 4-8 provides another example of an archival data item reflecting *supporting diversity* and *maintaining standards* and the context of advanced courses and enrichment programs contributing to this early formulation of the thematic category of *structural boundaries*.

In addition to *diversity* and *standards* as codes, and the emergence of *boundaries* as a category, or cluster of codes, the key codes of *privilege* and *exclusion* were sustained beyond the analysis of the archival and oral history data. These related codes also contributed to the extension of the category of *boundaries*. My study of boundaries underscored the depth of privilege associated with this community and its schools and the way in which privilege is preserved through exclusion. This interdependence of privilege and exclusion, already evident in my literature review, later showed up with frequency in the data. Data sources rarely used the word "boundaries," but the use of related words suggested a good fit with the code labeled *boundaries*. While participants narrated "belonging," "alienation," and being "stuck" in and "sucked" out of privileged sites of learning, archival sources noted "educational gates" and oral histories attended to course levels that were "open" to all or only accessible through parental vigilance, social networks, skin color, and socioeconomic class background. While data from the archives and oral histories introduced the code of *boundaries* and extended its meaning to include *geographical* and *structural boundaries*, it was not until data from the semi-structured interviews were collected that full dimensions of this category unfolded, introducing the third boundary code: *relational boundaries*.

The next section discusses how analytical codes and categories emerged from the semi-structured interview data in the desegregation study. There is an emphasis here on the strength of the semi-structured interview in eliciting data that are crucial to the study and on the power of the narrative, particularly among current and former students, in moving analysis forward.

ANALYSIS OF SEMI-STRUCTURED INTERVIEW DATA AMONG STUDENTS: RELATIONAL CONTEXT

The interview data allowed a rich exploration of thematic codes and categories and the emergence of thematic patterns across data sources, including archival and oral history data. The interview narratives consisted of words, phrasings, unfinished sentences, images, emotions, and stories. They were illuminating *and* mysterious. Often context-dependent and culturally bound, they were incredibly meaningful *or* outright inaccessible. They provided me with a glimpse into lived experience, offering particular words and meanings that tugged at my psyche and pushed me toward the formulation of a conceptual framework.

As noted earlier, my analysis of the interview data began during the transcription of the interview audiotapes. My early codes were straightforward and tied to the interview questions: experience of school, connections with racial ingroup/outgroup; experience of teacher expectations/opportunities/information about opportunities; comparison of experience to racial ingroup/outgroup; definition of racial equality; stories of racial equality/inequality. Manila folders held data reflecting these codes with pages of excerpts from interviews, archives, and oral histories. Also within these manila folders (and on electronic files) were additional reflections, questions, and musings associated with the code. These folders were often overflowing with pages of data sources and interview transcription, as I cast a wide net initially, not wanting to set parameters on meaning too early on in the analysis.

As I read through each interview transcript, I highlighted relevant text. Within the file for each interview, I recorded a list of codes emerging from the data and the pages on which the coded data could be found. These codes reflected ideas that were meaningful to the participant's narrative and addressed my research question on the *experience of racial equality* and *conceptualizations of equality* among participants in a desegregated school district. I completed some approximation of a code inventory, where I copied and pasted sections from the transcripts into the inventory, explored their meaning, and labeled them formally as a *code*, which allowed me to look for patterns across interviews.

For example, in my folder containing the transcript of a student interview, the following initial list of codes is provided, with page numbers where interview text reflecting this code would be found:

boundaries	92
parental vigilance	31
student comfort level	53–66; 67–72
scripts	31, 31–36; 37–38
teacher expectations	63–74
desegregation	88–92; 93–97

course levels	146–150
ingroup relations	38–45; 46–54
district reorganization	28–31
historical memory	16–17
relations of power	46, 66, 78
racial equality	180–190
school sites bringing outgroups together	23–25
segregation	35
connections between self and racial ingroup	12–15
connections between self and racial outgroup	9–10

Again, the analysis is iterative, so I found myself going back to data files as new codes emerged. As more instances of a code were located, and as the meaning of a code was tweaked, I updated my documentation of my analysis and returned to data files to check for a continued fit to existing codes. Some coded text was absorbed within other existing codes to provide greater nuance and meaning. For example, much of the data coded above under *desegregation, student comfort level, ingroup relations, relations of power, course levels, school sites bringing outgroups together,* and *segregation* eventually was absorbed within the code of *boundaries.* The *boundaries* code grew in strength and resiliency, and it ultimately became a broad overarching category that informed my interpretation of the data and my theorizing in response to my research question.

EMERGING CODE: SITE OF EDUCATIONAL PRIVILEGE

The interview data underscored the nature and scope of the district's educational offerings. Students, parents, and educators narrated the benefits of the educational experience that the district provided. Over time I was able to conceptualize what the archives, oral histories, and participant narratives suggested to be the full realization of an education in this district. This included the following: high teacher expectations influencing high academic outcomes; a rigorous and meaningful curriculum; opportunities to study and discuss academic work with peers; and relationships between students and educators that resulted in strong and productive connections inside and outside the classroom.

When students narrated the full benefits of the district's education, I coded their schooling experience as reflecting inclusion within these *sites of educational privilege.* These sites were not limited to classes. Extracurricular offerings that result in deeper connections with peers and adults in the school and opportunities to perform, debate, write, compete athletically, and provide community service I also grouped within this code. Sites of educational privilege could be racially isolated or diverse in race and class. When they were desegregated, they appeared to offer a specific set of experiences involving growth and loss, *a phenomenon I did not understand early in my analysis* and will discuss in the next chapter. Educational structures that could not be characterized by these factors I coded as *sites of educational exclusion.* These were rarely desegregated and they frequently served students of color, particularly low-income students of color. An analysis of archival, oral history, and interview data indicated that within the levels system, sites of educational privilege were not distributed equally at each course level, nor were they equally available to white and black students or accessed with the same frequency.

This coding of educational structures as reflecting *privilege* or *exclusion* allowed me to loop back into interview data and analyze the narratives of schooling experience. Gradually, patterns emerged across the student narratives: where some narratives reflected consistent student *access* to sites of educational privilege, others reflected *peripheral access*, and still others could be best analyzed as reflecting *sites of educational exclusion.* The differential access to sites of educational privilege, often by race and class, reflected patterns in the literature related to desegregation history, educational policy, and the social psychological study of group relations. The narratives of students located in very different educational structures, experiencing different levels of opportunity and expressing a range of views about access to opportunity structures, posed an analytic challenge as discussed in the following section.

ANALYTIC CHALLENGE: DRAWING MEANING FROM NARRATIVES

To illustrate the challenge in my analysis, I juxtapose two narratives in order to explore two differing paths through the school district. Jill, whose narrative is depicted on the left end of the arrow in figure 4-9, is

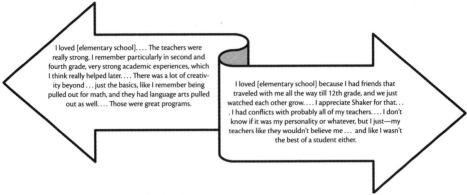

I loved [elementary school].... The teachers were really strong. I remember particularly in second and fourth grade, very strong academic experiences, which I think really helped later.... There was a lot of creativity beyond ... just the basics, like I remember being pulled out for math, and they had language arts pulled out as well.... Those were great programs.

I loved [elementary school] because I had friends that traveled with me all the way till 12th grade, and we just watched each other grow.... I appreciate Shaker for that... . I had conflicts with probably all of my teachers.... I don't know if it was my personality or whatever, but I just—my teachers like they wouldn't believe me ... and like I wasn't the best of a student either.

Figure 4-9. Experiences of schooling

white and from a middle-class, predominantly white neighborhood in the city. Diana, depicted on the right, is black and her neighborhood is predominantly black and working class. The juxtaposition is demonstrated in several key areas of their narratives, with an elaboration of the quoted text in the discussion that follows.

Both Jill and Diana, students graduating from the high school in late 1990 and early 2000, respectively, narrated affection toward the Shaker Heights City School District. However, Diana's and Jill's relationships with educators and educational structures varied considerably, as did their academic identity, or the extent to which they understood themselves to be academically engaged and successful. While Jill narrates "very strong academic experiences" and "creativity beyond . . . just the basics," Diana speaks of "conflict with probably all my teachers" who "wouldn't believe me," and she sees herself as "[not] the best student."

While both Diana and Jill narrated educational opportunity for themselves, the opportunity structures in which they participated and the relationships they sustained were considerably different, most evident at the high school and postsecondary level (see figures 4-10 through 4-14). For example, Jill was attending a competitive college at the time of the interview; Diana had recently graduated from high school with uncertain plans for the coming year.

While Diana's journey through the school system was characterized by conflict between herself and her teachers, she distinguished in figure 4-10 one year in middle school as vastly different and influential in helping her respond to later conflict with teachers. This year, unlike others, reflected a close brush with educational opportunity and the discovery within herself of her academic potential. Jill's narrative emphasized consistent opportunity, even when she bumped up against teacher distance and hostility, as noted in figure 4-11.

Interestingly, *sense of inclusion*, which emerged as a thematic pattern in the narratives, became nuanced in Jill's and Diana's descriptions of the coursework and academic settings in which they participated. Jill's sense of inclusion at the advanced placement level reinforces her persistence in the course. Diana also experiences a sense of inclusion in the Humanities program, serving students reading below grade level. Ironically, her sense of belonging in this remedial program supports her decision to remain there and not enroll in college preparatory courses.

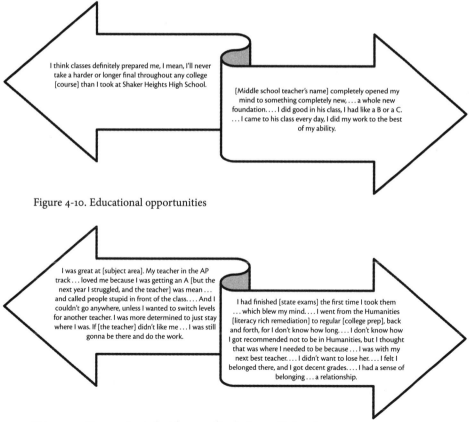

I think classes definitely prepared me, I mean, I'll never take a harder or longer final throughout any college [course] than I took at Shaker Heights High School.

[Middle school teacher's name] completely opened my mind to something completely new, . . . a whole new foundation. . . . I did good in his class, I had like a B or a C. . . . I came to his class every day, I did my work to the best of my ability.

Figure 4-10. Educational opportunities

I was great at [subject area]. My teacher in the AP track . . . loved me because I was getting an A [but the next year I struggled, and the teacher] was mean . . . and called people stupid in front of the class. . . . And I couldn't go anywhere, unless I wanted to switch levels for another teacher. I was more determined to just stay where I was. If [the teacher] didn't like me . . . I was still gonna be there and do the work.

I had finished [state exams] the first time I took them . . . which blew my mind. . . . I went from the Humanities [literacy rich remediation] to regular [college prep], back and forth, for I don't know how long. . . . I don't know how I got recommended not to be in Humanities, but I thought that was where I needed to be because . . . I was with my next best teacher. . . . I didn't want to lose her. . . . I felt I belonged there, and I got decent grades. . . . I had a sense of belonging . . . a relationship.

Figure 4-11. Nuances in students' sense of inclusion and belonging

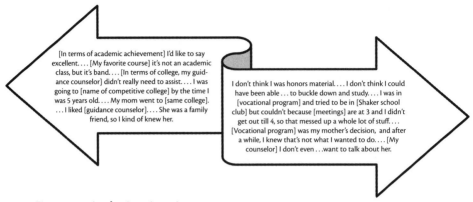

[In terms of academic achievement] I'd like to say excellent. . . . [My favorite course] it's not an academic class, but it's band. . . . [In terms of college, my guidance counselor] didn't really need to assist. . . . I was going to [name of competitive college] by the time I was 5 years old. . . . My mom went to [same college]. . . . I liked [guidance counselor]. . . . She was a family friend, so I kind of knew her.

I don't think I was honors material. . . . I don't think I could have been able . . . to buckle down and study. . . . I was in [vocational program] and tried to be in [Shaker school club] but couldn't because [meetings] are at 3 and I didn't get out till 4, so that messed up a whole lot of stuff. . . . [Vocational program] was my mother's decision, and after a while, I knew that's not what I wanted to do. . . . [My counselor] I don't even . . . want to talk about her.

Figure 4-12. Academic trajectories

In this sense, the educational structures within which the participants are located create some permanency. Movement out of these structures appears impeded by some sense of boundaries not to be transgressed. As these boundaries inform their academic identity, they also shape Diana's and Jill's academic trajectories, as noted in figure 4-12.

These excerpts from semi-structured interviews offer a window into the students' experiences of schooling, which varied by race and class, as evident most starkly in Diana's and Jill's narratives. The excerpts also illustrate an analytical movement within and across interviews to compare and contrast individual experiences of schooling within the school district. In keeping with my research question, I analyzed these experiences as they related to the students' conceptualizations of racial equality. My analysis of their views on equality often uncovered a discrepancy between what the participants narrated as racial equality and what their narratives revealed about their experiences *in relation to* structural and relational conditions. The following displays of narrative data reveal this discrepancy, particularly for Jill, who had consistent access to sites of educational privilege and who narrates equal educational opportunity for all students. While Jill narrates equal educational opportunity for blacks and whites, Diana does not see a similarity in the academic opportunities available to black and white students. The narratives are highlighted in the responses to my question, "I wonder if you could tell me, thinking now in the present, what racial equality in public education means to you?"

The experiences as narrated by Jill and Diana, and their perception of access to educational opportunity in the school system as noted in figure 4-13, reflected a pattern among many of the participants and raised questions for me. I was perplexed by the participants' understanding of what was accessible, not only for themselves but for others, within and outside their racial group. For example, what does Jill's narrative of a fairly straightforward view of racial equality within the school district suggest about students' experience of racial equality in a desegregated setting? Earlier in the interview, she concedes that many black students did not have a similar experience of schooling as she did, but she distinguishes this from opportunity, which she sees as equal for all students in the district.

In figure 4-14, Jill's narrative appears to rest most of the responsibility

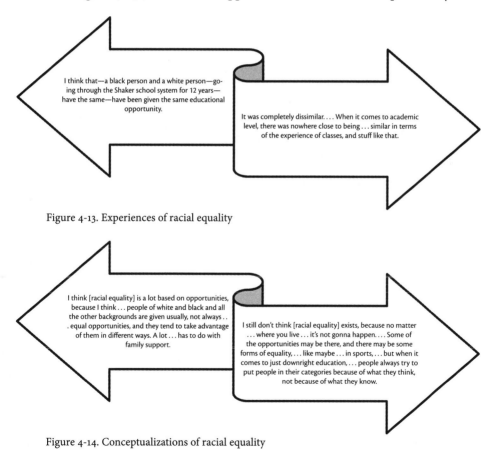

I think that—a black person and a white person—going through the Shaker school system for 12 years—have the same—have been given the same educational opportunity.

It was completely dissimilar. . . . When it comes to academic level, there was nowhere close to being . . . similar in terms of the experience of classes, and stuff like that.

Figure 4-13. Experiences of racial equality

I think [racial equality] is a lot based on opportunities, because I think . . . people of white and black and all the other backgrounds are given usually, not always . . . equal opportunities, and they tend to take advantage of them in different ways. A lot . . . has to do with family support.

I still don't think [racial equality] exists, because no matter . . . where you live . . . it's not gonna happen. . . . Some of the opportunities may be there, and there may be some forms of equality, . . . like maybe . . . in sports, . . . but when it comes to just downright education, . . . people always try to put people in their categories because of what they think, not because of what they know.

Figure 4-14. Conceptualizations of racial equality

for access on the individual student and his or her family, not the district itself. Diana, on the other hand, narrates inequality, but it is less directed at her particular experience and is more broadly connected to racial inequality in the district. Having narrated fondness toward the district, and the positive impact of a middle school teacher, Diana nevertheless noted teacher mistrust of her and conflict between herself and teachers. Diana describes her academic identity by noting she was "not honors material." Her participation in the remedial program followed by vocational education suggests that she did not realize the quality of education for which the district is known.

In many ways, Jill's and Diana's narratives served as exemplars for two categories of schooling experience in the district evident in the student narratives. The categories were informative in responding to my research question on the experience of racial equality. Buried in the data of the students, *whether they directly narrated it or not*, was evidence of a stark gap in access, or proximity, to sites of educational privilege. Table 4-1 depicts these contrasting patterns in the form of different dimensions of experience.

Table 4-1. Contrasting Patterns in Dimensions of Experience

Dimensions of "experience" within student narratives	Group 1	Group 2
expectations/opportunities/information	positive	positive and negative
inclusion in sites of educational privilege (mostly racially isolated)	yes	no
experienced compatibility of self as "student"— as having an academic identity	yes	yes for some
viewed experience as similar to racial ingroup	yes	yes
viewed experience as similar to racial outgroup	yes	generally no
narrated sites of educational privilege as equally available to white and black students	yes	generally no
view of racial equality	no inequality narrated; fairly straightforward	conflicted—"maybe it was just me" OR "clearly unequal" OR no narration of inequality

Two Emerging Categories among Student Narratives

In my coding of interview data, these two groupings increasingly began to take shape as follows: (1) narratives, to varying degrees, reflecting a full realization of the benefits of the education for which Shaker Heights was known, and (2) narratives, to varying degrees, reflecting a considerable lack of access to sites of educational privilege. The dimensions reflecting points of comparison and contrast, which are evident in the rows of table 4-1, served as codes (e.g., the extent to which the student was included within sites of education privilege; the student's view of racial equality in the school district). These codes were then collapsed into two categories, which I labeled *centrality* and *marginality*. The development of these two key analytical categories provided the basis for a conceptual framework focused on students' social psychological experiences of racial equality within a desegregated district.

The two groupings outlined in table 4-1 highlight contrasting experience at each level of coding, particularly in terms of access to sites of educational privilege and views about access, as well as their views on racial equality within this desegregated district. Ultimately, the distinguishing factor for these two groups was where the students were "located" in relation to the opportunity structures within the high school. Emerging in my interpretation, then, was an understanding of *the influence of opportunity structures* on both the students' experiences of schooling and on their academic identity. Access to sites of educational privilege influenced the nature of their experiences and their views on racial equality.

A Puzzling Third Category: Opportunity and Estrangement

However, there were some additional patterns to be teased out in the analysis. In looking closely at interview data, further informed by analysis of archival and oral history data, the appearance of a third group became evident. This third group was less distinct, revealing some blurring between groups 1 and 2. In this emerging and still analytically fuzzy category, a number of students narrated access to sites of educational privilege but some experiences of being on the periphery. Their narratives did not reflect a full view of self as centrally located within sites of educational privilege. Nor did they reflect a full sense of being outside of these sites. Additionally, they narrated considerable insight in terms of their views on racial equality within the district. These narratives held in common, with some variation, *greater complexity in their views of equality* and *some degree of agitation* as it related to their experiences of racial equality within the district.

As I moved further in exploring the nature of the experiences of students of color and of white students, in terms of their access to sites of educational privilege, I looked for some coding that would capture dimensions within the narratives of this third group, creating some nuance in the otherwise stark patterns of student narratives evident in groups 1 and 2. *How might I convey a thematic pattern that was emerging, among students across race and class, who accessed sites of educational privilege but whose narratives reflected their location more on the periphery?* The narratives of these students encompassed a phenomenon of *opportunity and estrangement*. They revealed an awareness of the contradiction between the discourse of equal opportunities and outcomes and their actual observations or experiences in the school system. How might I convey the kind of *edginess* within their narratives —some degree of insight into how privilege operated in the school system, which these students frequently narrated as unsettling their earlier view of the system as one of equality?

Summary

This chapter has outlined the ongoing and iterative analysis of data within qualitative research. It has described analysis as waves of interpretation, beginning with the organization of the data and assurances of the data's accuracy, followed by the documentation of emerging ideas from the data. These early ideas are labeled as codes and gain prominence as they increasingly are evident in the data sources. Codes that have a relationship with other codes are identified, with the nature of that relationship explored and labeled, forming categories. This process is facilitated by frequent close reading of the data and by looping back through data collection and ongoing analysis. Through the use of the desegregation study, the iterative and cumulative analytical process was illustrated, and two major categories, reflecting very different experiences of schooling and views of racial equality, were generated from a close study of empirical data. A third category remained fuzzy, requiring further exploration and perhaps a reconnection with theory, which is taken up in the next chapter.

In the next chapter, I discuss synthesizing study findings and theorizing for a wider public. This is an exciting phase within the research, as you move from coding and clustering ideas toward a more elaborate interpretation and the building of a conceptual framework. The synthesizing of your findings is likely to occur in fits and starts, as some elements of interpretation come sooner than others. The fullest realization of your thematic patterns is unlikely to occur until you have thoroughly mined your data in terms of their responsiveness to your research question.

Synthesizing and Interpreting Research Findings

5

Building Theory

It is relatively easy to write up individual stories as thick, local qualitative descriptions without revealing the webs of power that connect institutional and individual lives to larger social formations. Yet, if we do not draw these lines for readers, we render them invisible, colluding in the obfuscation of the structural conditions that undergird social inequities. It seems clear that researchers, as public intellectuals, have a responsibility to make visible the strings that attach political and moral conditions with individual lives. If we don't, few will. Rendering visible is precisely the task of theory, and as such, must be taken up by method.
—Weis and Fine (2004, p. xxi)

Like other phases of a qualitative design, the shift from analyzing to synthesizing thematic patterns is iterative and cumulative. The process of looping back through data collection and analysis begins to ease up as the constitutive analytical threads are secured in place. While some threads might still need reconnecting, or removal, there develops a gradual sense of having exhausted thematic possibilities at the level of coding and clustering codes into categories related to the research question. There is a bit of winnowing, too, as some thematic codes and clusters are placed on hold for later exploration.

In this chapter I discuss the progressive movement into synthesizing your research findings. I outline the process of drawing meaning from the products of your analysis toward articulating a conceptual framework. This is a very exciting phase of the research. The systematic collection and analysis of your data have yielded thematic patterns that now require you to further interpret their meaning and respond to your research question. As discussed here and illustrated through examples from the desegregation study, movement into synthesis involves drawing on the empirical and theoretical, and bringing them into conversation. It prepares you for communicating your findings to a wider public.

Conceptual Restlessness

As your analysis proceeds, you will be increasingly well positioned to attend to thematic *relationships*. Connections across thematic categories will become evident. Ideas drawn from the data themselves, and possibly from your experience with the research context, your autobiographical roots, and the literature that drew you into the research in the first place, are appropriately entertained at this phase of the research. The looping back into data collection is far less frequent, and there are fewer acts of description and far more shifts into inference. You may experience a sense of conceptual restlessness as ideas press for consideration.

Leading up to this point, your analysis has involved a repeated close reading of the data and locating instances that relate to your research question in some way—complicating your question, offering new meaning, raising additional questions. This required a parsing or segmenting of your data, breaking the data down into thematic codes. As this process unfolded, a new phase began, that of drawing thematic codes together into categories when they share common dimensions. As the research progressed, some thematic categories revealed connections and, in concert, appeared to offer some explanatory power as it related to your research question. These thematic categories, connected by key dimensions, have the potential to formulate a conceptual framework. This process—the ongoing collecting of data, breaking them down into coded material, and later uncovering relationships across the coded material—draws on both analytic and synthetic activities. As you increasingly articulate meaning from these acts of analyzing and synthesizing, you are engaging more fully in interpretation. Interpretive activities, as illustrated in figure 5-1, reflect the inductive power of qualitative research.

Several tools may assist you in drawing meaning from the thematic patterns that have emerged. These include graphic displays, reflective writing, and engagement of critical friends. Each of these tools will help

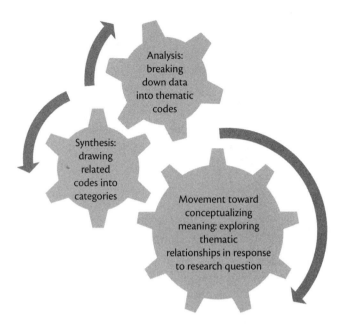

Figure 5-1. Interpretive activities

you to formulate explanatory possibilities, drawn from connections and contradictions evident across thematic categories. The intent here is to see how far you can take these thematic categories in conceptualizing a response toward your research question. As with every phase of the research, the strength of your conceptualizing depends on the degree to which you have systematically collected and analyzed the data, producing thematic patterns that offer analytical substance and resiliency. A summary of these steps is provided within figure 5-2.

Drawing pictures, or graphic renditions, helps you work toward conceptualizing relationships and meaning across key analytical themes. Such displays range from penciling configurations on your napkin at a local coffeeshop to utilizing computer software features to map out ideas. Graphics such as matrices and circles, sometimes connected through lines and arrows, are instrumental in exploring processes, hierarchies, and other patterns of relationships. Through this use of diagramming and drawing charts, you can document and explore connections, questions, partial leads, dead ends, and potential advances, working toward a good interpretive fit across thematic categories. A graphic display

Moving into Synthesis of Research Themes

assess the extent to which thematic coding and categorizing are fairly exhausted as they relate to your research question

explore the relationships across thematic categories toward generating sustained meaning and an increasingly dense network of ideas

attend to nuances and irregularities

use tools to assist interpretation: graphic displays, writing, member checks

consider what meaning is being generated in the synthesis of these key themes

formulate what synthesis offers in terms of responding to research question

Figure 5-2. Moving into the synthesis of research themes

moves you closer to conceptualizing the relationships across categories, and it contributes to the interpretation of your findings.

Similarly, writing is a useful vehicle for interpretive play across ideas (Richardson, 1994). Writing helps you sort out relationships and test possible connections in meaning. As in the early phase of your analysis of the data, it is good here to stay loose in your conceptualization —uncertainty is acceptable, and indeed very necessary, early on in synthesizing relationships across thematic categories. Efforts to integrate ideas require regularity in writing, as well as repeated close reading of your emergent text. At this point the writing is largely for your reading. Those who share a research interest *and* can tolerate the ambiguity, reversals, and tediousness of the writing may also serve as an interpretive community. In the long haul, the writing is a generative process, yielding new understanding of your study findings. It allows you to explore interpretive possibilities.

An additional tool in synthesizing thematic patterns is through some form of engagement with critical friends. This type of engagement typically involves individuals who are knowledgeable of the topic of your study. They may be intimately connected to the research context, or they may be outsiders to the particular context but not to the phenomenon of study. They may also bring a level of familiarity with the theoretical base from which the study draws. Discussing your synthesizing of thematic patterns with those who play the role of critical friends will press you to articulate the basis on which you are drawing your conclusions, will locate gaps in your thinking, and will strengthen your interpretation.

As you move into synthesizing thematic patterns, you may return to the literature from which the research drew its question, design, and analytical framework. Although never fully severed from theory, the research necessitates a reengagement with theory in the interpretation of study findings. This allows you to consider extant theory in relation to thematic categories. It is likely that you have entertained theory already, as noted in earlier chapters on data collection and analysis, even as you have sought immersion in the empirical data. At this point in the research, articulating connections across thematic categories and in relation to the literature is appropriate and necessary. From this you begin to craft a conceptual framework that will yield greater depth in understanding your research topic.

It would be misleading, however, to suggest that the interpretive activities of analysis and synthesis occur in stages or are linear. Instead, they are far more circular, with a process of looping through analysis into synthesis toward teasing out a possible interpretation in response to your research question, and frequently repeating this loop. As you move into synthesis of thematic categories you may be aware of unfinished work. In your use of graphic displays, writing, and engaging critical friends, you are pressed to make sense of themes and to begin to consider their representation to a wider public. This shift toward articulation of your findings within a conceptual framework is critical to interpretation. In the next section, I illustrate elements of looping and interpretative activities in the desegregation study as I moved toward synthesizing thematic patterns.

The Desegregation Study: Reengaging Theory—How to Interpret Narratives from Those "on the Periphery"?

In my exploration of relationships across themes in the desegregation study, I continued to puzzle over the third thematic category in my analysis of student narratives. As noted in the last chapter, the narratives in this third group reflected both opportunity and estrangement. In particular, narratives within this third category included some expression of dissonance and shock related to this group of students' experiences and views of racial equality in the school district. In my efforts to interpret this pattern of "shock," I understood the narratives to suggest that the students had bumped up against something impenetrable within the school system. Figure 5-3 excerpts some of this language of shock and dissonance among black, white, and biracial students.

Figure 5-3. Narratives from the third thematic category

In this third group of student narratives, I saw an emerging link between the expression of dissonance and shock and the conceptualization of a critical stage in racial identity development as theorized by the psychologists Janet E. Helms (1990) and William E. Cross, Jr. (1991). I found the black student narratives to reflect competing subjectivities of self in relation to other, where an event or series of events contested their understanding of themselves as black, smart, and appropriately positioned in sites of educational privilege. These narratives revealed connections with the stage of "encounter" in the development of black identity as theorized by Cross (1991). During this stage, individuals have an experience that catches them "off guard" and dramatically alters their worldview. Similarly, the white students' narratives of competing subjectivities, contesting their view of themselves as white, just, and within a system that distributed education equally, reflected the work of Helms (1990) on white racial identity development. Helms underscores "a personally jarring event" as crucial to white identity development and to understanding racial injustice. Both white and black students within this "periphery" category experienced a sense of racial equality that was agitated, in that they were uncomfortable with the contradiction between the discourse of equal educational opportunity alongside structures and relationships they had come to understand as unequal.

In this way, my reengaging with racial identity theory proved useful in *naming* my third thematic category: *encounter*. In referencing this stage of racial identity theory, I was able to capture dimensions of dissonance narrated by students concerning their experiences and conceptualizations of racial equality. I did not, however, pursue an analysis across the student narratives as the analysis related to other phases of racial identity development. Such a task would be appropriate for a subsequent research project. Instead I connected the data to theory, conceptualizing this "periphery" category in my analysis as a *social psychological space of encounter*.

FURTHER EFFORTS AT INTERPRETATION

As noted in the last chapter, I was perplexed by the way in which the narrative of equality among students who had been centrally located in sites of educational privilege *and* those who had been excluded in some way from these sites often reflected to some degree an eerie similarity

—equality was available to all of the students in the district, regardless of race and class. In some of the interview data, the normative view of course levels as predominantly white at the higher levels (advanced placement and honors) and predominantly black otherwise (college preparatory and general) was a recurrent theme. A good number of students whose narratives I analyzed as reflecting the first category of access (*centrality*) and those reflecting the second category of exclusion (*marginality*) spoke about the patterns of enrollment by race in the course levels as a given and an unquestionable dimension. For many of these students, there was little narration of incongruence between the district's discourse of equality and the students' narratives. How was I to interpret these narratives, given that my *theoretical* study of desegregation found equality of opportunity and outcomes was frequently constrained in some manner within desegregated school districts?

My interpretation of the data drew on a multilayered analytical framework that considered how individuals and groups were influenced by structural conditions and by the historical context during which they attended school. This analytical framework created the dialectical space characterized by individuals in relation to context. It created room for some degree of tension between the participants' narratives and the theoretically informed definitions of racial equality. It thus made visible the overlay of structural and sociopolitical conditions within the lives of students, *while not omitting* the actions taken and agency expressed among students within these conditions (Weis & Fine, 2004).

This textured interpretation complicated the discourse of "open" course levels and ample educational opportunity evident among some student narratives and also within some district documents. This discourse of access reflected a view of opportunity structures such as advanced course levels as being available to all students. This narrative of accessibility was contradicted by evidence of constrained access to sites of educational privilege by race and class. Repeated coding revealed the ways in which the course levels were racially identifiable, kept students apart by race and class, and shaped students' understanding of self and others, especially in terms of students' academic identity.

Pulling together the key relational and structural threads of coded material, I created a chart to help articulate an emergent conceptual framework. In doing so, I organized student narratives within the three thematic categories, theorizing *experience* as influenced by students' proximity to sites of educational privilege. Some student narratives reflected a proximity that was *centrally* or *marginally* located in relation to sites of educational privilege, while other student narratives reflected access to these sites at the *periphery*. This interpretation was strengthened by an in vivo code from my interview with Lorraine, a black student from the 1980s. Lorraine had offered the theme of positionality in her powerful statement, that "[educational] opportunity was there —how easily accessible it felt to people was not clear to me—*I wasn't in that position.*" Positionality provided the core interpretive thread through which other dimensions of student experiences and views of racial equality could be connected. These dimensions are evident in figure 5-4. In constructing this chart I developed a conceptual framework organizing the student narratives as reflecting three social psychological "spaces": marginalization, centrality, and encounter. Further interpretive work informed my understanding of how the educational structures narrated by students influenced their experiences of equality and their views on this topic. While narratives reflecting marginalization and centrality articulated a location in predominantly black or predominantly white educational settings, narratives reflecting encounter appeared to identify educational settings that were in some way racially

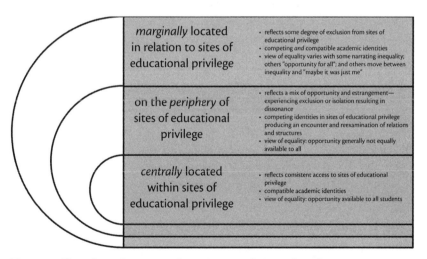

Figure 5-4. Three thematic patterns of experiences and views of equality

and economically diverse. Positionality as a thematic pattern in the student narratives offered some explanatory power in understanding how structural and relational conditions "located" students and influenced their views on racial equality. The coded material to the right of each thematic category helped build the framework from which I could begin to theorize about student *experiences* and *views of racial equality.*

Moving toward a Conceptual Framework

As illustrated in figure 5-4, graphic displays further your ability to build a conceptual framework. The framework is instrumental to your interpretation and ultimately will serve you well in reporting back to a wider public about your findings. As a conceptual framework takes hold, you will gain confidence in the way in which the relationships across thematic categories might be interpreted with greater complexity and depth. This is a period of considerable satisfaction. During this phase of synthesizing and interpretation, you are heavily involved in drawing meaning from the emerging thematic patterns. Increasingly, you are in a better position to conceptualize across these patterns toward articulating study results.

At the same time, your conceptual framework may fall short of encompassing all of the dimensions of your data. You may be aware of gaps in the explanatory power of your framework. These may be areas in your conceptualizing in which the categories do not fully accommodate the data. How do you address this and still hold onto the category and the emerging conceptual framework? The next section explores this more fully.

Addressing Interpretive Fit and Slippage

It is important to document where there is interpretive fit and where the conceptualizing falls short. Be explicit in your documentation about decisions you have made in your interpretation. Ask yourself if there is a conceptual stretch in your efforts to theorize. If so, is it substantial enough to undermine the trustworthiness of your interpretation? If you are able to make sufficient links back to your data sources, supporting the meaning you have drawn from those sources, then you can be fairly confident in your decision. Through your use of reflexivity, you can explore your concerns and scrutinize the interpretive choices you have made. These efforts to validate your emerging interpretation reflect the systematic nature and rigor of qualitative research. In this manner, consideration of interpretive fit and slippage will address questions a wider community may have about your research and will build confidence in your study conclusions. It will also mark areas for future study.

Documenting Conceptual Murkiness within the Desegregation Study

For example, in the desegregation study, there were some murky areas with which I struggled in terms of interpreting student narratives as appropriately reflecting one of the three categories in my conceptual framework. Many of the students narrated experiences that crossed some dimension of *each* category. Anthony, a black student from the 1980s, participated in the Ludlow School enrichment program, where he experienced a competing sense of academic identity between his view of himself as smart and his teacher's view of him as mentally troubled. While his narrative entailed opportunity structures, his overall story underscored his exclusion from these structures, including not graduating from the high school. I analyzed his narrative as reflecting marginality, and I positioned this experience as outside of sites of educational privilege. Michelle and Carol, black students from the 1970s and 1980s, respectively, graduated and continued postsecondary education through completion of master's degrees, yet their narratives revealed frequent depressed expectations of them by the school system. Their narratives are also analyzed as reflecting marginalization. Keith, a black student from the early 2000s, narrated little dissonance, yet I analyzed his narrative as reflecting encounter, because it revealed his deliberation in negotiating the racial isolation within the levels system. Kate, a white student from the 1980s, attended Moreland School, narrating an understanding of her contribution to racial equality by participating in the cross-enrollment voluntary desegregation plan. However, I did not analyze Kate's narrative as within the encounter category. Her narrative more generally reflected the centrality category of inclusion within sites of educational privilege with little narration of barriers of equality that were evident in the archival and oral history data of that period of time.

My conceptualizing about these thematic categories required that I document for each narrative why I included it within the particular thematic category. I made explicit, as much as possible, how I reached my interpretation. For several students in particular, I noted some ambiguity in "fit." *The conceptual "stretch," however, was not wide enough to undermine the interpretive claims of the study.*

In the section below I discuss the narrative of Karan, which was particularly challenging for me. As I indicate in this discussion, there are dimensions of her experience that reveal some thematic slippage in my interpretation of her narrative as reflecting encounter.

"the CP is for mostly blacks and honors is for mostly—white"

Karan is a white student who attended Lomond Elementary School and entered the high school in the early 2000s. In my analysis of Karan's experience, I found her narrative to suggest her experience as located in desegregated spaces of encounter, although in a very different manner from Mark, John, Samuel, or Matt. Karan's narrative, more than the other white students in this space of encounter, reflects an experience of contradiction without educational structures to support that experience. Karan responded high for the three questions on her experience in the high school: expectations ("very much"), opportunities ("a good amount"), and information and assistance (also "a good amount"). [Likert scale response for these questions is as follows: a great deal, a good amount, some, a little, none]. Karan felt that her experience was "somewhat similar" to other white students and also "somewhat similar" to black students. Karan's courses were at the college preparatory [CP] level, where she was in the minority. [Course level order, beginning with most advanced: advanced placement, honors, college preparatory, general.] When I asked Karan what classes or activities she felt brought groups of students together, she told me student council and the Student Group on Race Relations (SGORR). When I asked what set them apart, she responded,

Karan: Just, I think, the AP and honors, those kind of classes—just the CP is for mostly blacks and honors is for mostly—white.

Anne: OK, and what about kids who—who contradict that?

Karan: What do you mean, who go against, like the odd kind of—

Anne: Yeah or who are, who are not, you know, like—the black kids who go into the honors and the AP classes, the white kids who go into the CP classes.

Karan: What do you mean "what about them"—what groups they belong to?

Anne: Well, no, what, what experiences do they have? Like if, if, I mean, you may not know what a black student feels going into an honors or an AP class

Karan: No.

Anne: But, um—

Karan: I think—I'm a white student in the CP classes, and it's—it's —the *same*, I think, I mean, yeah, I don't think it really matters, I mean you might not have as many friends, but, you're fine.

While many white students cited "relationship with teachers" as an educational opportunity that the school provides, Karan was more mixed in her response concerning her teachers:

Anne: Would you distinguish educators as being different or are they pretty much just a group of educators?

Karan: I think it's just some are understanding and some aren't, I really think that's the major thing.

Anne: That's how you distinguish.

Karan: There can be mean, understanding teachers, but they're still understanding [but] . . . I think some teachers are just so out there and they frustrate every single student, and they don't do as well with their students.

Karan selected the highest level of connections in the Inclusion of Ingroup in the Self scale (IIS) for the strength of her connections to other whites and a fairly high level for the strength of her connections to blacks. For educational opportunities she felt she benefited from, she told me that she had a class, one period a day with a tutor in the subject with which she has the most difficulty. Karan told me she "loved" her tutor and the tutor was extremely helpful. An opportunity that she said she did not benefit from but would like to take advantage of was the tutoring center provided by the high school during after-school hours into the early evening. She noted that her strength was in the arts, and that was where she was taking her honors-level classes.

When I asked Karan about her thinking on racial equality in public education, she was very straightforward in her conviction that the playing field had been leveled. I asked her to define racial equality in public education, and her first response was "like teachers are a hundred percent fair. Teachers, counselors, they're, I think they're so fair. They don't care about race, I don't think at all." She noted that when teachers disciplined African American students, it was a result of the students' negative behavior and not of teachers' favoring white students. On her social map of the high school, she included a group which she labeled as "misbehaving students" and which she identified as predominantly African American. She told me that if you went into the assistant principal's office, "It's mostly African Americans in there. I think that if you give yourself that name in a classroom, then the teacher maybe starts to, to watch you more, but I think that if a white student was doing it, they'd watch them more, too. I don't think [it's] because they're African American."

I asked Karan if she could talk about a time she experienced racial equality or inequality and she told me, "OK, I think that African American students can push around the white people a little bit more . . ." While she did not say so, other responses in her interview suggested that her example was an experience of inequality to white students in general. Shortly after, when I ask if she had ever witnessed racial discrimination, she spoke further about her feelings of blacks not being disadvantaged by inequality, but quite the opposite: they were advantaged by a power they wielded in the social landscape of the school. We talked about this:

Anne: Have you ever been in a situation with an African American friend where the African American friend was discriminated against?

Karan: No—not at all, African Americans are not discriminated at all in our school [*thud*]. They, basically, they are, they don't, like, run the school, but no one [*voice drops*] messes with them, no one messes with them, it's something you don't do.

Anne: What about outside of school, like when you're out of school, going into stores and stuff like that?

Karan: No, no.

Although she would not likely agree with Karan's view on the absence of discrimination toward blacks, Nika, an African American student in the mid-1990s taking classes at the advanced placement level, relayed a similar terrain in terms of social relations at the high school while she was attending. The "power" ascribed to African American students was raised in a number of interviews. This theme emerged in other interviews. Its meaning was multilayered. It was evident in narratives describing a form of discomfort experienced by white students in a predominantly black college prep class on the part of white students and some black students. Or it was the experience of walking through the "black" door, an exit accessible to all students but used primarily by black students who lived on the southwest end of the city bordering Cleveland. In a related manner, the "socialization" pressure raised by Nika also revealed this notion of "power"—the way in which black students distanced themselves and even disparaged other black students taking higher-level courses . . .

While Karan narrated a school without racial prejudice, she also straightforwardly talked about prevailing stereotypes in the high school, as when she told me, "the CP is for mostly blacks and honors is for mostly—white." Karan herself, also, narrated exclusion from one activity. She had attempted to join a formal group in the high school, a group of African American students who work collectively and with educator guidance to increase study and content-area skills. Karan, encountering her own need for skill development and study skills, was seeking a place of belonging also, but she was excluded from one of these sites, which also had an explicit black identity component. [Karan told me that a student who was involved in this site indicated that she could not participate. Karan did not follow up with any educator who was supervising the site.] Karan described the exclusion as "unfair" because "I'm not allowed to go [because] I'm white." As a white student encountering exclusion, she was adamant about its unfairness. She told me, ". . . black people, yes, were enslaved, but, like, I had no control of that, no one in our school had control of it, like, you can't hold that against us, like, Jewish people —it has happened to almost every race, just because yours is more publicized and more, like, serious, I mean, yes, it's a very serious thing, and I feel extremely sorry for everything, but, like, it's not my fault, it's not anyone else's fault, it's not anyone else's fault that's still living—I mean, minorities don't achieve as well as white students, but still for the white students who don't achieve as well as the other white students, why can't we have something like that, or why can't we all be together?"

Karan, who told me in the interview "I think white and blacks have equal opportunity depending on how much they want it" and that

"African Americans are not discriminated at all in our school," did not see the utility in any efforts on the part of the students themselves or the institution of the school to offer black students additional support. Karan saw the distant history of slavery and the not-so-distant history of segregation as happening in the past and the responsibility of other white people, and therefore not an acceptable justification for educational efforts designed to facilitate racial equality, because in her eyes equality existed. While Karan benefited from the use of a tutor, she felt the additional support afforded this group of black female students would be helpful to her as well.

Karan's view is similar to that of Jill, a white student in the advanced placement classes in the mid- to late 1990s. Like Karan, Jill narrated an emphasis on race, when she said "race was a huge issue that year because the students made it so known, and made it such an issue." Like Jill, Karan saw race but not racial exclusion. Karan told me, "But I really do not see that anyone—has ever gotten discriminated against, like, that's just something that people don't do, like, it's—you don't do that anymore, like, it's, it's something that you don't do, and I don't—I've never, ever—I think whites and blacks have equal opportunity depending on how much they want it."

However, unlike Jill, Karan's academic and social experience in the high school contradicted the racial stereotypes. Like the black students in the higher-level classes, Karan was in the same position of isolation from her racial ingroup because of the enrollment patterns in the levels system. Similarly, she experienced isolation from her racial outgroup because of cultural distance and because she felt shut out of activities in which they participated, which were established specifically to help black students respond to their experience of exclusion in the higher levels.

Karan did not present her experience this way to me. She spoke of being grounded in a life outside the school of family and friends. She had friendships through extracurricular activities that drew black and white students together. Nevertheless, within the educational structures of the high school, she was "stuck between a rock and a hard place" as a black parent told me about her son in an advanced placement class. In her experience of a form of encounter, Karan struggled to find a space to "fit in" within the tightly constructed relational and structural boundaries in the high school. Additionally, because she did not "see" the boundaries about which African American students spoke, nor understand the enactments of exclusion they narrated, the supportive activities established for black students appeared to be exclusionary to her as a white student. Where she hoped to come together with black students in terms of a peer support program, she experienced exclusion. She did not see the inequality that created the need for the program, but she did see the program as unequally available to blacks and whites.

Karan narrated an unconvincing neutrality to her experience as a minority while a student in the majority black college preparatory classes when she told me, "and it's—it's—the *same*, I think, I mean, yeah, I don't think it really matters, I mean, you might not have as many friends, but you're fine." We talked about the stereotypes concerning race, achievement, and the levels system.

Anne: Has there ever been a time in your—you know, when you were going to school where—it may be even in your classes, discussing social studies, stuff like that, where kids in your class have talked about what is fair, and what's right and what's wrong—you know?

Karan: Not that I can think of, I mean.

Anne: Does the issue ever get raised, like, you know, the CP classes being—predominantly black, does that ever get raised in the school as an issue?

Karan: Um-hmm.

[*Slight pause*]

Anne: And, and how does it get raised, I mean, how is it talked about?

Karan: Like maybe a African American student will say, "Oh, us, like, black people always have to be in the dumb classes" or like—things like that, "all those smart white kids."

Anne: Um-hmm—OK, do—

Karan: Ah.

[*At the same time*]

Anne: teachers

Anne: respond to that?

Karan: No, they usually don't hear.

Like the black students in the higher-level classes, Karan's narrative suggested her maneuvering her way through her high school years, exhibiting a mix of nonchalance and vulnerability. In talking about her experience, Karan conveyed a complex view of schooling and equality.

Her lived experience informed her view of who was and was not appropriately located within the different course levels, which cut along racial lines. At the same time, she narrated a view of racial equality as having been achieved. Within this complex view was a phenomenon she struggled with later on in the interview, which had to do with the question of why African American students did not participate in the higher-level classes in the same numbers as the white students did.

Anne: Is that because black kids just don't want to be in those classes, I mean?

Karan: I don't know, I really do not know.

Anne: Um—OK [*slight pause*].

Karan: It really, I could not—I think maybe it's because they don't um —I don't know maybe because they don't think they will succeed in it —I don't know, 'cause I think there's a lot of African American students that could do well in it, but they don't, for some reason, either that's just the way they think it is, that's just the way it has to be, but—I think more and more, every year African Americans step up and say, "Hey I'll be in a honors class."

While Karan felt the black students with whom she was in college prep could participate in the higher-level classes, she puzzled over why they did not enroll in these classes. She felt that either they thought they could not succeed or that "that's just the way they think it is, that's just the way it has to be," reflecting the same statement she made earlier about her own views of the levels system as a practice that separated students: "just the CP is for mostly blacks and honors is for mostly—white." Here she explored alternative explanations for the absence of black students in the higher levels. However, from what she said in the interview, she did not see this phenomenon of underrepresentation of African American students in the advanced placement classes as related to racial inequality.

In sum, Karan narrated the isolating experience of contradicting stereotypes. She is white and she was in the college preparatory level, which defied the pattern of enrollment by race in the levels system. Like the African American students whose narratives I analyzed as within the category of encounter, Karan narrated the reinforcement of mutually exclusive racial stereotypes through enrollment patterns in the levels system and social psychological enactments of exclusion on the part of students. Her lived experience with dissonance resulting from her location outside the patterns of enrollment by race in the levels system is the basis for my interpretation, however awkward the fit. Furthermore, her experience was less one of privilege or centrality. The unevenness in quality of the college preparatory classes makes it difficult to analyze her position as fully within sites of educational privilege. Karan encountered isolation and to some extent racial exclusion, not from educators but from some of the black students with whom she was in classes. In some ways, her experience was similar to the students in the marginality category.

As a result, my analysis of Karan's narrative as in a desegregated space of encounter is somewhat problematic. Because her narrative does not suggest privilege but instead struggle and contradiction, it is unlikely that her experience would produce the kind of dissonance and reappraisal of opportunity structures as unequally available to students by race—common in the narratives of white students that I analyzed as within the desegregated space of encounter. Instead, her narrative illustrates in a compelling manner the powerful normative influence of the levels system on students' views of themselves and of the classes in which they feel they do or do not belong.

Toward Theorizing

As evident in the preceding excerpt from the desegregation study findings, the grounding of interpretive decisions within the data must be evident to an increasingly wider audience as you move toward writing up the results of your study. For this reason, it is very important to be clear about why you have coded data as you have, why you clustered codes into particular categories, and how you drew meaning from this synthesis. The trustworthiness of your interpretation requires you to continually weigh the strength of connections across your thematic categories for some degree of cohesiveness. During this phase it is important to articulate where the connections are strongest and where there may be some slippage. This articulation is necessary in making clear to a wider community the murkier areas of your interpretation. Additionally, this creates the potential for you or another researcher to pursue these more complicated areas in later research. Discussion of the basis of your interpretive decisions is crucial for the transparency of the research process and clarity of purpose. It sustains the rigor and systematic nature of the research and serves the public well in helping it understand how you have arrived at your conclusions.

As indicated in the example of the desegregation study, this phase of synthesizing your research themes focuses on building a conceptual framework. Your experience with the research context and your autobiography also influence the interpretive phase of your research as you draw meaning from relationships across key themes. The aim is to respond to your research question through the interpretation of your data. While theory has informed the study design, it, too, reemerges as a crucial source in conceptualizing the results of your study. From the conversation between data and theory, the conceptual framework is developed and often is given vitality through the language of the participants. Again, as in the analysis, your *naming* of key concepts emerging from the study is central to the next phase of the research: communicating your findings.

The Desegregation Study: Synthesizing History and the Study of Educational Structures

Returning again to the desegregation study, my design included a study of the district's desegregation history. In addition to studying the experience and views of racial equality among students, parents, and educators, I also explored educational policies and practices during the nearly 40-year period of the district's desegregation. In my study of interview, archival, and oral history data, I found considerable evidence of structural conditions that facilitated equality and drew students together in rigorous and meaningful learning opportunities, leading to positive academic outcomes and strong social networks. Educational programs and policies that reflected these dimensions were analyzed as transformative.

Moreover, I found that efforts to facilitate equality between students of color and white students were often accompanied by district assurances that high academic standards would be maintained. These assurances involved the establishment of programs, presented to the community as preserving academic excellence. Such action on the part of the district appeared to temper fears expressed among parents and community members about tarnishing the district's reputation for excellence as it became racially and economically diverse. Many of these programs contributed to the exclusion of students of color, particularly low-income students of color. While these policies, and their accompanying assurances of the maintenance of academic standards, did not appear designed to thwart racial equality, the group interest they served contributed to reinscribing privilege. In this manner, the study also revealed evidence of replicative educational change, which maintained inequality in terms of opportunities, outcomes, and social power between white students and students of color. This reflected my study of the school desegregation literature, which had revealed the tendency to protect the interests of those with the greatest social and economic investment in the public school system—primarily middle-class whites.

My analysis, then, revealed a thematic pattern in the district's desegregation history. The policies I analyzed as transformative were frequently established *in close tandem* with policies I analyzed as replicative. While I anticipated that my study would uncover both transformative and replicative change on the part of the district, I did not expect that the data would reveal the degree to which these efforts were intertwined. While the district sought to provide equal educational opportunity to African American students, particularly black students of low income, it also was compelled to retain the support of a predominantly white and black middle-class base through policies and practices that would benefit their children: gifted education, advanced course levels, and more recently a race-neutral approach to the problem of racial isolation. These policies and practices frequently yielded fewer opportunities for black students. Through the parallel enactment of these replicative and transformative structures, privilege and exclusion persisted.

In figure 5-5 is an excerpt of my email to the social psychologist Michelle Fine in which I summarized several points from our discussion of this thematic pattern. The message outlined our discussion of structural boundaries and their role in preserving exclusion by race and class within the district. As noted earlier in this chapter, the researcher's interpretation benefits from activities such as creating graphic displays, writing frequently on what has been learned thus far, and engaging those with familiarity toward the topic or context who might serve as critical friends in discussing the interpretation of the data.

In my efforts to develop a conceptual framework and theorize about my findings, I created a graphic display, shown as figure 5-6. The display included items symbolizing the way in which transformative educational structures disrupted normative routines and views about equality. I also noted those educational structures that limited access by race and class to opportunity structures, impeding racial equality. Constructing a graphic display tightened my thinking about relationships across the thematic patterns and offered additional explanatory power. It assisted me in developing a conceptual framework reflecting geographical, structural, and relational boundaries, through which I traced the parallel actions taken over the course of the district's desegregation history. As illustrated in figure 5-5, an email conversation with Michelle Fine in 2003 assisted me in my interpretation. Michelle brought up the analogy of *thickening*, efforts that alter but do not disrupt arrangements of power. Subsequent to our conversation, I named a process evident in the history of the district and in my study of educational structures within which students narrated their experiences. Referring to this phenomenon as *entanglement*, I theorized how each transformative action taken by the district to create access for black students precipitated another action, which led to the replication of inequalities. In terms of the

Thanks for the useful metaphor of "thickening" to describe educational change that is somewhere between replication (the "reinforcement" of relations of power ascribed to race and class) and transformation (the "disruption" of these relations of power). You described such change as that which "alters but does not disrupt social stratifications" and as change that "thickens but still preserves" privilege by race and class.

This notion of "thickening" is evident in the narratives and archival and oral history data, and illustrated in my chart of the emerging layers, or concentric circles, rigid at the center with increasing permeability at the perimeter. While black students were once excluded from the district, they can now access its opportunity structures. But students of color, particularly low-income students, are more likely to be located on the periphery of this site of educational privilege than at its center. Thanks so very much in helping me think through this! [Email correspondence with Michelle Fine, 6/28/03]

Figure 5-5. Advancing interpretation through conversations with critical friends

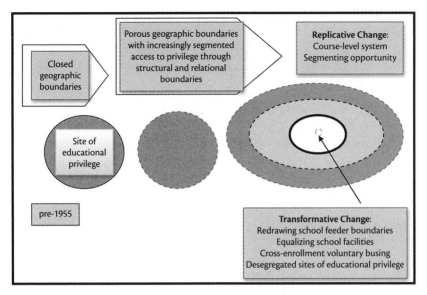

Figure 5-6. Conceptualizing entanglement

replication, these policy enactments sustained educational structures assuring white parents, and more recently black middle-class parents, of the preservation of academic standards, but they also contributed to *segmenting opportunity*, particularly for black students from families struggling to enter into or sustain their middle-class status. This conceptual framework on entanglement also allowed for theorizing more broadly on the nature of *relations of power* accorded to race and class in education.

Summary

This chapter emphasizes the process of synthesis, of weaving together the products of your analysis into one or several conceptual frameworks. The objective at this phase of your study is to generate meaning from the collection of themes that have emerged from the research. The semi-structured interview is particularly well equipped to get you there, bringing to the surface the multidimensional nature of lived experience and creating space for a dialectical conversation between data and theory. Because this phase is more open to direct conversation with theory, you are likely to return to the literature that generated your research question. Additional sources in the literature may be sought as certain thematic categories require further exploration. Synthesizing ideas as they relate to your key research themes is an intricate process that is best accomplished through waves of interpretation as you proceed throughout your research. The process of interpretation is very fluid as you "try out" various ways to make sense of potential connections across key themes and to locate gaps in meaning. Through the use of graphic displays, writing, and engagement with critical friends, you will increasingly develop ideas about what you have learned from your data.

As a result of your synthesis of study themes, you will develop a conceptual framework that will offer explanatory power in response to your research question. The task now is to present your work to a wider public and to share your findings. In the next chapter I discuss how you can now position your work in relation to the literature of your discipline and how you can engage communities invested in the implications and focus of your research.

6

Writing Up and Speaking Back to the Literature

How do we create texts that are vital? That are attended to?
That make a difference? One way to create those texts is to
turn our attention to writing as a method of inquiry.
—Richardson (1994, p. 517)

In carrying out a qualitative research project, you have been writing for
quite some time. Through writing, you followed up on the interviewing experience, noting particular ideas or questions that were evident to
you upon completing an interview. Writing offered a tool for reflexivity through which you could look back on decisions made during your
research and consider implications for the direction of the research.
As thematic patterns emerged, writing supported your articulation of
meaning and furthered your interpretation. Each step of the way, you
relied on writing as a means of reflecting back and moving forward
in terms of methods, ethics, and interpretation. Now, as you near the
phase of summarizing your research findings, your writing becomes
increasingly more public. This phase may begin tentatively through discussion with those who share knowledge of your study topic, through
additional member checks, and perhaps through a conference presentation of preliminary study results.

In this chapter I describe the process of writing up your work, sharing it with communities of interest, and positioning it within the literature. A major emphasis is the nature of research as an ongoing conversation within and across disciplinary boundaries. Additionally, I note the importance of finding ways to draw individuals and groups for whom your study is relevant into a discussion of the findings. Writing carries with it ethical demands, challenges of representation, and issues of interpretation and deliberation in responding to your research question. It raises as many questions as it seeks to answer. What is your obligation to your participants? How do you represent them in a manner that is complicated and not static? If your research is focused on an institution or organization, how do you communicate study findings but not reduce a site to a caricature? What is your commitment to the field in which you work, your discipline of study, your interpretive tradition? How do you engage a wider public with a language that is accessible and yet sufficiently complex in which to explore the depth of your findings? These are important questions that will be addressed—as best as possible—in this chapter.

Returning to the Anchor Document

In preparing to write up your findings, you should return to your original iteration of information on your research. This may be in the form of a research proposal, grant application, or dissertation prospectus. This document has likely served as an anchor throughout the research, keeping you connected to your research question, methods, analytical framework, and interpretive tradition. However, in the interim, so much has transpired. In many ways, you approach your anchor document with *new eyes*, having entered into the research problem with such intensity and focus. *How do you draw from the document and still recast it to accommodate research findings?*

Initially, sections from your existing document, such as your introduction to your study, literature review, and discussion of methods, can serve as a placeholder on the front end of your draft. While some form of these sections will be consistent in the final draft, the actual content will likely be revised to communicate more clearly from the front end your central message as it relates to your findings. To this existing document you will add a discussion of the following: research results, implications, relationship to the literature on the topic, and conclusion. The conclusion reminds the reader of the central ideas emerging from the research, and it often offers recommendations. It also notes thematic patterns not pursued within this study that serve as promising areas of future research.

What I have described thus far in terms of the organization of the final document reflects a fairly traditional format for summarizing research findings. Depending on your discipline, there may be a more specific structure for writing up your research findings. Or you may have considerable latitude in conveying results. Either way it is important to remember that this will *not* be your only opportunity to share your research findings. While this rendition fulfills obligations to your thesis or dissertation committee and/or the organization that funded the research, future opportunities may involve various presentation formats, writing styles, and creative ways to engage the public in your findings.

In this manner, as your discussion of the research continues to be a source of public engagement, your interpretation may extend beyond the original summary. The work remains a source of intellectual growth and a space within which you might continue to explore theory, methods, and ethics. In this way, your research produces a conversation over time, yielding additional insights and subsequent research. For the purpose of supporting your early efforts in writing up your results, however, this chapter focuses on the specific experience of communicating your findings at the conclusion of your research.

Writing for Clarity and Impact

After synthesizing themes and developing a conceptual framework, you are ready to share your work with a wider public. Having studied many narratives in your research, *you* are now in the position of narrator. What is the story you will tell? Equipped with data rich in imagery and meaning, your task is to produce an interpretive rendering of your study results. *How might you tell the story—well enough?*

In writing up your findings, you want to articulate the conceptual framework through the core elements that produced it: the thematic codes and categories from which you have drawn your interpretation.

The challenge is to write a document that provides readers with a sufficient discussion of the threads without their losing sight of the motif of your story. Your writing should be structured to achieve an elaboration of this motif. This means organizing the text purposefully, with an introduction that anticipates your conclusion. Chapters should be structured with attention both to documenting the analytical steps through which your interpretation was achieved and to articulating that interpretation. While the text must make clear the process of weaving, it must also focus on conveying a final product: a response to your research question.

Through your organization of the text, you can support your reader and make the story more accessible. A careful layout of chapters and subheadings within chapters will help to convey the material. Also useful can be the inclusion of displays, such as quotes from the participants, charts summarizing thematic patterns, and tables of important data. Perhaps the most direct form of impact is in your selection of a title. Here the challenge is to be succinct but also capture the many dimensions of your study in a few words or a phrase. The language and metaphors from your participants or archival materials are often effective in conveying an overarching theme. While the title is not sufficient to encompass the full story, it offers clues to important ideas associated with the research.

Used judiciously, footnotes also support your writing. They provide clarification, extend meaning, offer an important aside to your writing, and raise additional questions. Footnotes add dates, sources, related quotes, and statistical data. They introduce additional, and sometimes contrasting, expressions of meaning. These additional points may be sufficiently nuanced to interfere with your overall message in the main body of the text. Adding a footnote inserts a qualification in your interpretation, and it is important for you and your reader as it may signal the need for further research.

Framing Your Argument

In your writing, develop a structure that places front and center the prominent idea or set of ideas evident in your research. This forms your argument, and it is the basis from which you organize your text.

Crafting your published work may involve distinguishing between what information is integral to the manuscript and what might be accessible to the reader in other formats, made available through a citation, footnote, or appendix. Frequently, you write to convey one among several key ideas, referencing the full work elsewhere or suggesting more will be forthcoming. Regardless of whether your publication represents your full study or a dimension of the study, it should provide sufficient information regarding your data-collection methods, analytical framework, and findings. The extent to which you convey your argument effectively will rely on the consistency of the material you include and the manner in which you draw on this material to develop and sustain your argument.

Issues of Confidentiality

Should you have promised confidentiality in your research consent forms, you will need to assign pseudonyms to research participants if you name them in the writing up of your findings. The pseudonyms should convey some dimensions about your participants (gender and possibly cultural background) without revealing too much. This can be a challenge when context is important. It requires a bit of a balancing act as you trace your interpretation, which is often embedded in place, positionality, and conditions (Clandinin & Connelly, 2000), and at the same time protect the participants from being identified. This might require that you omit some information in order to keep your promise to your participants. Additionally, if your research involves a particular context, such as a town, business, or a school, you may need a pseudonym for the site as well. If you are affiliated with a university setting, your efforts to provide confidentiality to your participants and to the site will be outlined in your application to the Institutional Review Board (IRB) before the research begins.

Your participants may request that no pseudonyms be used. In research designed to be participatory, where there is considerable blurring between the "researcher" and the "researched," actual names may be used in the writing of the research as well as in its coauthoring. Such a decision should be established before the research begins and should be indicated on consent forms and in the IRB application. If deliberation with your participants midstream leads to changes in the original agreement, these changes should be clearly articulated between you and the participants and then reported to the IRB.

Should your research be focused on a particular setting, you will need to determine whether the site can be named or should be discussed by using a pseudonym. A person of authority at the site may indicate that it is acceptable to name the site in the research. It is useful to consider the benefits and drawbacks entailed in identifying the site by name. In terms of the disadvantages of naming a site, disclosure may cloud readers' full appreciation of study findings if they are familiar with the site. Assumptions often accompany familiarity, and this may constrain the degree of openness with which study findings are received. Pseudonyms keep the focus on study findings. On the other hand, if a site looks favorably on disclosure, this may allow for engagement in the study findings among the various constituencies affiliated with the site. Should your interpretive tradition favor an orientation toward action, identification of the site creates communicative space for deliberation over findings, direct interaction, productive conflict, and the potential for change in policy and practice. At the same time, "outing" your site requires considerable reflexivity in your writing and presenting your work. It presses you to balance reciprocity toward the site and your participants with your obligation to a wider community for whom your findings have important implications. In this way, the ethical dilemmas may be more salient *though not necessarily any more imperative* than if you used a pseudonym.

Representation of the Participants and Research Context

Considerable thought should be given to the way in which you convey your participants' narratives, and, if applicable, the research context. Your decisions are guided by your study findings, analytical framework, and your interpretive tradition. It is helpful to share your work with friendly critics who are knowledgeable about your research focus. They can review your text and ask questions about its organization, overarching message, and use of language and metaphor to convey meaning. The words you use convey implicit messages about individuals, groups, and institutions. While you cannot anticipate the range of possible responses to your text, you can be wise in considering how your writing might be misunderstood and how it might create or reinforce a static representation of individuals and/or institutions. The issue of representation of participants and the site is frequently challenging. In the next section, this is discussed further and illuminated through issues that arose in relation to the desegregation study.

The Desegregation Study: Representation of the Site

In the case of the desegregation study, the superintendent encouraged me to identify the district. This was a policy the district generally followed. In doing so, I was able to draw those within the district into discussions about policy and history as well as national trends impacting the district and the Cleveland metropolitan region. Nonetheless, naming the district created challenges for me. As a parent of children attending schools in the district and as a community member invested in the district's well-being, I felt a degree of tension in how the research findings were presented to a wider public. How might I represent the range of experience relating to racial equality over forty years of desegregation history at the district level? Furthermore, how might I situate the district within national history in order to tell a story larger than any single district?

In my writing up of the research results, I sought to portray participants in the study, particularly the students and alumni, in the complex manner through which I had studied their narratives, looking at their experiences in relation to historical and structural conditions. While my task in writing was to illustrate the conceptual framework of *centrality, marginalization,* and *encounter* as key social psychological spaces narrated by students, I also sought to portray the participants in the multidimensional manner evident in their narratives. My writing about students in the category of marginalization was particularly challenging. While students and former students narrated experiences of exclusion, they also revealed success through alternative pathways or through postsecondary education secured *despite* their experience of structural and relational boundaries. How might I convey their success and still analytically sustain my inclusion of their narratives within the social psychological space of marginalization?

For example, a participant in my study, Michelle, attributed her success to her mother, who completed high school after marriage and gained a nursing degree after she and Michelle's father divorced. Michelle is African American and grew up in the Moreland neighborhood, attending high school in the mid-1970s. In writing about Michelle's experience, I deliberately used a subtitle to highlight her point about her mother's support and Michelle's experience of marginalization. Integrating a direct quote from her interview transcript with her accompanying overarching message about her schooling experience, I titled the section discussing Michelle's narrative as *Race and Class Exclusion: "so **she** was my drive, it wasn't the school."* My writing moved between Michelle's narrative of experiencing racial inequality within the school system and the narrative of her persistence, her mother's support (and her mother's view that high school was Michelle's responsibility), and Michelle's academic success, including her completion of two graduate degrees. In this way, I wrote to convey marginalization as a thematic category within a conceptual framework. My hope was to reflect my analysis of student *narratives* and not to create a static representation of Michelle as a marginalized individual.

Additionally, it was important to me that the writing not represent the district in a one-dimensional monolithic manner. Because of the methodological choices made early in my research design, the inclusion of multiple methods revealed considerable depth and complexity of the district's desegregation history. While I analyzed a number of the district's efforts as transformative or replicative change, and I underscored the district's success at introducing counteracting mechanisms of inclusion, I located these policies and practices within the broader historical conditions that pressed upon the district. This was important in that it did not represent the district in isolation. In this way, I was able to tell the story of desegregation history that was not unique to a single district but reflected patterns across the country among districts similar to Shaker Heights. In the following excerpt, which comes from a particular section of writing focused on the history of the district in the 1980s, I illustrate my efforts to convey local history in a way that was not detached from broader sociopolitical conditions. As this chapter drew heavily on archival materials and the oral histories, there is considerable use of footnotes to clarify information, extend meaning, and identify sources from specialized archival collections in the district office and in the local public library.

The Mid-1980s: Precursors to Reorganization

The district reorganized in the 1987–1988 school year. The decision to do so emerged after a long period of discussion and several precursors. When Jack Taylor arrived as superintendent in the fall of the 1976–1977 school year, his early communications with other educators in the district focused their attention on the racial imbalance of the elementary schools. The U.S. Court of Appeals for the Sixth District ruled in the *Reed v. Rhodes* decision that the Cleveland Public School system, along with the State Board of Education and other state officials, was liable in having established practices that had "the purpose and effect of perpetuating racial and economic segregation."[1] Early in Taylor's administration, his communications to staff and the community spoke about "compliance" with the direction of the Supreme Court and avoiding any potential lawsuits as a result of continued racial imbalance, even with the Shaker Schools Plan, which might make the district vulnerable to lawsuits and federal intervention. While the Department of Health, Education, and Welfare (HEW) was not actively pursuing desegregation cases, the district courts, reflecting Supreme Court rulings, had focused on racial isolation in a number of cases in Ohio and Michigan, resulting in court-ordered desegregation rulings. Taylor held a community meeting that was widely attended in November of 1976. His particular concern at that time was to avoid having the Shaker Heights City School District included in a metropolitan desegregation plan as a result of the Cleveland desegregation ruling.[2]

While reorganization of the school system was always a possibility and several plans were suggested as early as the fall of 1976,[3] it was not seriously considered until 1983. In addition to expanding the Shaker Schools Plan in the 1977–1978 school year to include all of the elementary schools and the junior high schools, the district established a committee in November 1979 to study the use of magnet schools to attract more whites to the predominantly black schools.[4] The Ludlow Special Projects program began in the 1977–1978 school year and continued for nine years, until the district reorganized. In the 1981–1982 school year, a magnet was established at Moreland School, with a math and computer theme, and at Lomond School, with science and French as its theme. Mini-magnets were established at the predominantly white schools. In reviewing archival materials, the focus of staff energy and resources was invested in the predominantly black buildings, where the greatest concern about imbalance existed.

In the 1982–1983 school year, Peter Horoschak began as superintendent of the school system, taking responsibility for a system that had shrunk in size but still maintained all nine of its elementary buildings, and as a result was very costly to run. Concerns about racial balance continued. In addition, there emerged at that time an increasing sense of relative deprivation among whites, who questioned the utility and fairness of desegregation plans and began to speak in terms of inequity for their children. Concerns were expressed about the gifted program being in one building (Ludlow). Parents whose children were eligible, but who wanted their children to attend their neighborhood schools, were dissatisfied with this arrangement. In several superintendent professional advisory council meetings, during discussions about reducing expenses, a number of suggestions regarding ending the magnet program were raised, such as the "magnet program is not really working" and "unequal and extravagant expenditures at magnet schools,"[5] and at another meeting, during brainstorming about "possible future budgetary reductions," there were 12 comments to end magnets.[6] This level of critique toward the magnet programs, without sufficient appreciation for their role as race-conscious efforts for the purpose of increasing equality of opportunity and outcomes by race, was reflective of the direction of the country.

At the national level, there were signs of opposition toward race-conscious policies, beginning in 1978 with the *University of California Regents v. Bakke*, which involved the challenge by a white student of the constitutionality of affirmative action admissions policies at the medical school in the University of California at Davis. The Supreme Court's ruling on the Bakke case applied the language of Title VI of the Civil Rights Act to support its decision: "No person in the United States shall, on grounds of race, color, or national origin . . . be subjected to discrimination under any program or activity receiving Federal financial assistance." While Justice Lewis Powell wrote an opinion against the practice of setting aside a number of spaces for the inclusion of underrepresented racial and ethnic groups, he also indicated that universities' efforts to "take race into account" for the educational value of diversity were allowable. In this ruling, the argument of remedying past discrimination through present affirmative action practices failed to result in a decision that not only took race into account for the purpose of racial diversity but also for racial justice. From the standpoint of universities, however, it allowed some leeway in increasing the diversity of their campuses (Bowen & Bok, 1998).

As a result, the local context of Shaker Heights moving toward the mid- to late 1980s reflected contested views of racial equality and a muted sense of relative deprivation among some white parents, who felt excluded from sites of educational privilege, such as gifted education and adequately sized and resourced schools. There is the possibility that what emerged was a sense among these white parents of having been "disadvantaged" and excluded from "choice" in terms of programming, varied instructional approaches, as well as after-school and recess activities, all of which appeared to be lodged most heavily in the predominantly black elementary schools in the district's efforts to attract white parents and improve racial imbalance in the district.

Some Thoughts on Writing

As evident in the example above, the writing up of your research results is an additional iteration in the qualitative research endeavor, and it requires considerable thought in determining the structure and rationale in how you report your findings. The writing itself is generative. How might you arrange your discussion of thematic patterns in a manner that reveals the trustworthiness of your interpretation? How do you position your work in relation to extant theory in order to extend, challenge, or perhaps complicate research related to your topic? While the format and style of writing may be in keeping with disciplinary, departmental, or funding source requirements, the narrative of the text itself, your voice and that of your participants, and the angle of vision through which you make visible your findings are distinctly shaped by your deliberation. What do you intend readers to take away from your text?

In the writing up of my results for the desegregation study, participant voices were multiple, contradictory, provocative in their predictability, and delightful *and* troubling in their elements of surprise. Each dimension had implications for how I wrote up my results. How might I convey the diversity of experiences and views of equality while also communicating my interpretation and theorizing of this complex story? The findings necessitated two major sections of writing to address the two conceptual frameworks that had emerged from the study. As a result, I prepared a chapter focused on the district's history and a second chapter on thematic patterns in the student narratives. Both chapters were needed to convey the research findings. While the history chapter drew heavily on archival and oral history data, it was also informed by the data from semi-structured interviews with students, parents, and educators. The student narrative chapter relied largely on interview data from each of my student participants (those currently in the school system and those who had attended as far back as 1965), although it, too, was informed by archival and oral history data. My conclusion wove the two chapters together, creating a highly textured study of *experiences* and *views of racial equality* among students, parents, and educators over the 40-year period of the district's desegregation.

How did these two broad categories of history and narrative come together to communicate a full, deeply contextualized story? Taking seriously the theorizing of individuals nested in context and studying both structural and historic conditions as well as individual experiences, I worked toward a multilayered narrative. My use of the semi-structured interview, progressively moving participants from open-ended narratives of their experience, supported by tools and increasingly more structured and theoretically driven questions, produced rich material for interpretation and writing. My efforts to write aimed as much as possible toward reciprocity between myself and a participant as well as between data and theory. The use of the semi-structured interview, along with other methods, elicited considerable data and facilitated the analytical shift between narratives of *individual experience* and the *relational context* within educational structures and at particular moments in the district's history. This analytical shift informed thematic synthesis and writing. It produced waves of interpretation that were generative and advanced my understanding of what I needed to write and how I might do so in a way that told this story well enough.

To illustrate how I employed this analytical shift in crafting my writing, I highlight here two sections of text. Both sections drew on my analysis of Kate's narrative. Kate is a former student who attended the high school in the late 1970s and early 1980s. As a white student, when describing her early years in the school system, Kate spoke about the value of a racially diverse educational opportunity. Her parents volunteered Kate as a bused white student to Moreland in the early 1970s as part of the Shaker Schools Plan. In Kate's narrative, she revealed an appreciation for Shaker's racial integration at the same time she narrated her understanding of her position of privilege. However, Kate did not explicitly refer to her experience as privileged. Instead, she spoke about attending Moreland as a white student participating in racial integration. Her narrative reflected archival, oral history, and interview data from other white participants who took part in actions toward establishing educational structures that facilitated equality. The challenge in my writing was to represent Kate's narrative in a manner that conveyed her participation in transformative educational change *and* in the mechanics of privilege. While the former was most evident in Kate's expression of lived experience through her narrative, the latter was more evident in my use of structural and historical data to understand more broadly conceptualizations of equality among participants who were situated in school structures at particular historical moments in time. In the excerpt below from my chapter on the student narratives, I discuss elements of Kate's narrative.

> Although social ties with black students from Moreland Elementary School appeared generally to have weakened over her years of high school, Kate told me she felt she had an "advantage" as a result of having gone to Moreland, and then having those connections still in Woodbury Junior High School, and this advantage was that she was more familiar and comfortable with African American students: "I felt I had an acceptance from them—they knew I was cool: I did go to Moreland and had black friends and wasn't racist." In her narrative, it appeared that Kate's participation in the Shaker Schools Plan, desegregating the elementary schools in the 1970s, affirmed her sense of self as a white person connected to support for racial justice.
>
> Kate and I talked about her consciousness as a white student bused to Moreland and in a minority situation. She noted, "I was in the minority, skin-color wise, but I never felt less because as a kid you felt like you were

doing the right thing." During the interview she paused at this point and then told me, "Even as a kid I felt that blacks were not on an even ground [with whites]." She hesitated, and then added, "I know this is kind of arrogant, but I knew I was doing the right thing. Because there's such an inequality. I did not feel less because I had more." Kate continued to narrate her consciousness about this experience in a very transparent manner, noting that, although it was not pervasive, there was an element of her experience that viewed her participation as a white student at Moreland as contingent, allowing her to think, as she told me, "Hey, I'm doing you a favor—I could go back to my elementary school."

In Kate's narrative, then, was a powerful insight, even as a child, of the unequal relations of power ascribed to race and class. More significantly, her narrative reveals the implicit understanding of privilege that whites possess in desegregated settings particularly. Already in a position of privilege because her parents could choose where to live and where to send their children to schools, the school system preserved her privilege by the implicit power she wielded in being a critical player in the desegregation of Moreland.

The action taken by Kate's parents and other white parents participating in the Shaker Schools Plan reflected the shift from "privilege to responsibility" (Burns, 2003) as white and black parents and educators participated in efforts to make Moreland School a transformative educational setting in terms of facilitating racial equality. Her choice, or her parents' choice, to participate in the Shaker Schools Plan shaped her understanding of self in relation to others as white and as contributing to racial equality.

In this excerpt, I deliberately moved back and forth between Kate's story of what she gained as an individual from her experience of desegregation and the construction of a privileged stance within broader relations of power accorded to race and class. In the latter, I sought to connect her narrative to patterns of privilege narrated by other white participants and to the archival data that revealed similar sentiments. This underscored the ease of exit among whites, should a structural arrangement intended to facilitate equality not prove useful to them. In order to texture Kate's narrative, however, it was necessary to link her participation in the district's cross-enrollment desegregation plan with patterns of activism among white and black parents that contributed to the district's facilitation of racial equality. The actions of Kate's parents were underscored and connected with my analysis of the transformative actions taken on the part of the district and supported by some parents in an effort to collectively undertake responsibility for altering educational structures and disrupting past inequalities.

In including my analysis of these efforts to support racial justice, the interpretation is strengthened by a more in-depth understanding of the interplay between privilege and exclusion and the ways in which exercising privilege *and* supporting justice were *both* a part of Kate's narrative. This was the basis of the conceptual framework on boundary making from which I theorized *entanglement*, the competing enactments of transformation and replication evident in the district's history. Kate's story reflects the coupling of privilege and exclusion best understood in relation to historical and structural conditions within the district and across the country. In this way, my use of a multilayered analytical set of frames formulated explicit connections across history, policy, and relationship. These connections emerged from my analysis and writing, but they had their roots in the depth and richness of the data collected in the semi-structured interviews. Through this approach, the complexity of Kate's narrative could emerge, revealing her exercise of privilege *and* support for racial justice.

To tie together the threads of these highly textured data, I drew on Kate's insights again in my concluding chapter. In my conclusion, I reminded readers of my research question and of the study findings shaping my overall argument. I noted my focus on the experience of racial equality among students, parents, and educators and their conceptualizations of equality within the district's 40 years of desegregation. Connected to this question was my interest in situating the district in relation to broader national historical trends regarding desegregation. Were there junctures in the history of the district that reflected a willingness to *displace long-established patterns of race and class privilege* in order to reduce racial exclusion? Or were national trends of reluctance toward altering existing arrangements of white privilege evident in district policies and practices?

By bringing to the surface Kate's admission of contingency, "I could go back to my elementary school," I sought to underscore what I interpreted as "the power of the favor." This reconnected with the legal scholar Derrick Bell's convergence theory as it relates to racial justice (Bell, 1995), where privileged interests merge with demands for equality in a manner that advances legal and social change yet tethers it in some way to the maintenance of privilege. At a psychological level, Kate's statement reflected the work of the social psychologist Erika Apfelbaum (1979), who theorizes about relations of power and situates opportunity for marginalized groups within a sphere of conditionality. These were important theoretical connections that informed my interpretation and writing about patterns in the data. Kate's powerful statement took on greater meaning within the broader study of my data, beyond her individual experience and toward understanding entanglement in terms of the disruption *and* maintenance of race and class privilege within public education. To communicate this pattern in the data, I highlighted Kate's insights and elaborated on how they reflected patterns within and beyond the district, as indicated in the following excerpt from my concluding chapter.

A Split of Institutional Prerogatives: The Conundrum for Desegregated Schools

In the study of archival and interview data over the nearly 40 years of desegregation efforts, two competing and interdependent district prerogatives are evident. As the district has endeavored to retain those parents who keep the system racially and economically balanced through its cultivation of sites of educational privilege, it also has worked intensively, particularly in the current phase, to draw African American students into these sites. In its split of institutional prerogatives is reflected the commitment to academic excellence in a desegregated setting. At the same time, also reflected are the relations of power accorded to race in the larger society, in which the loss of white students portends the loss of resources and reputation for academic excellence.

It is the relations of power ascribed to race that were narrated in the experiences of students in their view of self in relation to other and in relation to educational structures. As a white student graduating in the early 1980s noted about her participation in the busing plan at Moreland, she was aware of both the significance of her presence there as a white student but also of a contingency in her presence, which she narrated as

"Hey, I'm doing you a favor—I could go back to my elementary school."
This provocative and introspective statement underscores the privilege of
those who have social mobility, facilitated by race, class and educational
background, and the privilege of "choice" or, as an educator narrated, the
ability to "control your own destiny." Implicit, then, in the relationship
between the white community, in particular, and its desegregated school
system is the power of "the favor."

In writing up the desegregation study, I aimed to write in a way that
was reflective of rigorous study, ethical in its representation of the participants and the site, and committed to clarity and impact. In reviewing the examples provided in this chapter, it is hopefully evident how
producing a written product from your research takes time, multiple
drafts, and discussions with critical friends. It also entails an ongoing
reflexivity toward the text, its audience, and the types of conversations
and actions generated from others' reading of your work. Keep in mind
that each published work or presentation will likely yield satisfaction
and a desire to convey this story differently or "better" the next time.
It is helpful to view your scholarship as an interpretive journey, where
further writing and engagement will yield greater clarity, additional
questions, and further opportunities to theorize.

Summary

Writing carries with it ethical demands, challenges of representation,
and issues of interpretation and deliberation in responding to your
research question. Writing up your results takes time. It is often useful to return to the anchor document, such as your dissertation prospectus or funding proposal. You will revise this text considerably, as
your research findings will now shape how you construct your introduction and subsequent chapters. You will convey your findings more
effectively when you support them with the use of quoted material from
your interviews and other data sources, as well as charts, tables, maps,
and images that supplement your discussion of the findings. Careful
planning in the organization of your text, selection of a title, and use
of subtitles also assist in communicating your key points. Footnotes
can help to clarify and qualify points, identify sources, and introduce

additional nuances. Consideration of your audience is important as it will influence the style and format of your writing. Nonetheless, there are some basic elements to consider in communicating to others about your study findings. Generally, the writing should be clear about your research purpose, questions, methods, analytical framework, and interpretive tradition. It should aim for coherence but not be shy about the dimensions of the study that remain in question and are still perplexing.

Writing requires thought on your part in terms of the representation of study participants in your text and of the representation of the study site if your research involves an organization or institution. Sharing your work with friendly critics will provide useful feedback and guidance. Continuing to engage in reflexivity is important as you prepare to share your work with communities of interest. The degree to which you have maintained rigor and a systematic approach to data collection and analysis will strengthen your ability to tell the story emerging from your research. While writing up your findings signals the completion of your research, it also sets the stage for further inquiry, as some thematic codes and categories will require additional study.

After your initial effort to write up the results, you will want to look for opportunities to share your work in other venues. You may also be thinking about ways in which this work might impact policy, practice, and the discourse concerning the focus of your research. In addition to writing, your communication of findings may also be conveyed through performance, such as poetry or a dramatic script, as well as other creative works, as in film or music. Each rendition of your work will deepen your understanding of what you learned from your study. Questions raised within your discipline and among those invested in your topic may send you back into the data in search of further clarification and interpretation. You also may be compelled to address new developments in scholarship and in policy making through your work.

Writing up and presenting the results of your research has the potential to connect you with a broad sphere of individuals and groups who share your research interests. Public engagement of your research will contribute to the knowledge base within your field. Over time, your work will continue to evolve with subsequent iterations of interpretation, writing, and peer review. In this way, your theorizing on a topic is not a singular event but instead an ongoing scholarly journey.

Afterword

Loose Threads

We have to examine the psychological dimensions of our societies, conscious of the fact that this examination itself is involved—and has a stake—in the very processes and conflicts it is analyzing.

—Martín-Baró (1994, p. 49)

This aim of this book was to invite you to consider the possibilities that are available to you in conducting qualitative research. I emphasized the inductive nature of qualitative research, the use of reciprocity and reflexivity, and the systematic and iterative steps involving data collection, analysis, and interpretation. The semi-structured interview is a qualitative research method that is frequently underestimated in the social sciences. The versatility and strength of this method can allow for an exploration of specific dimensions of your research question. The semi-structured interview is instrumental in creating openings for a narrative to unfold, while also including questions informed by theory. As such, this method is particularly suited to assist you in attending to the depth and complexity of your data.

In order to ground the abstract discussion of methods and interpretation, I used a completed research project as an example. This study, referred to throughout as the desegregation study, was not meant to be an exemplar but a means through which you might imagine the possibilities in qualitative research as it relates to your research interest. At the same time, I had a stake in telling the desegregation story. As a result, I wrote this book with the hope that the text might *carry a story* while *communicating a method*.

What is at stake in your efforts to explore a topic, to locate gaps in existing theory, or perhaps pursue a phenomenon tied to your autobiography? How might you bring your creative and scholarly interests to bear on a broader conversation about an important social issue? What do you do with questions that won't go away?

In addition to serving as a resource for your research endeavor, I hope this book has inspired you to take seriously the nagging questions, the unease you experience in sensing an underexplored dimension of a pervasive social problem, the desire to probe more deeply into dilemmas that are deeply entangled and within which your research topic may be situated. Pursuing a question that has been a source of conceptual restlessness for you is likely not only to offer you a research project but also to set you on a trajectory within your discipline as you produce new insights and promising opportunities for further research.

To provide an illustration of the direction of scholarly work subsequent to one's initial study, I have included in this text a book chapter completed after the desegregation study. In 2007, William E. Cross, Jr., approached me about coauthoring a response to the late anthropologist John U. Ogbu, who had published a study of the black community in Shaker Heights entitled *Black American Students in an Affluent Suburb: A Study of Academic Disengagement*. Ogbu's study was published in 2003, and, at the time, I had just completed my research. Over the next year or two, it became clear that there was considerable potential in our conversing across the two studies of the same school district.

In our response to John Ogbu's study of Shaker Heights, Bill Cross and I raised important questions about Ogbu's reliance on the study of the black community as a single frame for understanding the black-white achievement gap. Our analysis complicated the research on the gap in educational outcomes. Through the study of the experiences of students, parents, and educators within an analysis of history and policy, we revealed a broader web of structures and relations that created a gap by race and class in the social psychological experience of schooling. Combining Bill's study of black achievement motivation from a historical lens, which traced the historical evidence of black support for education and investment in building and sustaining schools from Reconstruction onward, and my study of the district's desegregation history and student narratives, we challenged Ogbu's analysis. This work, included in a volume edited by the psychologist Andrew J. Fuligni, is reprinted and located in appendix B. My inclusion of this book chapter also serves as an illustration of the promising points of collaboration that may exist as you share your work with a wider public in local, national, and international settings.

In writing this text, I hope you anticipate many exciting opportunities to conduct qualitative research. This work is central to the advancement of your discipline and the efforts to solve persistent social problems. Your use of qualitative research and the completion of a research project will offer you and those with whom you engage in your research findings a level of reciprocity and reflexivity. It will likely provide a good deal of satisfaction and an edgy sense of needing to do more to explore complex social topics and important dimensions of the human experience.

Appendix A

Sample Protocol for Student Participants

Interview Protocol: Current Phase Student (1988–2003)

Segment One: Opening Narrative

1. Community Context

Were you born in Shaker Heights? [*if not, probe for where moved from and what year*]

How would you describe the community of Shaker Heights?

2. School Context

What elementary school did you attend? How would you describe your elementary school?

How would you describe Woodbury? [*probe for dimensions of experience, such as favorite teachers, opportunities they accessed and those they did not, meaningful learning experiences, adult and peer relationships that facilitated their academic success, and those relationships and educational policies and practices that constrained educational opportunity*]

How would you describe the middle school?

HIGH SCHOOL CONTEXT: MAPPING THE SOCIAL LANDSCAPE

The remaining questions in this interview will deal with your high school experience. However, if you have an experience at the elementary school level or junior high school level that relates to any of these questions, please bring it up. It's not a digression and it will likely contribute to the wide range of experiences you talk about during the interview. [*Keep narrative moving—use materials to generate stories about self and other in the social landscape of high school.*]

We will use some materials to make a map of the social landscape of your high school.

Materials include:
oval-shaped cardboard paper as social map of the high school
small circles as representing social groups in high school
"sticky" notes marked "self" to place besides groups with which participant feels socially connected
blue pipe cleaners for encircling influential social groups among students
red pipe cleaner for encircling influential social groups that wield influence with adults
"sticky" notes marked "black/African American," white/European American," and "racially mixed" to indicate social groups' racial backgrounds

Formation of Groups
Within the high school, could you use these small circles here to show the various groups, or small communities, of students that you think made up your school? Could you place on the oval-shaped cardboard some circles that represent social groups in the high school?
For example, you could depict various groups
　　by friendship;
　　by particular classes or clubs;
　　by student interests, such as sports, music, academic interests;
　　by their neighborhoods; or
　　by another activity or other influence that helped to form groups in the high school.

Relationships between Groups
What kinds of relationships did these groups have to each other:
Did some have more contact with each other during the school day?
Were some more socially close to each other?
Were there any particular classes or extracurricular activities that brought these different student groups together?
Were there any particular classes or extracurricular activities that set these different student groups apart?
Were there any groups that were more isolated than others?

Relation of Self to Other Groups in School

Think about your own experience in school. Are there groups of students already on this map that you had *contact* with and/or were *socially affiliated* with?

Use these "sticky" notes labeled "self" and put these on the map near the groups you had contact with or with whom you socially affiliated.

Are there additional groups of students, which are not already on this map, that you had contact with and/or were socially affiliated with?

[*Add groups.*]

[*Place "self" label beside groups in relationship with self.*]

Group Influence

In looking at this map of the high school, could you talk about what kind of influence you think some or all of these groups of students, educators, and parents had in the high school at the time you attended it?

By influence I mean the strength of their voices or opinions in the decision making of the school. While all of these groups made up the school, some of them were likely to exert more influence in school activities, policy decisions, the way the school was presented to the larger public, and the overall direction of the school.

Could you indicate from among these groups of students, which group or groups were the most influential:

in terms of policy decisions and the activities/direction of the school?

[*red pipe cleaner*]

in terms of influencing their peers? [*blue pipe cleaner*]

Racial Makeup of Groups

In looking at this map of the high school, and the student groups that you have identified, what can you tell me about the racial makeup of these groups—were they predominantly African American? White? Racially mixed?

[*Apply stickers to circles to identify the groups' racial makeup.*]

3. Sense of Connection to Racial Ingroup (Self-Identified)

Part of my interest is in the relationship between groups of people and how strongly connected people feel to each other.

Before we move into the next section of the interview, I'd like to now ask you a bit about yourself and your relationship to other groups.

Could you tell me what racial group would you identify yourself as belonging to?

[*Show the participant the Venn diagram with the Inclusion of Ingroup in the Self (IIS) scale (Tropp & Wright, 2001) for the racial group for which the participant did identify him/herself as a member.*]

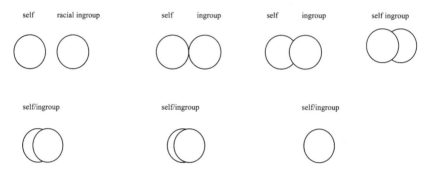

On this page is a set of circles, or Venn diagrams, that show the strength of one's sense of connection with racial groups.

What set of circles would you select that best represents the strength of your own sense of connection with this group that you identify yourself as belonging to?

Where in school are you most likely to share these connections?

4. Sense of Connection to Other Racial Group
[*Show the participant the sheet of paper with the Inclusion of Ingroup in the Self (IIS) scale (Tropp & Wright, 2001) for a racial group for which the participant did not identify him/herself as a member.*]

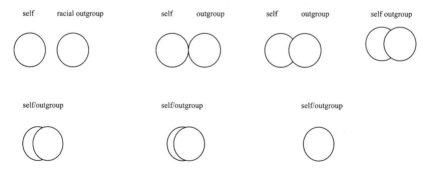

Using this set of circles depicted on the previous page, what set of circles would you select that best represents the strength of your own sense of connection with _____ [*name other racial group*]?

Where in school are you most likely to share these connections?

Segment Two: Questions of Greater Specificity

Let's talk a little more specifically about your experience as a student in the high school, class of _____.

5. Expectations

Think about your parents' expectations for you as a student in the high school. What goals do they expect you to have reached by the time you graduate?

How much do you think that the high school shares the same expectations as your parents did for you?

☐ very much   ☐ a good amount   ☐ some   ☐ a little   ☐ none

6. Educational Opportunities

I want to ask you about educational opportunities for you in the high school.

Educational opportunities provide students with the kind of teaching, courses, and opportunities to study and discuss academic work with their peers that is necessary to prepare them, academically and socially, for college and a career. Educational opportunities include academic classes and extracurricular activities.

How much have you benefited from the opportunities available in school?

☐ a great deal   ☐ a good amount   ☐ some   ☐ a little   ☐ none

Could tell me what educational opportunities in particular you have benefited from and in what way?

Are there opportunities you would like to benefit from that you did not? What would have to happen to make this possible?

7. Information

Students are more likely to take advantage of educational opportunities when they know about them and get help in choosing classes and participating in activities, such as:

learning about the kinds of classes needed to be accepted into a competitive college; getting extra help in a class; changing from a college prep class to an honors or advanced class or from an honors or advanced class to a college prep class.

Given this, how much information and help do you feel you have in terms of learning about and taking advantage of the educational opportunities that are available?

☐ a lot   ☐ a good amount   ☐ some   ☐ a little   ☐ none

8. Academic Outcomes

How well do you do in terms of academic achievement?

☐ excellent   ☐ very good   ☐ good/average
☐ needing improvement   ☐ failing

What level of coursework do you generally take classes in?

_____

How do the use of different course levels influence your educational opportunities and achievement?

Did they enhance your learning?

Did they impede your learning?

What, if anything, would be necessary for you to achieve at a higher academic level?

9. The Parents' Sense of Control over the Child's Education[1]

If your parents are dissatisfied or concerned, what would they do to see to it that the high school, or the school system, responded to their dissatisfaction?

Do you have an example of a time they felt concern and sought a response from the school system?

What were the different steps your parents took to ensure that action was taken by the school system on behalf of their children?

[*Probe: parents' and/or students' use of face-to-face responses with a teacher or administrator; appeal to a higher authority (Board of Education or district office); group response; exit or resignation.*]

Given what you've just spoken about, how much control do you think your parents have over your education?

☐ a lot   ☐ a good amount   ☐ some   ☐ a little   ☐ none

10. Experiences Within and Across Racial Groups[2]

How similar or dissimilar would you say your experience as a student in the high school was to the experience of other _____ [*indicate person's self-identified race here*] students?

☐ very similar   ☐ somewhat similar   ☐ similar
☐ somewhat dissimilar   ☐ very dissimilar

What about _____ [*indicate other major racial group (white or African American) here*] students? How similar or dissimilar would you say your experience was to the experience of _____ [*identify other group*] students?

☐ very similar   ☐ somewhat similar   ☐ similar
☐ somewhat dissimilar   ☐ very dissimilar

And biracial students? How similar or dissimilar would you say your experience was to the experience of biracial students?

☐ very similar   ☐ somewhat similar   ☐ similar
☐ somewhat dissimilar   ☐ very dissimilar

Segment Three: Exploring the Opening Narrative in Relation to Questions of Theoretical Significance

In 1954, the *Brown v. Board of Education* decision of the Supreme Court ruled that public schools that were racially segregated and operated under a "separate but equal" premise were unconstitutional and "had no place in public education" (*Brown v. Board of Education of Topeka*, 1954).

Can you tell me what racial equality in public education means to you?

11. Racial Equality and Its Facilitators

In thinking about your experience as a student, is there a particular story that comes to your mind of an experience you might have had —either one of racial equality or inequality? Perhaps something that happened to you that might have made you pause and think about racial equality in the schools?

What helped this experience take place?

If an experience of racial inequality:

What do you think got in the way of the facilitation of racial equality in this situation?

12. Engendering/Fostering Equal Power Relations[3]

An additional area in making racial equality possible is in bringing about equal social influence, or power, between whites and African Americans. By this, I mean that people in the community and the school system, white and black, recognize the historical advantage whites have had in education. Also, the community and school system try not to sustain this advantage within its schools.

In what way would you say the school system has paid attention to bringing about equal social influence or equal power between blacks and whites?

In what way has the system not paid attention to this?

13. Extent to Which Participants Have Experienced Transformative Educational Change

When a school system pays attention to racial equality, it creates the possibility of transforming its schools, that is, interrupting a history of unequal education and making schools a very different place for white and black students.

To what extent have you experienced the Shaker schools as a setting that is transforming education for white and black students?

What else would have to happen to transform it more?

14. Other Comments, Thoughts, Reflections

Is there anything else you would like to add before we end this interview?

Appendix B

Past as Present, Present as Past: Historicizing Black Education and Interrogating "Integration"

One of the objectives of the works included in this volume is to interrogate the so-called achievement gap between mainstream white and Asian American students as compared to minority students in general and black students in particular. The current chapter focuses on the latter, although our analysis has implications for the general discourse on the achievement gap. The intractability of the problem within the black community moved the late and renowned anthropologist John Ogbu to search beyond racism in his efforts to pinpoint the origins of the gap, and instead to probe the dynamics of black culture and traditions (Ogbu 1987, 1998, 2003, 2004). Ogbu noted that blacks entered America on an involuntary basis, and during the nearly two hundred and fifty years that the institution of slavery lasted, captive Africans evolved various forms of psychological resistance to protect their humanity. In forging an "oppositional identity," the captive Africans, according to Ogbu's interpretation, achieved a modicum of self-definition, with a cost of cultural alienation from aspects of the dominant "white" culture. Ogbu believed that by anchoring blackness as the opposite of whiteness and by including schooling and education under the rubric of whiteness, blacks initially developed a cynicism, estrangement, and resistance to achievement that stemmed from the slavery experience.

Since slavery was followed by years of legally sanctioned racial segregation or the era of Jim Crow (circa 1890 to 1954), Ogbu concluded that historical circumstances never made possible an intervention, transformation, or corrective drift toward high achievement. Consequently, over time, what was originally a "healthy" response to slavery and the crude realities of life in the Deep South during the first half of the 20th century "ossified" and became an anachronistic aspect of black culture. According to this perspective, blacks continue to "resist" and be "oppositional" even when they are nested in educational environments characterized by opportunity, equality, fairness, and choice rather than exclusion, stigma, inequality, and racism.

In his recent study of academic disengagement among black students in the Cleveland suburb of Shaker Heights, Ohio, Ogbu (2003, 2004) extends his theory of oppositional identity and black underachievement beyond poor and working-class black families to middle-class blacks in an affluent suburb. In locating oppositional identity and black underachievement among the black middle class, his theory gained greater credence, because in the face of the freedom and multiple "choices" afforded middle-class status, he could point to blacks who were conducting imaginary battles with racism, even when such vigilance seemed unnecessary and the resulting depressed achievement levels dysfunctional. Thus, Ogbu thought it critical to demonstrate the existence of academic oppositionalism among both poor and middle-class black students and its omnipresence or ubiquity became a pillar undergirding his theory that oppositionalism and underachievement were endemic to black culture and the likely were the "legacy" of slavery and years of post-slavery oppression.

Historicizing Black Education: Black Achievement Motivation Following the Civil War

John Ogbu was not the first person to isolate, document, and theorize the existence of black educational oppositionalism, for in many ways his theory is an extension of observations made years earlier by Kenneth Clark in his ground-breaking text of the 1960s, *Dark Ghetto* (1965), or, reaching back still further, related themes can also be found in Carter G. Woodson's classic, *The Miseducation of the Negro* (1934). Shortly, we shall reveal the discovery of instances of academic oppositionalism and "planned" underachievement in our own research, but it is one thing to come to terms with the actual existence of academic oppositionalism in the behavior of today's black students and another to draw a straight line between the present and past by invoking the legacy-of-slavery thesis. We contest the legacy argument and show that contemporary displays of oppositionalism and muted achievement by black students are more readily traceable to structural elements and educational policies that define integrated schooling. But before deconstructing what is meant by "integrated schooling," let us step back in time to debunk the legacy-of-slavery myth.

In the late 1950s and early 1960s, there was considerable historical evidence that the ex-slaves became involved in educational activities almost immediately following the collapse of slavery (Bullock, 1967; Butchart, 1980; Du Bois, 1935; Woodson, 1919). At first, historians concluded the ex-slaves' educational agenda was suggested, imposed, or made possible by external influences such as key leaders from the Union Army as well as white teachers and white benefactors, who flooded the South to assist in helping the slaves transition to freedom. In this scenario, the ex-slaves had to be "shown" or convinced of the value of formal education. Whatever interest or enthusiasm they displayed toward schooling was thought to have been triggered by outsiders.

The image of the post–Civil War black community as neutral, passive, or at best naïve to the value of education extends into the history of black education in the 1930s, as evidenced by the fact that wealthy white northern philanthropists, such as Julius Rosenwald, were depicted as having to prod the rural black communities of the 1920s and 1930s to build schools for their children. The Rosenwald agents would enter a rural black community, help the community organize itself for the purpose of building the first schools to service blacks in the county in question, and put up funds which the community had to "match" as a demonstration that it agreed with the educational thrust being pressed by the Rosenwald Foundation. This theme of black attitudinal underdevelopment drives the historical record on the evolution of black education up to the late 1960s, and it is central to the standard text on the topic, *A History of Negro Education in the South: From 1619 to the Present,* by Henry Allen Bullock. It should be noted that although Bullock and others did not speak explicitly of a legacy of slavery, their depiction of ex-slaves as passive, crude, and naïve and their description of rural blacks of the 1920s and 1930s as being in need of conversion to the value of education come very close to saying that from the end of slavery into the 20th century the value of education was not organic to black culture.

In 1935, W. E. B. Du Bois, one of the leading intellects of the 20th century, published a radical critique of the then current mainstream perspectives on America's failed attempt to proactively transition blacks from the status of slave to citizen. In his controversial text, *Black Reconstruction in America*, Du Bois accords greater *agency* to blacks themselves. Du Bois paints a picture of the average ex-slave "demanding" education for black children; however, because Du Bois was at the time an avowed Communist, his depiction of the ex-slaves as agentic, focused, and *self-motivated* toward education was considered "radical" history. *Black Reconstruction* was a masterfully written history of the reconstruction period that reflected the application of state-of-the-art historiography and for this reason it could not be summarily dismissed. However, by depicting blacks as the social equal of others, it became a thorn in the side of mainstream history, never to be dismissed but never to be fully accepted either.

Observers of the black experience would have to wait until 1988 and the publication of *The Education of Black Americans in the South, 1860–1935*, a groundbreaking work by James D. Anderson, before they could fully comprehend that the adult ex-slaves and their children transitioned from slavery to freedom holding attitudes toward the value and importance of education that not only were positive and reflective of high achievement motivation but matched the positive attitudes toward education once associated only with ethnic white immigrants, who would not hit America's shores for another 20 to 40 years. Anderson traces the origins of high black achievement motivation (BAM) to the worldview developed by blacks within the context of slavery. Even without the benefit of literacy, the slave community was able to decipher how formal education helped explain the social hierarchy found among whites, in that landless, poor, and politically vulnerable whites were typically those who had little or no education, while the plantation owners, school teachers for the owners' children, and key figures in the larger white society evidenced the benefits of formal education. Though they were but a tiny fraction of the slaves' ecology, there were often pockets of free blacks near the plantation, and the free black community teemed with educational activities. It was not uncommon for educated free blacks to assist in the formal education of the slave owner's children, and clearly this made an impression on the average slave. From time to time, a literate black would fashion a pamphlet urging blacks to rise up and overthrow the owners, and near the end of slavery, the Abolitionist Movement provided written as well as living icons, such as Frederick Douglass, that clearly guided the average slave toward a nuanced understanding of the "power" of literacy and formal education.

Anderson shows how such experiences and observations helped shape the educational attitudes of the slaves such that when they left slavery, one of their most potent assets was a positive attitude toward education. From Anderson's research we see the ex-slaves beginning the education of their children before friends from the Union Army and teachers and supporters of black freedom from the North even came into contact with the ex-slaves. However, when the ex-slaves and white sympathizers did eventually make contact, the fusion of the ex-slaves' desire for formal education and the immense resources of the northern Army in conjunction with the aid of northern sympathizers, including many black teachers willing to return to the South at risk of life and futures, exploded into a social movement for black education (Cross, 2003). William E. Cross, Jr., has shown that had the drive for education and meaningful freedom been allowed to run its natural course, by the beginning of the 20th century, some 40 years after the end of the Civil War, blacks would have been disproportionately represented across all levels of the public education establishment in the South, including higher education.

Finally, Anderson was able to link BAM to black educational activities in the South up to the beginning of the Great Depression in the 1930s. Black tenant farmers were the poorest of the poor, yet so motivated were they to educate their children that they in effect double-taxed and in some cases triple-taxed themselves to make it happen. Anderson points out that, during the Jim Crow Era, southern rural blacks seldom saw a fair share of their tax dollars spent on the education of their children. So blacks would impose on themselves a second tax by holding a festival where people volunteered their labor, bartered goods, and gave money to build rural schoolhouses. The schools were built on land given to the black community by one of its land-owning members. Yet another festival might be scheduled to raise funds to pay the teachers' salaries and buy books. Anderson also uncovered historical documents showing that when, in the 1920s and 1930s, the Julius Rosenwald Foundation injected its presence into a black community, there was no evidence of the community having to be prodded to embrace the education of its children. If anything, Anderson showed that the fund's importance has tended to be exaggerated, for in looking at the projects supported by it, time and again the black community itself provided the larger sum of funds and material support in the building of a "Rosenwald" School. With equal force and clarity, he also documents the way in which the larger white-controlled society systematically turned its back on the black community by segregating it and, where possible, radically underfunding black education. "Separate" never approached "equal."

In summary, there is no legacy of slavery that explains the educational attitudes found among contemporary blacks, whether they be the children of the poor or of the middle class. Given that Anderson's work and the follow-up research that gave it even greater credibility did not appear until 1988 and later, it is understandable how Ogbu and others might have entertained the legacy-of-slavery thesis. More difficult to comprehend is why Ogbu held on to this discredited thesis long after the historical studies that disprove it were readily available. There simply is no straight line between the educational attitudes slaves embraced when they exited slavery and the evolution of oppositional attitudes held by a significant portion of black youth in the present. The origin of such attitudes is much more recent than Ogbu and others have been able to comprehend.

Interrogating "Integration": Attending to Policy and Student Experience of Systemic Factors

Fast forwarding to the present, the second part of this chapter draws on new work (Galletta, 2003) that focuses on the history of school integration within the Shaker Heights, Ohio, school district (referred to henceforth as the Galletta study). The study synthesizes archival materials, original school documents, newspaper reports, interviews with key teachers and administrators, and interviews with different cohorts of both white and black parents as well as interviews with youths and alumni who attended the Shaker Heights schools between 1965 and

2003. The Galletta study offers a fine-grained discussion of the policies, practices, strategies, and narratives linked to the Shaker Heights integration experience, and a book-length version is in preparation (personal note to 2nd author, Galletta, 2005).

The Galletta study was never meant to be a counterpoint to the late John Ogbu's important work on the Shaker Heights schools, as Anne Galletta's original motivations for undertaking the dissertation were grounded in her own personal history as a resident of Shaker Heights and mother of children who continue to attend the district schools. In fact, she made the Shaker Heights–John Ogbu connection after much of her own data collection was completed. Reflecting a desire to capture the frames of reference of informants on their own terms, and guided by an interdisciplinary base of desegregation history, educational policy, and social psychological theory, the Galletta study engaged grounded data and extant theory in the analysis of the data (Lather, 1986; Weis & Fine, 2004). Nevertheless, the Galletta study now stands as an important counterpoint in that it complicates, rather than negates, the Ogbu thesis, by showing it underestimates the power of certain integration policies and practices and exaggerates the role of black culture in explaining the origins of black student oppositional attitudes. In light of his recent and premature passing, we regret not being able to engage him directly, but we hope our discourse reflects the high esteem with which we approach his scholarship.

Brown and the Shaker Heights Integration Experience: 1965 to the Present

America's response to the 1954 Brown v. Board of Education Supreme Court decision—with its mandate to provide and "equal" and integrated education—varied by state, region, and school district. Virginia simply shut down those schools in which black and white children would attend classes together (Irons, 2002), and other southern states came close to instituting the same strategy of resistance. As noted by Orfield (1978), white students in the South were serviced by top-quality "alternate" systems, while the public schools, now the province of mostly black students, were grossly underfunded, understaffed, and cut off from key components of the larger society. Northern as well as southern urban centers saw whites simply abandon urban districts and moved to distant suburbs, creating a form of American Apartheid (Massey & Denton, 1993). Many whites did not change their place of residence but simply pulled their children out of the public schools and enrolled them in private schools.

Other school systems—such as Hyde Park in Chicago; Evanston, Illinois; Montclair, New Jersey; and Shaker Heights, Ohio—struggled to define proactive strategies that let integration happen by positive design, courage, and good planning. In Shaker Heights, there was a powerful drive among educators to carry out the mandate of Brown. On the other hand, the school district sought to sustain itself financially and preserve its stellar reputation. These dual needs in effect translated into not only stemming white flight but also building white confidence in the district's capacity to sustain quality in the face of integration. The double institutional prerogative also reflected the views of the students, parents, and educators in this city. While some white residents on the school board and in neighborhood meetings supported and even brokered desegregation efforts, others opposed them outright or accepted desegregation conditionally. In this situation the social and material capital of this historically affluent community has been a powerful lever in supporting the district's commitment to racial diversity and good schools, but it has also served as a drag on the extent to which educational policies designed to facilitate racial and economic equality are actually carried out.

In this sense, education is truly a "property of power" (Ng, 1982) and as a source of social advantage its distribution is frequently contested. This is key to our deconstruction: that desegregation has meant access to a privilege once enjoyed only by whites. In this sense, privilege is intimately tied up with exclusion, since what has historically contributed to the school system's privileged status is the exclusion of others by race and class. While notions of "equality" were explored and debated, terms like "standards" and "excellence" remained impervious to scrutiny, creating a firewall around those policies and practices presumed to sustain "quality," while simultaneously replicating race and class inequalities.

The Galletta study of the integration history in Shaker Heights explored four principal areas: (1) *Racial balance or literal integration* —these are efforts to make it possible for black and white children to attend the same schools, regardless of the racial composition of the immediate neighborhoods where their individual households are located; (2) *Enactments of quality and excellence*—the policies and practices, such as the levels system and various enrichment and remedial programs, meant to sustain the district's pre-integration historical reputation for educational excellence; (3) *Adjustments, interventions, and "fixes,"* which are actions taken when some aspect of the original integration policy or strategy causes unintended, negative consequences; and (4) *Narratives,* the stories told by students, in their narration of the integration experience.

Racial Balance or Literal Integration

Shaker Heights, an upscale, and newly developed affluent suburb of Cleveland, was incorporated in 1912. Until 1955, the city and its school system were segregated. Shaker Heights used restrictive racial and religious covenants in its property sales, until the Supreme Court ruled these practices unconstitutional in 1948 in *Shelly v. Kraemer*.[1] Still, realtors encouraged or pressured their clients to abide by these now-illegal covenants through the 1960s.[2] The first neighborhood within Shaker Heights to desegregate was Ludlow, bordering on Cleveland; it drew middle-class and professional African Americans in the late 1950s from the Cleveland area. This neighborhood, through the work of its community association, engaged financial institutions and realty firms in crafting policies that stemmed white flight. However, in the nearby Moreland neighborhood, working-class white families abandoned the area upon the arrival of middle- and working-class African American families, and Moreland resegregated. Other Shaker Heights neighborhoods to the east remained predominantly white and middle class, with very affluent families located along the wooded northern boundaries of the city in the Boulevard and Malvern areas. Moreland and Ludlow, or the neighborhoods reflecting significant demographic change, were often referred to as "the other side of the tracks," whereas the areas to the north and east were viewed as "deep Shaker," all-white and impenetrable to blacks.

These distinctions are both historical and contemporary, and they carry race and class signifiers evident in the narratives of students, parents, and educators. Also evident in the data is the classification of the "pioneers" for the black families who first desegregated Ludlow. Implicit in the story of the "pioneers," however, is the story of the "trespassers," black families stretching beyond their working-class means to move their children into middle-class status. This group in particular has experienced the greatest struggle in fully realizing the educational opportunities available in the Shaker Heights City School District. Nevertheless, even the pioneers' educational and economic standing did not fully ensure access to the same sites of educational privilege as it did for white students.

From 1965 to the present, the school district has struggled to make racial balance or "literal integration" a reality in all the elementary and middle schools, regardless of whether the neighborhood site of the school was "deep Shaker" or "the other side of the tracks." Integration took place fairly quickly at the high school, because there was and continues to be only one high school servicing the entire district. However, at the elementary and junior high schools, racial balance would be a new venture. The school district has reconfigured its racial-balance strategy to stay ahead of demographic shifts through mandatory and voluntary policies as well as a district-wide reorganization in 1987. Currently, nearly all elementary schools are racially balanced, while the upper elementary school, middle school, and high school serve the entire district. To a certain extent, the fact that Shaker Heights continuously struggled to make "literal integration" a reality was a victory for the black community and progressive and moderate whites. Being admitted to the same schools and entering the same buildings meant to many that black and white children would experience the same classes, the same teachers, the same curriculum, and the same overall quality education.

Quality Education and Excellence: Sustaining the Shaker Heights Tradition for Educational Excellence

Not only was the Shaker Heights educational establishment victorious in the promotion of an aggressive racial-balance program at the level of practically every school building, even in the face of objections from segments of the "deep Shaker" population, but it also was prohibited from equivocating on how quality and excellence would be sustained within each building and across the system as a whole. The strategy for programmatic quality also involved change. Before 1964, the district offered a few advanced-placement classes and provided a rigorous college preparatory program for most of its students. Then, at the very same time the district was experiencing high migration of black students into the district, the high school introduced a new five-category "levels system."[3] Subsequently, the junior highs, particularly the more economically and racially diverse Woodbury, instituted "individual pupil scheduling."[4]

The district introduced the levels system as an educationally sound practice and an indicator of excellence.[5] It distinguished course levels from academic tracks and tracking in the following manner: ". . . the system is unique in Shaker Heights, though many schools have instructional tracks, a closely allied method of ability grouping. Students . . . are not frozen at any level in any subject, but may choose in time to move to another level."[6] In a manner of speaking, the upper tracks would service gifted and advanced children and the middle and lower tracks the less gifted and regular students. In this light, the new system would provide quality and continuity to satisfy white and black middle-class families, and theoretically, at least, provide access to other students who might start out at one level and progress over time to a higher level. A full-fledged levels system did not make educational sense in elementary schools, but what evolved were special enrichment programs for the gifted that had the effect of being precursors or feeder programs designed to funnel students into upper levels in junior high (later, the middle school) and high school.

Early on, placement into programs and levels in the junior high and high school relied heavily on some combination of testing and teacher recommendation. Use of tests was considered part of a fair and color-blind way of administering quality and excellence. Over time and with increased scrutiny, enrollment at the higher levels became increasingly "open" and did not require testing or teacher recommendations. However, participation in enrichment programs at the upper elementary school (now Woodbury School) requires students to achieve a designated high score on standardized tests.

The program of testing and placement in the early grades and the district's policy of "open" levels at the middle and high school exemplify quality control strategies common in desegregated school systems such as Shaker Heights. The racial-balance strategy made literal integration a reality within each school building, while the combination of enrichment programs and the high school levels system met or exceeded the demands of "deep Shaker" that the district as a whole continue its legacy of excellence for all children (Bell, 1995, 2004). The many white and small number of black parents saw in these educational programs a clear pathway for their children to socially and educationally reproduce their privileged status. They also took for granted that for those "trespassers" with the right stuff, the system also made possible social mobility to the extent that black working-class students took advantage of the various programs and course levels.

Program Adjustments, Fixes, and Interventions:
Addressing the Achievement Gap

Early in the district's experience with integrated education, officials publicly and privately expressed concern about the gap between standardized test scores of black students and white students. Differences in test scores translated into differential participation in programs for gifted children at the elementary level and in the higher-level courses in the upper grades. Black and white students were entering the same buildings, but once in school, they separated and headed for classes that were racially identifiable (Mickelson, 2001; O'Connor, DeLuca Fernandez, & Girard, 2007). At the elementary and middle school levels, white students dominated the enrichment programs, save for a few black children of the middle class. At the high school, black students predominated in the lower and middle levels and the higher levels were largely white.

Archival materials from the period 1965 to 1980 reveal little debate among officials and the general public concerning the relationship between racially identifiable course levels and the gap in test scores by race and class. The gap was discussed in isolation from the levels system. Beginning in 1980, questions about the levels system and racial isolation in the system came into focus, particularly at the initiative of African American parents, but so far the system remains in place.

Enrichment programs and the levels system continue to be seen as race-neutral, and even the standardized tests are viewed as color-blind (Peller, 1995; Schofield, 1982). Race-neutrality emerges in the narrative data as well. A white educator, who reflected on how her style of teaching may once have excluded black students, noted that she and many of her colleagues often equated color-blindness with equality. From this perspective, race "differences" pointed not to problems in teaching methods, curriculum, access, or the school system, but to problems within the students themselves. She noted it was not uncommon for teachers to affirm (perhaps not out loud) "I'm treating everyone equally . . . I don't see what their problem is."

In 1997, the achievement gap between black and white students at the high school took on added significance through the publication of a report in the *Shakerite*, the student newspaper, dramatically presenting the "races" as distributed by tracks, with blacks at the middle and bottom and seldom represented at the top levels, which were occupied mostly by whites. The event reveals the high degree of contestation of beliefs concerning the causal factors for the gap. While some teachers and parents felt the urgency of the issue justified the article's publication, others, particularly African American parents and students, were angered by the one-sided portrayal of all black students as underperforming (Patterson & Bigler, 2007).[7] The article appeared during Black History Month, and many resented that as well. The lack of representation of black students on the *Shakerite* staff also contributed to black students' and parents' suspicions about the intentions underlying the article. Additionally, the power of such unnuanced reports served to reinforce racial stereotypes concerning achievement and motivation, as evident in the comments of one white student's reflection on the data provided in the article:

> It [the article] was factual information that they were presenting, it was not an opinionated article. It was these are the scores, there is a problem that there is this racial difference in test scores, and these kids are coming from the same elementary schools, and the same middle schools, the same high schools, there shouldn't be—such a discrepancy in who's in the AP classes and who's in the general classes and who's scoring this and who's scoring that, um, so I think it was a very eye-opening article that

sort of got started this initiative of trying to—bring up the scores and bring up the level of achievement of African American students, and I think that one of the things that was focused on there was that family involvement, that if the education is not supported in the home, then it's not—gonna—go very far.

Many black parents voiced a different point of view. They longed for a "report" that interrogated the system, which in their eyes, made it nearly impossible for their children to perform at their best. A black middle-class father noted that he encountered teachers who questioned the academic competence of his child on the basis not of his child's performance, but of the teachers' acceptance of racial stereotypes. Although his children attended school in the 1970s, his frustration reflected similar experiences narrated by black parents in more recent years. He summarized the teachers' attitudes toward black students as follows: "I don't believe you read this book, I don't believe you are supposed to be in this class, I don't believe [this or that]—[now] prove yourself!" This parent noted that after repeated encounters with such enactments of exclusion, it became increasingly difficult for him to support the authority of the school system. Although his son was eligible for the advanced classes, he experienced racial isolation within these classes. Ultimately this parent chose to transfer his son to a private school, noting:

> I believe teachers should be respected and trusted, and once you say that teachers are going to make decisions that you believe are unjust, it's hard to trust [them], [and] I had to come out [take my child out of the public schools] . . . If the school system is elevating some [kids] . . . because of one variable or another, then it's very hard for a parent to avoid buying into the same system, ok, because you're gonna be suggesting to your kids that somehow they're not as bright, or they're [other kids] not as fast. . . . [So taking your kid out is] a matter of self-defense.

One black mother whose children were also in the high level classes in the 1970s recalled the distraught nature of a black father's response to the school system, when he declared, "They're killing our students!" and described his children's experience as "Murder in the classroom!" This parent continued:

And I thought, "Gee, this man is crazy!" That was before our kids went to school . . . He had had some experiences [and] . . . it was trauma for him. I mean, and so, people just sort of looked at him, like he was not with it. Until you *really* found out that there were some of these attitudes [about our kids in the schools].

Another mother who was African American and whose child graduated from high school in the 1990s told the story of her child coming home and saying of some other black boys, "Those kind of kids are always bad—they always have to sit in the corner." She visited her child's classroom and observed various forms of inappropriate behavior on the part of a number of the boys in general but she noticed it was the "very kinetic black boys" who were singled out for punishment. She noted that the teacher depicted the black but not the white boys as being "out of control." The same parent said that later, in high school, it was this group of boys who were enrolled in alternative classes, often located in the basement of the high school, or taking "CP" class[8]—that is, class for "colored people." She felt these students had lost interest over the years and did not want to learn.

The concerns of the black parents, particularly the activism, in the 1970s of Concerned Parents and of Caring Communities Organized for Education in the 1990s continuing to the present, coupled with the targeted efforts of a number of black and white educators, resulted in the implementation of new programs focused on student support, intense skill building, and the development of study skills. The first example of this occurred in 1979 with the establishment of the tutoring center for junior high and high school students,[9] providing free tutoring by certified teachers after school in the afternoon and the evening four days a week. More recently, there was a coming together of teachers in the high school to respond to their concerns about the differentials between white and black students in accessing educational opportunities and producing academic outcomes. The faculty achievement committee at the high school was formed around 1983, and their study of the gap, which included the participation of a number of high-achieving black male students, led to the formation of the Minority Achievement (MAC) Scholars, beginning in 1991, with the MAC Sisters following several years later and then the establishment of both programs reaching down to fifth grade in the 2000–2001 school year. In the late 1990s, through the work of a white educator, study circles were established, based on research conducted by Urie Triesman at the University of Texas at Austin on engaging students of color in math and science education. This program, designed to provide support for students enrolled in the advanced classes, particularly African American students, expanded to include the middle and upper elementary schools in the 2002–2003 school year. In 1999, with 14 other urban and suburban school districts, the school system also formed a consortium called the Minority Student Achievement Network (MSAN) "to improve the academic achievement of students of color."[10]

Student Narratives: Integration as a Lived Experience

We now turn to narratives told by white and black students. To fully study the enigma of the "gap," the experience of both groups of young people must be analyzed. There is diversity within these narratives, but there also are disturbing patterns and trends by race and class. Here, we discover black students narrating how they maintained an academic sense of self in the face of school experiences that were ambiguously if not openly racist. We also come to understand the narrations of white students who express either uncomplicated privilege or an uneasy awareness that notions of merit, choice, and an "open" levels system have effectively obscured their race and class advantage.

JILL

Jill, a white student who graduated from the high school in the late 1990s, began high school enrolled in all high-level classes. She felt she gained a lot from the school system's academic excellence and its racial diversity. At Lomond Elementary School and in the upper elementary Woodbury School, she participated in the gifted program, which she characterized as a strength of the Shaker Heights schools. She noted these were "great programs," and that they provided "a lot of creativity beyond just the basics" in math and language arts.

While Jill's experience reflects an experience central to sites of educational privilege, she did tell of a struggle in high school she had with a teacher in an advanced-placement class. She received an A in this class early on, but after earning a B, Jill noted the teacher exhibited persistent antagonism toward her. She considered dropping down a level, but ultimately decided she did not want to leave the AP level nor sever her social ties with the cohort of students she had traveled with throughout her years in Shaker Heights. She stated, "Once you get into that [high] track, you're with the same people, for most of the same classes . . . those are the people that you're seeing and doing stuff with."

It is important to look at Jill's reasoning for remaining in her AP class and the factors that reinforced her sense that she belonged there. Jill narrated a compatible subjectivity as "student" that had been fostered over her many years of experiencing inclusion in sites of educational privilege. There was no previous experience of dissonance to compound this particular encounter with a teacher's negativity toward Jill. Toward this end, there were no racial stereotypes about achievement and motivation to threaten her position as an advanced-placement student in the high school. In fact, the stereotypes affirmed her position in the predominantly white class and helped her ward off this teacher's enactment of exclusion toward her (Good, Dweck, & Aronson, 2007). If the negative stereotypes about black students acted as a social psychological boundary for their movement upward to higher tracks, the positive stereotypes concerning whites meant that these students were far less likely to exit the higher tracks. In Jill's case, the social and structural factors support her implicit assignment to the high levels in the district's "open" levels system. In a manner of speaking, Jill was "stuck" within the higher track.

MARK

Mark, a white student of the early 2000s, entered the system as a transfer student, coming from a nearby suburban district. Early on he had trouble keeping up in his higher-level courses, but his parents were in contact with his teachers, who provided support. In his own struggle to "belong" in the higher-level classes, Mark narrated an understanding of the racial stereotypes about achievement and motivation that white and black students absorb. He indicated that for a white student, the assumption was that the student took honors or advanced placement. And if a student was enrolled in advanced-placement classes, others assumed that student to be a good student. Hence, white students were good students, "even if you haven't proved yourself to be." When asked about the assumptions attached to students who take college preparatory classes, he noted that students' views another student's enrollment in these classes depended on the student's race. Here he most clearly articulated the difficulty of resisting a racial stereotype that was reinforced in the enrollment patterns by race evident in an "open" enrollment system. Calling it a "battle," he noted that many students were unwilling to fully explore the complex factors at work in the school system such that fewer black students accessed educational opportunities such as the higher-level courses:

> I think the general judgment is, if you're in, if you're a white kid in CP classes, you're lazy, and if you're a black kid in CP classes—[tap] it's expected . . . I guess that's it, if you're a white kid in CP classes, they assume you're lazy or you don't, you don't want to try hard. But if you're a black kid, they won't really judge you because they don't, you know, people really don't—they don't want to get in that battle or whatever it is.

Mark's father, Matt, also attended Shaker Heights Schools and had participated in one of the early integration programs. Matt talked about his interactions with teachers in making them aware of Mark's struggle to complete assignments under very short deadlines. Matt reported that teachers responded positively and were supportive of his son. However, he also discussed how he felt racial stereotypes were operating within parent-teacher interactions, and these stereotypes made it more likely that teachers would perceive Mark's difficulty as a learning problem, a solution to which the teacher and parent could support. Matt noted that he felt African American parents presenting a similar case were more likely to have their children's difficulty interpreted as a motivational problem.

STEPHEN

Black students sometimes narrated what can be called the zigzag storyline in that they bounced from one academic frame to another and sometimes back again. Stephen, an African American student, grew up in the predominantly black Moreland area and graduated from high school in the early 1990s. He spoke very fondly of the Moreland School and was "proud to be from Moreland," because they were "doing big things there"—the school had won an award for its academic excellence and educational activities. It was "the black school in the district,"[11] and its principal was an African American man. Stephen recalled that at the close of the school day, the principal, who knew his students well, would say goodbye to the students by name. Stephen's academic performance was above his grade level, so he took some subjects in classes with students in the older grades. He was also one of the very small number of African American students who participated in "Moreland's Math Projects" class, an advanced math class offered as part of the school's magnet program.

When Stephen reached the upper elementary grades, his father thought there might be more opportunities in a predominantly white school, and his parents transferred Stephen from Moreland to a predominantly white school through the Shaker Schools Plan for voluntary school transfer. He said he "hated" his experience at this school. "I felt alienated, being [a] new kid, but also being [from] Moreland." He stated his teacher had a negative attitude toward him. It seemed to him that his teacher, also African American, "disciplined black kids differently," and was more lenient with white children. Like several other African American students interviewed, Stephen wondered aloud whether he could be imagining this. There was a noticeable drop in his school performance.

He described a split in a formerly coherent view of himself as a "student." At the middle school and in his early years in high school he did not enroll in higher-level courses. He was not focused on classes and grades, although he was active in the high school band, which he enjoyed very much. He said, "I saw how much attention I was getting and that was my focus. [My] focus [was more] being popular than being smart." He noted that a lot of this solidified for him while he was in the predominantly white school, saying, "To be black was to be—you had [to] be more cool than smart, you had to know how to fight." He stated that if you "succumbed to academia, you were an Oreo." He said, "I had been alienated at [name of predominantly white school]; [I] didn't want to be alienated again."

Stephen's trajectory from within sites of educational privilege to outside them was dramatically halted the year he learned he would be held back from a grade and would not enter high school. "That was the day the world stood still." Several educators became closely involved with his academic progress and made strong connections with him during the year he repeated, and he was able to make further connections with more educators during the years that followed. These individuals deflected the enactments of exclusion and competing subjectivities that he continued to encounter as a black student, particularly a black male student re-entering sites of academic privilege. Stephen stated that in the one advanced-placement course he elected to eventually take in high school, he experienced inclusion and a compatible subjectivity as "student." He described the teacher of this AP class as someone who valued his opinion and in whose class, where he was the only African American male student, he felt fully supported and included. Additionally, Stephen noted that the principal of the high school was "very influential, very powerful" in engaging him in academics. At the same time, Stephen dreaded meeting with his high school counselor. His counselor did not discuss opportunities at the different course levels and was "rather reluctant" to let him take an advanced-placement course. Stephen "blew the counselor out of the water" when the counselor saw how well Stephen performed in the advanced-placement course. In the end the counselor wrote him a recommendation for college, but only, in a sense, only after Stephen "proved" himself by scoring high on tests.

DIANA

The zigzag pattern narrated by Stephen is echoed in Diana's narrative but the outcome is in a downward trajectory. Diana is an African American student who graduated from high school in the early 2000s. Her experience with schooling had been an uneasy one. She loved her elementary school but she had "conflicts" with all her teachers. In her interview, she noted that she did not think the teachers accepted what she said as truthful, but then, like Stephen in a predominantly white school, she wandered in a less defensive stance, concluding, "I don't know, maybe it was just me." In middle school, however, she had a class with a teacher whom she described as having "just completely opened my mind to something completely new." She noted that she felt very comfortable with this teacher, who was also African American, a person for whom she had "great respect and admiration." She invested a lot of effort in his class, saying, "I came to his class every day, I did my work to the best of my ability."

When Diana entered Shaker Heights High School, she was enrolled in the Humanities Program, a less demanding program, even though she had passed the state-mandated proficiency tests in eighth grade[12] and thus qualified for higher placement. Predominantly black students are enrolled in this program. Diana loved her teachers, who supported and encouraged her, and ironically, she was reluctant to move up from the Humanities Program to the "regular" program, because, "I got decent grades, and I was, I had a sense of belonging, I had a relationship with the teachers." Here, her strong connections with teachers in the Humanities Program evolved into a rationale as to why she should not move upward to a higher track. In addition, she did not see herself as "honors material" or "book-smart." When asked for a definition of "honors material," she said that it meant dedicating time outside of school studying and doing homework. She was quite adamant about her unwillingness to do this, but she noted that she might make an exception for a teacher she had in the middle school, noting that her attitude in his class was "I'm gonna do it because I, I don't want to let him down." Though Diana was comfortable in what can be called sites of educational exclusion, characterized by strong student-educator relationships within less academically rigorous settings, she also knew them to be inferior to the sites in which most white students participated. Therefore she did not view education as equally available to black and white students within the school system.

NIKA

Nika, an African American female student who graduated from high school in the middle 1990s, was in the gifted "track," beginning with the Ludlow Elementary School Special Program for the gifted, followed by advanced classes in the fifth through eighth grades, and advanced placement in the Shaker Heights High School. Although she was the product of educational privilege, she narrated what it was like to be caught between black and mainstream white experiences, located within sites of educational privilege but on the periphery.

Originally, Nika was not bothered by the negative vibes she felt coming from the African American children who remained in the regular as compared to gifted classes, noting, "It was the black girls . . . maybe they were jealous . . . they would like call me an Oreo, stuff like that, just because I was in those classes." She stated that she ignored the harassment, saying she did not care, and "I'm gonna interact with the people I spend the whole day with." In high school, Nika noted differences between herself and many of the black girls, particularly in terms of what she saw as their undue attention to clothing and appearance. Nika reported that she felt no such distance from of dislike of African American boys her age. Her friendships with white students also continued through the middle and high school.

Nika's somewhat naïve attitudes about race and the role played by the system in discouraging the black students who were sometimes her harshest critics, changed in the vortex of an experience—an encounter, if you will—that took place in middle school:

> [The educator] called all the black students' names and told us—in front of the whole class—that we were in the wrong class, that we were supposed to be in the other teacher's and [the educator] said [the other teacher's] name, and the other kids in the class knew that wasn't the enriched class, and I'm, and I'm thinking to myself, this is wrong, this is not—how could that be? And we were all kind of like embarrassed, you know, because why are you like singling—you're singling us out, number one, and then, you don't have to say, you can just say, "Oh, I need to see these students," you don't have to say, "You're in the wrong class" . . . and all of us were like, "What?!" Like [*hands come down lightly on desk*] and that doesn't make any sense, and I was—*mad*, I mean I was like *livid*.

Nika knew the information was incorrect. She noted that the other black students in the class likely did, too, because many had taken advanced classes together. She quickly surmised that the error was tied to the racial stereotype that claims African American students are academically inferior—"I knew it was racial the moment every single black student in that class, no one else's name, only—not—and it wasn't like they called all but one black student, it was every single one." According to Nika, most of the black students who were removed from the class did not return, even those who rightfully belonged in the class. She recounted the academic repercussions for these students: "When I got to ninth grade, they weren't even, they weren't in my AP classes, it's like they were, like de-tracked."

That night she discussed the incident with her parents. In a separate interview, Nika's mother, Lynne, revealed she, too, had experienced acts of exclusion when she was a student in the Shaker Heights schools. Lynne's ability to handle the demands of advanced classes had also been called into question when she was a Shaker Heights student, so her daughter's story hit close to home. Lynne and her husband immediately responded by calling the school and a correction was made. The next day Nika and only one other black student returned to the class. None of the other black students ever attempted to rejoin the class. The experience of re-entering the classroom for the first time felt odd, surreal to Nika. It was the first time she understood how a black person can achieve "token" status in the perceptions of white teachers and students alike. The experience shattered Nika's sense of comfort with the system:

> That's when I saw like the light, I saw really what was going on in that whole school system, it's like, they showed their face pretty much, and, I mean, if you don't really, if you don't get hit like that, then you're naïve, you don't even know, and you just let it go, you don't do anything because you think there's nothing to do, you think you're in the right place and you're not.

The experience opened Nika's eyes to the way academic levels and enactments of exclusion reinforce each other to create a powerful deterrent for African American students accessing sites of educational privilege in an "open" enrollment system. Nika continued: "They tried to *suck* the black males out, at, in the middle school, so that you can't even get in, like I said, it's like either you're in or you're out, so they want them out, before they even get to the high school." There also was a lack of clarity as to when prerequisite courses were necessary and when they could be waived. She noted, "I mean, like, some, some students that I knew—could do that work but they were in CP because no one ever sat there and told them that they *could* take that class, they made you think that if you didn't start with AP in the ninth grade, or if you weren't in enriched in the eighth grade, you couldn't get in, kind of like, it's this exclusive club membership—you know if you're not a member by this time, then you just can't be at all."

Nika remarked that the group of mostly white students in the AP track remained the same year after year: "A lot of those students that were in that 12 AP, were the ones that were in AP chem, and those kids were the same ones that I went to Ludlow with in Special Projects, the same ones in my pull-out program for the advanced . . . [classes] at Woodbury . . . but it was interesting, I mean it's interesting because they all just stuck together."[13] Her perceptions are similar to Jill's, presented earlier. Moving beyond the outline of sites of privilege, Nika also marked the three major groups among African American students: Black students in the honors classes and advanced-placement classes, those in the college preparatory classes, and "the Cru."[14] The latter she depicted as a group of about 100 students across grades in the high school who hung out together in school and after school. Her description of the exclusive nature of this group sounded vaguely familiar to her description of the exclusivity of the advanced-placement track:

> It was kind of like, an *exclusive* club, like you couldn't get in—if you weren't already in from the beginning, you couldn't be pulled in by association or anything because they had already labeled you the way that you were.

As a "token" black among whites, and an Oreo in the eyes of fellow blacks, she felt estranged from both blacks and whites. As with other African American students interviewed who participated in one or all higher-level classes, the experience of access to the high-level classes did not guarantee encounters of inclusion but were likely to involve racial isolation. Things changed for Nika during her senior year, and black students reached out and expressed how proud they were of her accomplishments and success. She indicated that it did not make up for the more difficult times, but she was nonetheless appreciative of their newfound support. Her own experience had vividly inscribed in her mind the rigidity of social and structural boundaries for black students seeking access to sites of educational privilege. Looking back, Nika expressed the opinion that racial equality did not exist in the Shaker Heights schools or in the larger society.

Summary of Narratives

Black students tended to narrate various forms of self-concept "splitting." For students like Stephen, the split was along the fault lines of the Du Boisian (Du Bois, 1903) double consciousness: There is the self-image I have constructed for myself, but what do I make of the image reflected back to me in the eyes of the "other"? Diana shared essentially the same dilemma. Nika's predicament took on a four-part structure: There was her personally constructed self-image; the "token" status in the eyes of the other; genuine acceptance in the hearts of some white friends; and the estrangement from other black students who sometimes pestered her with taunts of "Oreo."

As for their educational development, black students were subject to a "zigzag" pattern. At times, they relied on one dimension of their split image and at other times shifted back to another image. Key shifts from one identity to another were sometimes elicited by at least one teacher —sometimes black, sometimes white—who challenged them to dig deeper into their sometimes self-neglected or self-repressed academic sense of self. The nature of the relationship with such a teacher took on the dynamics of an academic "intervention." Thus, whereas white students depicted fairly continuous support from a broad range of teachers across all grade levels, black students narrated the discovery of their academic potential through only one or a limited number of teachers. Ironically, these few supportive teachers helped black students learn to negotiate interactions with less supportive teachers so that they could maintain high achievement motivation in the face of less than optimum conditions (Stanton-Salazar, 1997).

In the grand scheme of things, Stephen and Nika were successful students but at what cost? Are the test scores and grade point averages for black students who zigzag from kindergarten to twelfth grade as "high" as the scores recorded by white students whose student self-image has been consistently reinforced? Might their "depressed" scores and slightly subpar grade point averages be mistakenly understood as "self" inflicted? In Diana's case, might her self-conscious decision not to participate in a higher educational track be interpreted as defiant oppositionalism? We saw that what appeared to be Diana's resistance to higher achievement was connected to the sense of belonging she experienced in the Humanities Program, something she did not want to risk losing by moving upward. What stories had she heard that made her think a black student's sense of belonging would be different in the higher tracks? The need to belong is, of course, not unique to black students, for we saw in Jill's case, that she, too, made decisions driven by her sense of belonging within the upper track; Mark struggled to "belong" in the higher-level courses, and parent and teacher support helped him maintain his placement. Finally, are test scores and GPAs related to the total number of teachers who express support across K–12? Aside from the issue of conscious and unconscious racism, how does one measure the effect of going through a school system where students experience teacher support and educational structures that reinforce racial stereotypes about achievement and motivation?

At some points of entry into the narratives of Stephen, Nika, or Diana, one can find evidence in support of oppositional identity, but at other points, these same students are exemplars of high achievement motivation. The evidence that flows from the Galletta study can be used to negate or affirm notions of oppositional identity and oppositional "culture." However, taken as a whole, the Galletta study complicates and shows to be simplistic any explanation for the origin of the achievement gap that is not ultimately "ecological" and systemic, rather than personological, individualistic, and noninteractional. The Galletta study makes it possible to predict that over and above issues of gender, family structure, and socioeconomic status, variables such as splitting of the self, zigzag performance, and the existence and perception of everyday racism in the classroom should predict less than optimal academic performance for most black children. Such factors are explored in the empirical studies in this volume; like the Galletta study, they do not necessarily reject Ogbu's thesis, but it is most certainly *complicated* (see Good, Dweck, & Aronson, 2007; Lawrence, Bachman, & Ruble, 2007; Moje & Martinez, 2007; O'Connor, DeLuca Fernandez, & Girard, 2007).

Finally, Galletta reported that although white students voiced almost unreserved appreciation, affection, belonging, and pride to be or once to have been students in the Shaker Heights school system, a cohort within this group also narrated dissonance toward the arrangement of educational opportunities and academic outcomes that they had come to understand as unfairly distributed by race and class. This knowledge did not, however, jeopardize the academic achievement of those students. Black students also shared a deep appreciation for the school system. Even among those black students who recognized the inequality of the system, whose academic standing *was* jeopardized by this understanding, their pride in being Shaker Heights students was high. Galletta was caught off guard by this finding. When she dug deeper she found the reference point the black students were using was not the white community and white students, but black students caught in the malaise of inferior educational settings in urban Cleveland. For all that they endured in the Shaker Heights integration experience—that is, identity splitting, the acts of discrimination, the moments of estrangement from other blacks, or the sense of being a token to many whites —all of the students suggested with considerable certitude that they would be far "less" educated today, had they attended low-income predominantly black schools in nearby school districts.

Conclusion

Our efforts to historicize black education and interrogate "integration" situated the experience of African American students in general and black students in the Shaker Heights City School District in particular within a broad analysis of history, educational policies and practices, and individual student narratives of the educational experience. Our organization of the chapter itself shifts across time and contexts. We started with a historical analysis that revealed the high level of achievement motivation blacks embraced upon exiting slavery. We underscored how the social movement for education spearheaded by former slaves contests John Ogbu's interpretation of low-achievement attitudes found among many of today's black youth as being historically linked to whether a group entered the United States under voluntary or involuntary conditions. In the next section we fast-forwarded to the present, and deconstructed the history of integration based on Galletta's research conducted in the same school system studied by John Ogbu, where he collected data in support of his oppositional identity concept. After first casting doubt on part on the legacy-of-slavery thesis, we showed that Ogbu underestimated the role played by policies and practices associated with school integration in the social production of black youths' oppositional attitudes. In so doing, we sought to illustrate the complexity of social identity development among youths in desegregated schools and its influence on the nature and extent of their educational participation.

NOTES

NOTES TO CHAPTER 1

1. *Shaker Heights High School 2002–2003 School Year Report Card* (Columbus, OH: Department of Education, p. 3). Data also indicate that 11.1% of the high school students were economically disadvantaged, 0.9% were limited in their English proficiency, and 13.2% were students with disabilities.

NOTES TO CHAPTER 6

1. *Reed v. Rhodes*, as quoted in *The Cleveland Desegregation Decision: Reed v. Rhodes. Prepared for the Study Group on Racial Isolation in the Public Schools and Its Member Organizations*. Shaker Heights Public Library Local History Collection.
2. See Shaker Heights Public Schools *INFO: Intra-Staff Communication*, September 1976. See also "A Further Statement on the Battisti Case" (September 30, 1976), Shaker Heights Public Schools Intra-Staff Communication, Shaker Heights Public Library Local History Collection.
3. In her November 2, 1976, memo to Jack Taylor ("Subject: Information for November 18th Meeting"), Beverly Mason proposed several plans for a systemic response to the racial imbalance, and some elements of this proposal were implemented over the next 10 years. See also two related documents: R. C. Blue (March 3, 1981), "A Special Report on the Princeton Plan or Grade Level Organization: A Desegregation Strategy for the Shaker Heights City School Schools"; *Alternative Plans for Achieving Racial Balance in Schools*, a document written under the direction of Dr. Guy M. Sconzo by a committee and issued around March or April of 1981. Both documents are in the Shaker Heights Public Library Local History Collection.
4. Administrative council meeting summary, November 20, 1979, page 1. District archives.
5. Superintendent's professional advisory council meeting, March 9, 1983. District archives.
6. Superintendent's professional advisory council meeting, April 8, 1983. District archives.

NOTES TO APPENDIX A

1. Data from this question revealed stark variation among parents as to their interpretation of "control." A good deal of this variation appeared to correspond to parents' racial and socioeconomic backgrounds. My use of these Likert-scale

questions was not for quantitative purposes, and my data collection relied on the qualitative data elicited during and following the participant's selection of a Likert-scale response. This question in particular, when used in my parent interviews, required considerable probing to understand parents' interpretation of "control."

2. The options presented in question 10 were white/European American and black/African American as racial ingroups or outgroups. The study design acknowledged the need for future work to explore connections with other racial and ethnic groups, which, within the district from 1965 to 2003, were considerably smaller in comparison. Some time into the study, a third option was added to question 10, which also included biracial students, as evident in this protocol.

3. The student protocol provided here in differs from the protocol for parents and educators. The parent and educator protocols included an additional question that delved into participants' view of equality of academic outcomes. This question was located between question 11 and 12. It asked the parent and educator participants to view charts depicting the gap in scores between white and black students from state standardized tests and to discuss their thoughts on the gap in the test scores. Please see chapter 2 for a discussion of the decision not to include this question with high school students and recent graduates from the district.

NOTES TO APPENDIX B

1. *Shelly v. Kraemer*, 334 U.S. 1 [1948]. In 1968, following Dr. Martin Luther King's assassination, Congress enacted the Fair Housing Act. According to Keating (1994), there was little to no enforcement of the Fair Housing Act. In 1988 the Act was amended, giving Housing and Urban Development (HUD) "the power to initiate complaints" (Keating, 1994, p. 196).

2. Weeks (1968). Interviews with study participants also indicated these practices continued for some time after the 1948 Supreme Court decision had ruled them unconstitutional.

3. According to Kaeser and Freeman (1981, 1982), the percentage of African American students *across the district* was 10.5% in 1964–1965, the first year enrollment by race was documented. This rose to 14.5% in the 1965–1966 year, which records indicate was a 42.3% increase in the change in enrollment.

4. "Woodbury inaugurates individual pupil scheduling," *School Review*, October 1966, p. 3. There were some enrichment courses established in the late 1950s in the junior highs in math and science, but it was not as extensive as the program Woodbury put in place in the 1966–1967 school year (*School Review*, March 1956; *School Review*, May 1957, p. 2).

5. "Levels of instruction inaugurated in Shaker," *School Review*, November 1964, p. 3. Also "High school principal reports to school board: Portrait of the present . . . prophecy of things to come," *School Review*, March 1965, p. 2.

6. As noted in "Levels of instruction inaugurated in Shaker," p. 3. Level 1 was

eliminated in the 1970–1971 school year, according to J. Lawson, "Answers to questions on balance, ballots, and levels," *School Review*, October 1970, p. 3.

7. Much of this event was captured in a film, *Struggle for Integration*, which was produced and directed by Stuart Math (Stuart Math Films, Inc., Cleveland, OH). Shaker Heights Public Library Local History Collection.

8. Current course levels include the following: advanced placement, honors, college preparatory, general education.

9. According to the *Selected Initiatives to Improve Student Achievement in the Shaker Heights City Schools* (January 15, 1997, p. 11), a tutoring center in the high school library opened in 1979. A tutoring center for elementary students was established in 1980.

10. See Ferguson (2002) for details on the MSAN, as well as a summary of data on the achievement gap from participating districts.

11. During 1980–1981, one of the several years Stephen was at Moreland, the elementary school was 72% African American. Because of the district's voluntary busing program, a percentage of black students elected to attend predominantly white schools elsewhere in the district, and a percentage of white students from predominantly white schools elected to attend Moreland. The projected percentage of enrollment of black students at Moreland without the busing plan was estimated to be 96 percent. This is per a memorandum and attachments from Jack P. Taylor, Superintendent of Schools, to Members of the Board of Education, January 5, 1981, regarding State Guidelines for Desegregation. Shaker Heights Public Library Local History Collection.

12. State proficiency tests, in existence since 1990, consist of a test in math, reading, writing, citizenship, and science. The overall passing rate in that first year was 51% of the 373 ninth-grade students, with the percentage of whites passing in the first year at 81% and for blacks, 22%. See B. Sims, "Proficiency test results disappointing," *Shakerite*, February 7, 1991, p. 3. Diana took the test a number of years later, and passing rates for black students did show improvement. A study and preparation program for the proficiency tests, PROBE, was instituted in 1991 for students who failed the test.

13. In transcribing this statement, Galletta found Nika used the word "they" instead of the "we" Galletta expected, revealing a level of distance on Nika's part toward the predominantly white advanced placement class with whom she spent most of her school-age years.

14. A review of yearbooks through the mid-1990s indicates students used various renditions of the social designation "the crew" to describe what may be different social groups of students.

REFERENCES

Anderson, J. D. (1988). *The education of black Americans in the South, 1860–1935.* Chapel Hill: University of North Carolina Press.

Apfelbaum, E. (1979). Relations of domination and movements for liberation: An analysis of power between groups. In W. G. Austin & S. Worchel (Eds.), *The social psychology of intergroup relations* (pp. 188–204). Belmont, CA: Wadsworth.

Apfelbaum, E., & Lubek, I. (1976). Resolution versus revolution? The theory of conflicts in question. In L. Strickland, K. Gergen, & F. Aboud (Eds.), *Social psychology in transition* (pp. 71–95). New York: Plenum.

Bagnoli, A. (2009). Beyond the standard interview: The use of graphic elicitation and arts-based research. *Qualitative Interview, 9*(5), 547–570.

Bell, D. A., Jr. (1995). Brown v. Board of Education and the interest convergence dilemma. In K. Crenshaw, N. Gotanda, G. Peller, & K. Thomas (Eds.), *Critical race theory: The key writings that informed the movement* (pp. 20–29). New York: New Press.

Bell, D. A., Jr. (2004). *Silent covenants: Brown v. Board of Education and the unfulfilled hopes for racial reform.* New York: Oxford University Press.

Bowen, W. G., & Bok, D. (1998). *The shape of the river: Long-term consequences of considering race in college and university admissions.* Princeton: Princeton University Press.

Brown v. Board of Education of Topeka, 347 U.S. 494 (1954).

Bullock, H. A. (1967). *A history of Negro education in the South from 1619 to the present.* Cambridge: Harvard University Press.

Burns, A. (2003). *Academic success as privilege: When privilege becomes responsibility* (Unpublished master's thesis). City University of New York, New York.

Butchart, R. E. (1980). *Northern school, Southern blacks, and Reconstruction, 1862–1875.* Westport, CT: Greenwood.

Carspecken, P. F., & Apple, M. (1992). Critical qualitative research: Theory, methodology, and practice. In M. D. LeCompte, W. L. Millroy, & J. Preissle (Eds.), *The handbook of qualitative research in education* (pp. 507–553). San Diego, CA: Academic.

Chase, S. E. (2008). Narrative inquiry: Multiple lenses, approaches, voices. In N. K. Denzin & Y. S. Lincoln (Eds.), *Collecting and interpreting qualitative materials* (3rd ed., pp. 57–94). Thousand Oaks, CA: Sage.

Clandinin, J., & Connelly, M. (2000). *Narrative inquiry: Experience and story in qualitative research.* San Francisco: Jossey-Bass.

Clark, K. B. (1965). *Dark ghetto.* New York: Harper & Row.

Collins, P. H. (1998). *Fighting words: Black women and the search for justice*. Minneapolis: University of Minnesota Press.

Cross, W. E., Jr. (1991). *Shades of black: Diversity in African-American identity*. Philadelphia: Temple University Press.

Cross, W. E., Jr. (2003). Tracing the historical origins of youth delinquency and violence: Myths and realities about black culture. *Journal of Social Issues, 59*(1), 67–82.

Dollard, J. (1949). *Caste and class in a Southern town*. New York: Harper.

Du Bois, W. E. B. (1903). *The souls of black folk*. New York: Dodd, Mead & Company.

Du Bois, W. E. B. (1935). *Black Reconstruction in America*. New York: S. A. Russell.

Ferguson, R. F. (2002). *What doesn't meet the eye: Understanding and addressing racial disparities in high-achieving suburban schools*. Retrieved from http://www.ncrel.org/gap/ferg/

Freire, P. (1970/2000). *Pedagogy of the oppressed*. New York: Continuum.

Galletta, A. (2003). *Under one roof, through many doors: Understanding racial equality in an unequal world* (Doctoral dissertation). The Graduate School and University Center of the City University of New York, New York.

Galletta, A., & Cross, W. E., Jr. (2007). Past as present, present as past: Historicizing black education and interrogating "integration." In A. J. Fuligni (Ed.), *Contesting stereotypes and creating identities: Social categories, social identities, and educational participation* (pp. 15–41). New York: Russell Sage Foundation Press.

Giroux, H. (1988). Critical theory and the politics of culture and voice: Rethinking the discourse of educational research. In R. Sherman & R. Webb (Eds.), *Qualitative research in education: Focus and methods* (pp. 190–210). New York: Falmer.

Good, C., Dweck, C. S., & Aronson, J. (2007). Social identity, stereotype threat, and self-theories. In A. J. Fuligni (Ed.), *Contesting stereotypes and creating identities: Social categories, social identities, and educational participation* (pp. 115–135). New York: Russell Sage Foundation Press.

Helms, J. E. (Ed.). (1990). *Black and white racial identity: Theory, research, and practice*. Westport, CT: Praeger.

Hirschman, A. O. (1970). *Exit, voice, and loyalty: Responses to decline in firms, organizations, and states*. Cambridge: Harvard University Press.

Irons, P. (2002). *Jim Crow's children: The broken promise of the Brown decision*. New York: Viking.

Jackson, J. P., Jr. (1998). Creating a consensus: Psychologists, the Supreme Court, and school desegregation, 1952–1955. *Journal of Social Issues, 54*(1), 143–177.

Jefferson, C. (1991). *An historical analysis of the relationship between the great migration and the administrative policies and practices of racial isolation in the Cleveland Public Schools: 1920–1940* (Doctoral dissertation). Cleveland State University, Cleveland, Ohio.

Jones, J. M. (1998). Psychological knowledge and the new American dilemma of race. *Journal of Social Issues, 54*(4), 641–662.

Kaeser, S. C., & Freeman, M. (1981). *A review of school and housing integration data in*

Shaker Heights and strategies to improve school integration through housing policy. Shaker Heights, OH: Shaker Heights City School District.

Kaeser, S. C., & Freeman, M. (1982). *A special report on data and data needs related to school and housing integration.* Shaker Heights, OH: Shaker Heights City School District.

Keating, W. D. (1994). *The suburban racial dilemma: Housing and neighborhoods.* Philadelphia: Temple University Press.

Kincheloe, J. L., & McLaren, P. (2000). Rethinking critical theory and qualitative research. In N. K. Denzin & Y. S. Lincoln (Eds.), *The SAGE handbook of qualitative research* (2nd ed., pp. 279–313). Thousand Oaks, CA: Sage.

Kohl, H. (2009). *Herb Kohl reader: Awakening the heart of teaching.* New York: New Press.

Ladson-Billings, G., & Donnor, J. (2005). The moral activist role of critical theory scholarship. In N. K. Denzin & Y. S. Lincoln (Eds.), *The SAGE handbook of qualitative research* (3rd ed., pp. 279–302). Thousand Oaks, CA: Sage.

Lather, P. (1986). Research as praxis. *Harvard Educational Review, 56*(3), 257–277.

Lawrence, J. S., Bachman, M., & Ruble, D. (2007). Ethnicity, ethnic identity, and school valuing among children from immigrant and non-immigrant families. In A. J. Fuligni (Ed.), *Contesting stereotypes and creating identities: Social categories, social identities, and educational participation* (pp. 136–159). New York: Russell Sage Foundation Press

LeCompte, M. D., & Schensul, J. J. (1999). *Designing and conducting ethnographic research.* Walnut Creek, CA: AltaMira.

Martín-Baró, I. (1994). *Writings for a liberation psychology.* Cambridge: Harvard University Press.

Massey, D. S., and Denton, N. A. (1993). *American apartheid: Segregation and the making of the underclass.* Cambridge: Cambridge University Press.

Mickelson, R. A. (2001). Subverting Swann: First and second generation segregation in the Charlotte-Mecklenburg schools. *American Educational Research Journal, 38*(2), 215–252.

Moje, E. B., & Martinez, M. (2007). The role of peers, families, and ethnic-identity enactments in educational persistence and achievement of Latino and Latina youths. In A. J. Fuligni (Ed.), *Contesting stereotypes and creating identities: Social categories, social identities, and educational participation* (pp. 209–238). New York: Russell Sage Foundation Press.

Ng, S. H. (1982). Power and intergroup discrimination. In Henri Tajfel (Ed.), *Social identity in intergroup relations.* Cambridge: Cambridge University Press.

O'Connor, C., DeLuca Fernandez, S., & Girard, B. (2007). The meaning of "blackness": How black students differentially align race and achievement across time and space. In A. J. Fuligni (Ed.), *Contesting stereotypes and creating identities: Social categories, social identities, and educational participation* (pp. 183–208). New York: Russell Sage Foundation Press.

Ogbu, J. U. (1987). Variability in minority school performance: A problem in search of an explanation. *Anthropology and Education Quarterly, 18*(4), 312–334.

Ogbu, J. U. (1998). Voluntary and involuntary minorities: A cultural-ecological theory of school performance with some implications for education. *Anthropology and Education Quarterly, 29*(2), 155–188.

Ogbu, J. U. (2003). *Black American students in an affluent suburb: A study of academic disengagement.* Mahwah, NJ: Lawrence Erlbaum.

Ogbu, J. U. (2004). Collective identity and the burden of "acting white" in black history, community, and education. *The Urban Review, 36*(1), 1–35.

Opotow, S. (1995). Drawing the line: Social categorization, moral exclusion, and the scope of justice. In B. B. Bunker & J. Z. Rubin (Eds.), *Conflict, cooperation, and justice: Essays inspired by the work of Morton Deutsch* (pp. 347–369). San Francisco: Jossey-Bass.

Orfield, G. (1978). *Must we bus? Segregated schools and national policy.* Washington, DC: Brookings Institution.

Orfield, G. (1983). *Public school desegregation in the United States.* Washington, DC: Joint Center for Political Studies.

Orfield, G., & Eaton, S. E. (1996). *Dismantling desegregation: The quiet reversal of Brown v. Board of Education.* New York: New Press.

Patterson, M. M., & Bigler, R. S. (2007). Relations among social identities, intergroup attitudes, and schooling: Perspectives from intergroup theory and research. In A. J. Fuligni (Ed.), *Contesting stereotypes and creating identities: Social categories, social identities, and educational participation* (pp. 66–87). New York: Russell Sage Foundation Press.

Peller, G. (1995). Race-consciousness. In K. Crenshaw, N. Gotanda, G. Peller, & K. Thomas (Eds.), *Critical race theory* (pp. 127–158). New York: New Press.

Pettigrew, T. F. (1986). The intergroup contact hypothesis revisited. In M. Hewstone & R. Brown (Eds.), *Contact and conflict in intergroup encounters* (pp. 168–195). New York: Basil Blackwell.

Plessy v. Ferguson, 163 U.S. 53, 551 (1896).

Pollock, M. (2004). *Colormute: Race talk dilemmas in an American school.* Princeton: Princeton University Press.

Reed v. Rhodes, 422 F. Supp. 708 (1976).

Richardson, L. (1994). Writing: A method of inquiry. In N. K. Denzin & Y. S. Lincoln (Eds.), *The SAGE handbook of qualitative research* (2nd ed., pp. 923–948). Thousand Oaks, CA: Sage.

Ryan, W. (1971/1976). *Blaming the victim.* New York: Random House.

Schofield, J. W. (1982). *Black and white in school: Trust, tension, or tolerance?* Westport, CT: Praeger.

Schofield, J. W. (1986a). Black-White contact in desegregated schools. In M. Hewstone & R. Brown (Eds.), *Contact and conflict in intergroup encounters* (pp. 79–92). New York: Basil Blackwell.

Schofield, J. W. (1986b). Causes and consequences of the colorblind perspective. In J. F.

Dovidio & S. Gaertner (Eds.), *Prejudice, discrimination, and racism* (pp. 231–254). San Diego, CA: Academic.

Sewell, W. H., Jr. (1992). A theory of structure: Duality, agency, and transformation. *American Journal of Sociology, 98*(1), 1–29.

Shelly v. Kraemer, 334 U.S. 1 (1948).

Sirin, S. R., & Fine, M. (2008). *Muslim minority youth: Understanding hyphenated identities through multiple methods.* New York: NYU Press.

Stanton-Salazar, R. D. (1997). A social capital framework for understanding the socialization of racial minority children and youths. *Harvard Educational Review, 67*(1), 1–40.

Strauss, A., & Corbin, J. (1998). *Basics of qualitative research: Techniques and procedures for developing grounded theory* (2nd ed.). Thousand Oaks, CA: Sage.

Stupay, D. S. (1993). *The Shaker Heights City Schools: An overview.* Shaker Heights, OH: Shaker Heights City School District.

Sweatt v. Painter, 339 U.S. 634 (1950).

Tajfel, H., & Turner, J. C. (1979). An integrative theory of intergroup conflict. In W. G. Austin & S. Worchel (Eds.), *The social psychology of intergroup relations.* Monterey, CA: Brooks-Cole.

Tropp, L., & Wright, S. (2001). Ingroup identification as the inclusion of ingroup in the self. *Personality and Social Psychology Bulletin, 27*(5), 585–600.

Weeks, K. M. (1968). *A suburb faces the future.* Unpublished manuscript presented to the Shaker Public Library and the Shaker Housing Office.

Weis, L., & Fine, M. (2004). *Working method: Research and social justice.* New York: Routledge.

Wells, A. S., & Crain, R. L. (1997). *Stepping over the color line: African-American students in white suburban schools.* New Haven: Yale University Press.

Wells, A. S., Holme, J. J., Revilla, A. T., & Atanda, A. K. (2009). *Both sides now: The story of school desegregation's graduates.* Berkeley: University of California Press.

Whyte, D. M. (2003). *African-American community politics and racial equality in Cleveland Public Schools: 1933–1973* (Doctoral dissertation). Case Western Reserve University, Cleveland, Ohio.

Woodson, C. G. (1919). *The education of the Negro prior to 1861.* Washington, DC: Associated Press.

Woodson, C. G. (1934). *The miseducation of the Negro.* Washington, DC: Associated Press.

Annotated bibliography, 15
Apfelbaum, Erika, 12, 39, 188
Apple, Michael, 2, 70, 93
Archival study, 25–26; as part of desegrega-
    tion study, 23, 26–29
Atanda, Awo Korantemaa, 14

Bagnoli, Anna, 49
Bell, Derrick A., 13; and convergence theory,
    13, 188
Bok, Derek, 183
Bowen, William G., 183
*Brown v. Board of Education of Topeka,
    Kansas*, 10, 13–14, 68
Brown II, 13
Burns, April, 186

Carspecken, Phil, 2, 70, 93
Categories for data analysis, 127–128; in
    desegregation study: clustering codes into
    "boundaries" category, 132–134; emergent
    categories of "experience" and "views of
    equality," 142–144
Chase, Susan E., 45
Clandinin, Jean, 177
Codes for data analysis, 122–128; assessing
    durability of coded material, 129–130; in
    desegregation study, emergence of codes,
    131–133; viability of, in addressing research
    question, 127–128. *See also* Categories for
    data analysis; Data analysis
Collins, Patricia Hill, 2, 60
"Color-blindness" or race-neutrality, 12–13.
    See also Eaton, Susan; Orfield, Gary; Pel-
    ler, Gary; Pollock, Mica; Schofield, Janet;
    University of California Regents v. Bakke
Communicative and conceptual spaces of
    engagement, 77–78
Conceptual frameworks, 158–159, 167–
    168, 171–172; *See also* Social psycho-
    logical spaces . . . in desegregation study;

entanglement as conceptual framework in
    desegregation study
Conceptual murkiness in desegregation
    study, 159–167
Confidentiality issues in writing up research
    results, 177–178
Conflict, as revealing inequality, 12. *See also*
    Apfelbaum, Erika; Lubek, Ian; Pettigrew,
    Thomas F.
Connelly, Michael, 177
Corbin, Juliet M., 119
Crain, Robert L., 14
Critical friends: in desegregation study, as
    tool advancing interpretation, 169–170;
    engagement with, as interpretive activity,
    153
Critical pedagogy, 19
Critical race theory, 19
Critical reflection: in desegregation study,
    95–104; as a means of researcher-partici-
    pant reciprocity, 76–78, 93–95; risks asso-
    ciated with critical reflection, 99. *See also*
    Communicative and conceptual spaces of
    engagement; Critical theory; Dialectical
    theory building as . . . reciprocity; Lather,
    Patti
Critical theory, 2, 18–19; in desegregation
    study: as interpretive community, 19, 60;
    as influencing third segment of semi-
    structured interview, 70–71; as related to
    engaging participants in critical reflection,
    93–95. *See also* Fine, Michelle
Cross, William E., Jr., xi–xii, 13, 113, 155,
    192–193; in Galletta and Cross (Appendix
    B), 203–230

Data analysis, 17–18; analysis of archival
    and oral history data, 128–134; analysis
    of interview data, 134–144; cluster-
    ing of codes for analysis, 127–128; in
    desegregation study: interpretive shifts

Data analysis (*continued*)
  between empirical and theoretical
  sources, 16–17; locating and labeling
  codes, 122–127; multiple levels of analysis,
  18–21; preparing data for analysis, 120–
  124; uncovering thematic relationships,
  150–153
Desegregation, as study context, 10–11;
  literature, 12–15; local policies in Shaker
  Heights, Ohio, in relation to national
  events in 1980s, 181–183; reflecting split of
  institutional prerogatives, 188–189; as discussion of local Shaker Heights history in
  Past as Present, Present as Past, 203–230.
  See also Shaker Schools Plan
Dialectical theory building as a form of
  researcher-participant reciprocity, 77–78,
  94–95; as conversation between data
  and theory in articulating conceptual
  framework, 171–172; in desegregation
  study: as used in formulating research
  question, 16–17; in designing interview
  protocol, 70–71; as related to analytical
  framework, 20, 156. *See also* Communicative and conceptual spaces of engagement; Critical reflection; Critical theory;
  Lather, Patti
Dissonance in desegregation study: as an
  analytical code, 92–93; as experienced by
  researcher, 109–113; as related to analytical
  category of encounter, 154–155
Donnor, Jamel, 2

Eaton, Susan E., 13, 14
Entanglement, as conceptual framework in
  desegregation study, 168–171; 187–189

Feminist theory, 19
Ferguson, Ronald F., 233n10
Fine, Michelle, 2, 21, 49, 149, 156, 169–171,
  194. *See also* Critical theory; Oscillation in
  interpretation; Thickening, as altering . . .
  stratifications
Frankfurt School, 19
Freeman, Mark, 232n3 (Appendix B)
Freire, Paulo, 94

Gaining access to research site, 40–42
Giroux, Henry, 2
Graphic displays: in desegregation study: as
  a tool for exploring relationships across

"experience" and "views of equality," 156–
  158; as an interpretive activity, 150–152; as
  a tool for conceptualizing entanglement of
  replicative and transformative educational
  policies, 170–171

Helms, Janet, 113, 155
Hirschman, Albert O., 14
Holme, Jennifer Jellison, 14
Horoschak, Peter, 182

Inclusion of Ingroup in the Self (IIS) scale:
  in desegregation study, 61–65; use of IIS
  with biracial student, 110–111; within
  interview protocol, 197–199. *See also*
  Tropp, Linda R.; Wright, Stephen C.
Institutional Review Board (IRB), 40–41,
  177
Interpretive activities, 149–154
Interpretive fit and slippage, 158–168
Interpretive tradition, 18, 44, 48, 49, 72, 76,
  99, 174

Jackson, John P., 13
Jefferson, Carolyn, 14
Jones, James M., 37

Kaeser, S., 232n3 (Appendix B)
Keating, W. Dennis, 232n1 (Appendix B)
Kincheloe, Joe L., 2
Kohl, Herb, 103

Ladson-Billings, Gloria, 2
Lather, Patti, 2; and dialectical space for
  analysis, 17; and dialectical theory building, 94–95; and reciprocity, 77–78
Lawson, John, 80–81, 232–233n6. *See also*
  Shaker Schools Plan
LeCompte, Margaret, 34
Levels system in Shaker Heights Schools,
  Ohio, 34–36, 55–57, 59–60, 101; in desegregation study: as related to analytical
  code of structural boundaries, 132–134;
  informing core interpretive thread of
  positionality, 155–158; reflecting codes of
  privilege and exclusion, 136–137; as related
  to experience of racial isolation, 160–167;
  as replicating inequality, 171
Liberation psychology, 19
Likert scale responses, 66; in desegregation
  study interview protocol, 199–201

Literature review, 11–12; and development within desegregation study, 12–15
Lubek, Ian, 12

Martín-Baró, Ignacio, 2, 94, 191
Marx, Karl, 19
McLaren, Peter, 2
Member check, 30, 127, 173
Multimethod research design, 2, 22, 126; analysis, 128–129; multiple methods in desegregation study: design, 22–23; in writing, 180–181

Ogbu, John, 192–193
Opotow, Susan, 39
Oral history, 29–30; as a method in desegregation study, 30–32
Orfield, Gary, 13, 14
Oscillation in interpretation, 21; as means to study individual, structural, and sociopolitical analytical levels, 149, 156. *See also* Fine, Michelle; Weis, Lois

Participant recruitment, 33–34; within desegregation study, 34–40
Peller, Gary, 13
Pettigrew, Thomas F., 12
Plessy v. Ferguson, 13
Pollock, Mica, 12–13
Positionality, as core interpretive thread in desegregation study, 100–103, 157–158
Powell, Justice Lewis, 182
Privilege and exclusion, as desegregation study analytical code, 107–109, 134, 169–171, 187
Pseudonyms, 177–178

Queer theory, 19

Racial equality in desegregation study: as analyzed across methods of data collection, 137–144; as connected back to research question through interpretation of positionality, 154–158; as reflected in analytical category of encounter, 155; as theoretical construct, 16; as third segment in interview protocol, 68–71
Racial identity development: and Janet E. Helms, 113, 155; and William E. Cross, Jr., 113, 155

Reciprocity, 77–78; and critical reflection, 93–103; through communicative and conceptual spaces of engagement, 77–78; as engaging participants in clarification, 78–84; generating meaning, 84–93
Reed v. Rhodes, 181, 268n1 (Chapter 6)
Replicative educational change in desegregation study, 14–15, 169–171
Representation of participants and research context, 178–183
Research question, formulation of, 15–16; in desegregation study: development of, 16–17
Researcher as instrument, 75, 103–104
Researcher bias, 11–12, 41–42, 65–66, 104–105; in desegregation study, 116–117. *See also* Researcher reflexivity
Researcher reflexivity, 12, 18, 22, 104–105; relationship between researcher-participant reciprocity and, 103–104, 117–118; in desegregation study, 42–43, 65–66, 105–117
Researcher's autobiography, 10, 11–12, 168, 192
Researcher's race in desegregation study: as source of ethical consideration, 42–43; as interfering with data collection, 105–108, 109–113; as a lens through which emergent themes might be explored, 112–113, 116–117
Revilla, Anita Tijerina, 14
Richardson, Laurel, 152, 173
Ryan, William, 39

Schensul, Jean J., 39
Schofield, Janet, 13. *See also* "Colorblindness" or race-neutrality
Sewell, William F., 19
Shaker Schools Plan, 80–81, 109–110, 181, 185–186, 221. *See also* Lawson, John
Shelly v. Kraemer, 130, 232n1, 2 (Appendix B)
Sirin, Selcuk R., 49
Social psychological spaces of centrality, marginality, and encounter in conceptual framework in desegregation study, 157–158
Strauss, Anselm, 119
Sweatt v. Painter, 14; and intangibles, 14
Synthesizing research themes, 149–153; 171–172

Tajfel, Henri, 94
Taylor, Jack, 181, 233n11
Telephone interviews, 101–102
Theory building: and engaging critical friends in synthesizing thematic patterns, 153; through graphic displays, 151; and writing towards interpretation, 152
Thickening, as altering but not disrupting social stratifications, 169–171. *See also* Fine, Michelle
Thomas, William, 45
Tools for eliciting participant responses, 48–49; in desegregation study, 57–59, 69–70
Transformative educational change, as defined in desegregation study, 14–15, 168–171
Triangulation of data sources and methods, 21. *See also* Trustworthiness of interpretation
Tropp, Linda R.: and Inclusion of Ingroup in the Self (IIS) scale in desegregation study, 61–65; use of IIS with biracial student, 110–111; within interview protocol, 197–199. *See also* Inclusion of Ingroup in the Self (IIS) scale; Wright, Stephen C.
Trustworthiness of interpretation, 21; as achieved through member checks, 30, 127; to address conceptual murkiness, 159–160; in addressing interpretive fit and slippage, 158–159; in conveying results, 183–184; in desegregation study: through multiple methods and frames of analysis, 21, 29; and engaging participants in meaning making, 93; in ensuring systematic study and rigor in research, 167–168. *See also* Triangulation of data sources and methods
Turner, John, 94

University of California Regents v. Bakke, 182–183

Validity. *See* Trustworthiness of interpretation

Weeks, K. M., 130; 232n2 (Appendix B)
Weis, Lois, 2; 21, 149, 156. *See also* Oscillation in interpretation
Wells, Amy Stuart, 14
Whyte, Donna M., 14
Wright, Stephen, C.,: and Inclusion of Ingroup in the Self (IIS) scale, in desegregation study, 61–65; use of IIS with biracial student, 110–111; within interview protocol, 197–199. *See also* Inclusion of Ingroup in the Self (IIS) scale; Tropp, Linda R.
Writing: in desegregation study: as a tool for reflexivity, 10, 42–43, 107–108, 116–117; as an interpretive activity, 152; issues of confidentiality, 177; organization and framing key ideas, 175–177; representation of site, 179–183; representing research site and research participants, 178–179; on returning to anchor document to write up research results, 174–175; writing up results, 183–189

Znaniecki, Florian, 45

Anne Galletta is Associate Professor at the College of Education and Human Services at Cleveland State University. As a social psychologist, her research focus includes the study of social relations and the structural arrangements influencing these relations. Dr. Galletta collaborates with community-based organizations and public school systems in conducting research toward creating more humanizing and equitable educational practice and policies.